JOHN BROWN'S BODY

John

Brown's Body

SLAVERY, VIOLENCE, & THE CULTURE OF WAR

FRANNY NUDELMAN

The University of North Carolina Press

Chapel Hill and London

© 2004
The University of North Carolina Press
All rights reserved
Set in Ruzicka and Melior types by
Tseng Information Systems, Inc.
Manufactured in the United States of America
The paper in this book meets the guidelines for
permanence and durability of the Committee on
Production Guidelines for Book Longevity of the
Council on Library Resources.

Library of Congress Cataloging-in-Publication Data
Nudelman, Franny.
John Brown's body : slavery, violence, and the culture
of war / by Franny Nudelman.
p. cm. — (Cultural studies of the United States)
Includes bibliographical references and index.
ISBN 0-8078-2883-1 (cloth : alk. paper)
ISBN 0-8078-5557-x (pbk. : alk. paper)
1. United States—History—Civil War, 1861-1865—Social aspects.
2. United States—History—Civil War, 1861-1865—African Americans.
3. United States—History—Civil War, 1861-1865—Literature and the war.
4. Body, Human-Social aspects—United States—History. 5. Body,
Human—Symbolic aspects—United States—History. 6. Death—Social
aspects—United States—History—19th century. 7. Death—Symbolic
aspects—United States—History—19th century. 8. Violence—Social
aspects—United States—History—19th century. 9. Racism—United
States—History—19th century. 10. War and society—United States—
History—19th century. I. Title. II. Series.
E468.9.N84   2004
973.7′1—dc22   2003027753

cloth   08 07 06 05 04   5 4 3 2 1
paper   08 07 06 05 04   5 4 3 2 1

A portion of this book was previously published, in
somewhat different form, as "'The Blood of Millions':
John Brown's Body, Public Violence, and Political
Community," *American Literary History* 14, no. 4
(2001): 639-70. Used with permission.

FRONTISPIECE: Confederate dead gathered for burial.
Alexander Gardner, Antietam, Maryland, September 1862.
Library of Congress.

For Carolyn Porter and in memory of Michael Rogin

CONTENTS

ILLUSTRATIONS

ACKNOWLEDGMENTS

The love and generosity of friends, family, colleagues, and students made it possible to write this book. It is dedicated to my teachers, Carolyn Porter and Michael Rogin, who taught me how to learn and how to teach, and convinced me that this work matters. Finishing the book in Mike's absence has reminded me that speaking to the dead is a poor substitute for conversing with the living.

My faithful longtime friends have buoyed me up across large distances: Thalia Stanley, Steven Sugarman, Kimberly Moses, Stephanie Hochman, Marcus Verhagen, Carol Lloyd, Hank Pellissier, Gary Wolf, Alan Lyons, Andreas Killen, Johanna Schenkel, and Marlene Saritzky. In New Haven, Charlottesville, and points between, I have been blessed with generous, inspiriting colleagues. My thanks to Nancy Cott, Jean-Christophe Agnew, Michael Denning, Richard Brodhead, Ann Fabian, Matthew Jacobson, Jon Butler, David Waldstreicher, Michael Levenson, Alan Howard, Greg Colomb, Chip Tucker, Elizabeth Fowler, Deborah McDowell, Ed Ayers, Gary Gallagher, Steve Cushman, Gordon Hutner, Carolyn Karcher, Karen Sánchez-Eppler, Susie Gillman, and Jackie Goldsby, all of whom have offered vital support, advice, and feedback along the way. Over the years, Jill Campbell, Lanny Hammer, Forrester Hammer, Laura King, Laura Wexler, Bryan Wolf, Beverly Gage, Mike Wigotsky, Marion Rust, Bob Geraci, Dan Rosenzweig, Julie Jones, Matthew and Suzanne Crane, Chris and Brenda Yordy, Susan Fraiman, Eric Lott, Alison Booth, Vicki Olwell, and John O'Brien have sustained me with their conversation and friendship. In Corvallis, David Robinson urged me on, while Janet Winston and Laura Belmonte kept me sane and happy. A special thanks to Walter Michaels, who offered indispensable encouragement early on, and to my collaborator Grace Hale, who enabled this work with her careful reading and infectious commitment to intellectual endeavor. From his first warm greeting years ago, Alan Trachtenberg has proved an unparalleled friend and mentor; his faith in the project helped to coax this book into being.

Conversation with countless students informs every page. I owe a special debt to Jaclyn Reindorf, who brought "John Brown's Body" to my attention, to my research assistants Joshua Rowland and Emily Grandstaff, and to Sarah Hagelin for her help with the manuscript in its final stages. I am grateful to Yale University for a Samuel F. B. Morse Junior Faculty Fellowship and to the University of Virginia for a Sesquicentennial Associateship as well as other forms of support. I had the good fortune to complete this book at Oregon State University's Center for the Humanities, where I found intellectual companionship, as well as material and emotional support, in abundance. Communities as well as individuals have brought the work along: the Nineteenth-Century American Women Writers Study Group provided inspiration as I began this project, and the Charlottesville Center for Peace and Justice has helped me to put some of the ideas expressed in this book into practice.

John Brown's Body has been in sure hands at the University of North Carolina Press. My editor Sian Hunter has offered invaluable insight and guidance at every turn; David Hines has been unfailingly helpful; and Paul Betz has brought his remarkable ear for language, and eye for detail, to the project, making this a better book.

Finally, I thank my family: my brothers, Aaron and David Nudelman, for playing rock music with unbelievable nerve; my dad, Stanley Nudelman, for his love and support; Martin Klein and Suzanne Silk Klein, for their sterling example; Holly and Gerry Wilson, Andrew Norman, Margaret Norman and Geoff Holton, Susan, John, and Sarah Holton, for their warmth and generosity. My mom, Jane Cutler, taught me how to read and write, and how to find meaning in the world around me. Our lifelong conversation gives my work its very shape. If the love of friends and family made it possible to undertake this project, my son and husband have made it possible to finish it. Leo, buoyant and determined, reinvents life from the ground up each day, while David, with unparalleled sweetness and grace, makes this topsy-turvy world feel like home. Together, they have schooled me in the spirit of improvisation and the sense of hope I needed to write this book.

JOHN BROWN'S BODY

INTRODUCTION

Narration closes histories, narration heals; and for the
activist, histories must always remain open, like a wound.
—James Dawes, The Language of War (2002)

In 1862, Unitarian minister John Weiss predicted that after
the Civil War the United States would be "the most dangerous country on the face of the earth." He explained that "it
will see its own ideas more clearly than ever before, and long
to propagate them with its battle-ardors," and concluded,
"We have the elements to make the most martial nation in
the world."[1] In the years following the Second World War, as
the United States built its massive nuclear arsenal, Weiss's
prophecy was fully realized: capable of destroying the planet
many times over, this arsenal allowed the United States to
achieve global dominance. The Civil War contributed to the
development of technologies, and the centralization of federal power, that would eventually lead to the emergence of
the United States as a superpower during the Cold War. But
as Edmund Wilson, grappling with the Civil War in light of
the bomb, contended, culture played a vital role in this process. He remarked, "Everything, past, present and future,
takes its place in the legend of American idealism." Fascinated by the power of abstraction—specifically the opposition between good and evil—to obscure, and enable, the exercise of state power, Wilson sought to give an "objective
account of the expansion of the United States" by way of the
largely idealistic culture of the Civil War.[2]

My study, similarly concerned with the relationship between Civil War culture and state power, investigates the
process of abstraction that enabled the living to rededicate
themselves to the project of war in the face of stunning loss
and destruction. Indeed, the Civil War's most difficult practical effect—the presence of so many dead bodies—became
the source of its greatest abstraction: national union and re-

birth.[3] The song "John Brown's Body," from which I take my title, provides a succinct and memorable example of this transformation. Singing "John Brown's body lies a mouldering in the grave, his soul goes marching on," soldiers celebrated the process of decomposition through which Brown's actual body was transformed into a diffuse, inspiriting presence. In this way, the popular tune exemplifies the tendency of nationalist culture to abstract the effects of violence. Reassuring soldiers who contemplated imminent death that their pain would serve a transcendent purpose, the song also inspired Julia Ward Howe's "Battle Hymn of the Republic," which continues to fortify the American public in times of sorrow.

This book aims to reverse the song's trajectory by returning to the material contexts that gave John Brown's corpse and other dead bodies their figural meanings. Throughout, my efforts are indebted to the wealth of recent scholarship that can be loosely grouped under the rubric "Violence Studies." As this field grows, we come to recognize that violence is, as Joseph Roach puts it, a "form of cultural expression" that produces exclusion and generates a profound sense of belonging.[4] Like other cultural forms, it admits close analysis; scholars have begun to identify, however tentatively, a vocabulary of violent practices and the concepts that govern them. This makes it possible to interrelate different kinds of violence—slavery, murder, war, genocide—and begin to comprehend the ways that particular acts of destruction reverberate across time and space.

By contextualizing the belief that violence regenerates, I mean to interrogate the assumption that bloodshed is the necessary, unrivaled means of periodically reenergizing our commitment to national life. In the absence of suffering—so the story goes—people grow complacent, taking the many privileges of citizenship for granted. Through violence, by contrast, they come to experience the depth and intensity of their relation to a larger community. The idea that violence breeds national unity and, indeed, harmony, has allowed U.S. citizens to elevate the violence they inflict on others and imagine that such aggression is the condition of national belonging. This narrative must coexist, however, with the devastating consequences of combat—the ruin of body, mind, and spirit. Imagining that the battlefield dead nourished the earth as they decayed, Civil War artists and politicians cultivated a potent figure for the process through which death creates life. At times, however, the corpse—contorted, dismembered, unrecognizable—could not be idealized; instead, the dead revealed that war, far from producing a sense of belonging, stripped away the conventions, beliefs, and certainties that allowed people to love their dead and, by extension, to love one another.[5]

In order to offer an alternative account of the Civil War dead, in which violence appears neither transcendent nor foreordained, I study the bodies of martyred soldiers in relation to antebellum precedent. I focus on three discursive contexts: sentiment, science, and punishment. Each allows us to understand the cultural significance of dead soldiers in relation to prewar conventions for representing, studying, and disciplining African American bodies. Antebellum mourners beautified the corpse and crafted surrogates for it, tokens that might fortify and expand the bonds of community. The corpses of marginal people, by contrast, were frequently dismembered and denied the privilege of a proper burial. The mutilated bodies of soldiers, abandoned on the battlefield or hastily buried in unmarked graves, recalled the indignities inflicted on the corpses of the poor, African and Native Americans, and criminals. Thus the effort to elevate the corpses of dead soldiers worked not only to sanctify the war but also to disentangle it from the violence traditionally visited on powerless people.

In the context of a war initially fought to stem the spread of slavery into the territories and, eventually, to emancipate slaves, the potential resemblance between the plight of slaves and that of soldiers, both subject to extraordinary forms of violence, was especially acute. Even as Civil War culture tends to avoid the problem of slavery, perceptions of the war dead cannot be extricated from debates over slavery. During the antebellum years, reformers, doctors, artists, and politicians, among others, used the bodies of powerless people, most often black, to shape consensus concerning the nature of violence and its social applications. Both those who sought to justify slavery and those who sought to resist it exerted a mighty influence on wartime reactions to the crisis of mass death.

In light of a history of institutionalized violence directed against free and enslaved African Americans during the prewar years, wartime carnage does not appear to be an inevitable manifestation of the urge to collective renewal but rather the expression of particular interests and beliefs. Likewise, remembering the dead is a matter of deliberation and craft. I scour the culture of slavery and war to find those rare moments when the dead appear unavailable to transformation—beyond redemption—because I want to make the simple point that far from breeding life, or strengthening community, violence wreaks havoc on our physical and conceptual worlds. At times, the corpse, in all its grim materiality, calls the idealization of death in war into question and suggests a less inspiriting account of the relationship between death and national community.

Commemorative Objects

From the moment John Brown was sentenced to death, his body became a source of controversy and political struggle. Realizing the potential significance of Brown's demise, interested parties in the North and the South had designs on his corpse and, more broadly, on the meaning of his insurrectionary violence. Supporters hoped that the public display of Brown's body would secure his status as a martyred hero. W. J. Jarvis, for example, encouraged Wendell Phillips to buy Brown's body so that it might be paraded through major Northern cities with face and hands, still tied with rope, on display.[6] Detractors, by contrast, sought to remove Brown's body from public view. Anticipating the cult status of Brown's body, Southern physician Lewis Sayre wrote to Virginia's governor, Henry Wise, suggesting that in order to avoid a "triumphal procession through all the Eastern states," which would surely make Brown a "hero martyr," Brown's body be taken to a Southern medical school for dissection.[7]

The struggle over Brown's body suggests the significance of the corpse —actual and imagined—to the formation of political community in the nineteenth century. In private settings, mourners used corpses to dramatize an intimate and enduring relationship between the living and the dead that, in turn, provided a model for social harmony. While Puritans viewed the rotting corpse as a reminder of pervasive sin, nineteenth-century mourners beautified and domesticated the dead. By washing, grooming, and posing the corpse, mourners made it look more lifelike and familiar. Taking photographs, painting portraits, clipping a piece of fabric or hair, they produced commemorative objects that served as analogs for the dead body. These artifacts objectified the mourner's attachment to the dead. Circulating among friends and relatives, they also established mourning as an opportunity to identify with others who had experienced similar grief. As they passed from hand to hand, commemorative objects, which embodied the residual vitality of the dead, bound the living to one another.[8]

Mourning not only fortified local ties in the wake of death but also served as a model for sentimental exchanges that ideally structured society as a whole.[9] Just as individual sorrow might span the divide between life and death, compassion—sorrow felt on behalf of others—bridged seemingly insurmountable forms of social difference. While mourners used corpses to help them materialize the intimacy between the living and the dead, reformers applied the precepts of death culture to the problem of inequality.

Antislavery writers, for example, used scenes of loss and mourning to structure their appeal to an unenslaved readership. In *Uncle Tom's Cabin*, the emotional suffering of grieving parents interconnects a large cast of characters—white and black, enslaved and free, Northern and Southern—allowing Stowe to dramatize the national character of slavery.[10] Eliza Harris and her son Harry arrive at the Birds' house one short month after the death of the Birds' son Henry. In light of their recent loss, Senator Bird and his wife feel a particular sympathy for Eliza, who has fled the Shelby plantation after learning that her son has been sold to a slave trader. Senator Bird expresses his sympathy not only by spiriting Eliza and Harry away to the relative safety of the Quaker settlement but also by asking his wife to give some of their dead son's clothing to Harry.

Henry's clothes at once embody the dead boy and signify all that Harry and Henry have in common. The shoes—"worn and rubbed at the toes" —bear the imprint of Henry's own feet.[11] At the same time, they will fit either boy. In the tradition of commemorative objects, Henry's shoes objectify his parents' grief and provide a medium of exchange. Demonstrating the interpenetration of reformist rhetoric and mourning ritual, these garments cross the social divide between black and white children as well as the epistemological divide between the living and the dead. Thus they manage both the problem of inequality and the cognitive difficulty of death itself. When the Birds give clothes to Harry, they express their concern for the slave child while also finding a way to affirm the ongoing presence of their own dead son. Dressed up in a dead boy's clothes, Harry realizes the utopian impulse at the heart of memorial culture: he gives living form to the enduring and ineffable presence of the dead.[12]

Antebellum death rituals objectified the dead and, in doing so, affirmed their ongoing influence. During the Civil War, however, it was impossible to honor the dead in customary ways. Dead soldiers were rarely transported home for burial. Instead, they were buried in haste, if at all. Often their corpses went unidentified. Northerners found well-tried rituals suddenly antiquated as they grieved for dead soldiers in the absence of corpses. These conditions threw people back on conventions as they attempted to construct what Drew Faust has called a "Good Death" out of inadequate circumstances. At the same time, it led them to develop new concepts and rituals that might accommodate the mass of unburied and anonymous dead.

In the face of such difficulties, wartime artists searched for a way to commemorate dead soldiers that reflected, even elevated, the corpse's absence and, by extension, the mass scale of death in war. Whitman's wartime writing grapples with the challenge battlefield death posed to memorial conventions, and signals the emergence of new ways of conceptualizing the dead. In *Specimen Days*, he tries to find a way to honor the "thousands, north and south, of unwrit heroes, unknown heroisms, incredible, impromptu, first-class desperations." Describing the death of the "typic one of them" that stands "no doubt, for hundreds, thousands," he imagines the soldier who "crawls aside to some bush-clump, or ferny tuft, on receiving his death-shot—there sheltering a little while, soaking roots, grass and soil, with red blood . . . the last lethargy winds like a serpent round him—the eyes glaze in death—none recks—perhaps the burial squads, in truce, a week afterwards, search not the secluded spot—and there, at last, the Bravest Soldier crumbles in mother earth, unburied and unknown."[13] Celebrating the decay of the soldier's corpse, Whitman's wartime writing makes a virtue out of necessity. As Gary Laderman observes, during the antebellum period attention shifted away from "the corruptibility of the dead body," as the "process of disintegration" was subordinated to an "idealized spiritual continuity."[14] Yet during the war the body's decomposition emerged as a powerful figure for the subordination of identity, indeed the sacrifice of life itself, in the name of national community. While commemorative objects defied the process of decomposition, helping people to remember the dead as if they were unchanged, organic imagery described decay as a benevolent force.

Civil War culture nationalized a sentimental view of the enduring and benevolent influence of the dead. By way of the "mouldering" corpse, wartime representations of battlefield death expanded on the belief, common to death ritual and reformist discourse, that in sorrow one might discover forms of connection that transcend difference and inequality. Favoring abstraction over objectification, these descriptions abandon an antebellum investment in commemorative objects. Like the song "John Brown's Body," *Specimen Days* takes the corpse's gradual disappearance to best describe the way that individual death radiates through a larger community. Drawing on an evangelical commitment to the ongoing presence of the dead, wartime nationalism frees itself of reliance on actual bodies or their surrogates, turning one of the crises of war—the corpse's absence from the scene of commemoration—to advantage.

Specimens

W. J. Jarvis hoped that Brown's corpse would function as a commemorative object, strengthening collective ties as it passed through city streets. As it turned out, Brown's body was neither dissected nor paraded through Northern cities. Instead, it was turned over to his widow, Mary Brown, who carried it back to their home in North Elba, New York. Six days after Brown's execution, family and friends held a small memorial service, and Brown was buried beneath his grandfather's headstone in the place he loved most. Two weeks after Brown's execution, four of his coconspirators—two African American and two white—were put to death on the same scaffold. While the bodies of Edwin Coppoc and John Cook were, like Brown's, turned over to their families, Governor Wise refused to relinquish the bodies of the two black raiders, John Copeland and Shields Green. Instead, their bodies, after a brief burial, were dug up by a group of medical students and taken to the Winchester Medical College for dissection.

The middle-class parlor was only one of the settings in which nineteenth-century views of death took shape. In the medical school classroom, the anatomical museum, and the illustrated volumes of ethnologists, the corpse was objectified not in the service of memory but of science. As anatomy became increasingly important to the study of medicine, medical schools employed grave robbers or drafted medical students to obtain the corpses needed to stay in business. Most often they plundered African American cemeteries and potter's fields where the poor were laid to rest; the bodies employed by anatomists typically belonged to criminals, African and Native Americans, and the poor. For these people, death brought further subjugation to a violent social order; postmortem dissection was the final insult directed at bodies long subject to abuse.[15]

Dissection instrumentalized the body, narrowing rather than expanding its social significance. In this way, it severed the bonds of identification and neutralized the power of the corpse to generate community. While domestic death rituals employed the corpse's materiality as an expressive medium intended to manifest the relatedness between the living and the dead, the anatomist enumerated parts of the body without offering any context for their interrelatedness. Thus he demonstrated the irredeemable physicality of the dead and repudiated the body's social nature. Lifting the corpse out of social and religious contexts and establishing it as a source of valuable knowledge, dissection not only excluded the dead from a religious narrative of burial and resurrection but also from forms of community that depended on the body as a figure for common experience.

Subject to forms of violence typically reserved for the disenfranchised, dead soldiers were dismembered, objectified, and studied in the name of the greater good. The Army Medical Museum, founded by the federal government in 1862, employed a utilitarian view of the dead as a source of state authority. As Civil War surgeon John Hill Brinton remembered it, the attack on Fort Sumter transformed life in the North as "discussion ceased, political arguments were at an end, and almost absolute unanimity prevailed." Despite this popular consensus, however, the power of the government was far from secure. The "only question," Brinton writes, "was how best to establish the supremacy of the Government, and how to vindicate its authority."[16] Brinton's own war work was part of a larger effort to strengthen federal power by way of system-building that would ensure efficiency during the war and obedience in its aftermath. In June 1862, Brinton was asked to prepare "the Surgical History of the Rebellion" (169). He began collecting specimens—limbs, bone fragments, bullets—as well as devising a system for classifying them. Brinton used these specimens to establish the Army Medical Museum.[17]

In his *Personal Memoirs*, Brinton laments that at the beginning of the war information concerning wounds was "meager." All gunshot wounds were lumped in "one great comprehensive category" and reported without "real information of a precise character" (173). This problem was compounded by the chaotic circumstances of war. How to ensure that single wounds were not reported multiple times, or that the wounded man was properly identified? "One of the chief difficulties at this time," Brinton recalls, "was that of procuring truthful and full histories of the specimens" (186). Brinton's work, as he describes it, was to produce a detailed context for every bone fragment or bullet he could find and in doing so transform the generic nature of wartime injury into a field for differentiation and classification that resembled other systems for ordering large quantities of men, supplies, and information.

Brinton insists that his museum does not represent a "collection of curiosities" but rather the acquisition of "objects and data of lasting scientific interest," which will, in time, "be productive of real use" (186). But when push comes to shove, he is forced to acknowledge that these limbs and bones enhance the government's authority not only by demonstrating that war is the source of useful knowledge but also by showing that the government can claim possession of the bodies of its citizens. Brinton describes men who visit the Army Medical Museum looking for their lost limbs. One soldier, a private, insists that his limb is "his own property" and that he wants it back. Brinton reminds the soldier that he enlisted for the duration of the war and that until the war is over "the United States Government is entitled to all of you" (190).

Who can claim possession of the dead body? The question of self-ownership, so central to debates over slavery, was generalized during the Civil War. Antebellum death ritual rested on the assumption that interiority was simply embodied; commemorative objects had meaning in the eyes of survivors because they were infused by the aura of a particular dead person. Thus the corpse, and the meaning produced from it, remained closely associated with a given individual. Dissection, by contrast, was a form of racial violence that represented the power of the anatomist to divorce body and identity, thus rendering the corpse useful to the community. It resembled slavery, which employed the threat of violence to extract the body's resources and deny self-possession to the enslaved individual. In the context of the emerging science of anatomy, the meaning of the body after death—hardly a matter of experience, identity, or essence—was determined by professionals able to extract knowledge and, by extension, authority from it.

The Scaffold

Although John Brown was a celebrated martyr during the war years, in December 1859 he was executed as an enemy of the state. Deciding to have Brown hanged, Governor Wise of Virginia defied those who warned that execution would turn the traitor Brown into a hero. As he told the Virginia legislature, "the threat of martyrdom is a threat against our peace, and demands execution to defy such sympathy and such saints of martyrdom."[18] In this instance, the logic of martyrdom, in which the criminal becomes a hero of the people, trumped the state's effort to use the scaffold to exert power and control. Brown used his trial and execution to speak out against slavery and condemn the country that was preparing to put him to death. From the scaffold, he prophesied apocalyptic violence that would punish the errant nation in retribution for the suffering inflicted on generations of slaves. Slavery, he predicted, "will never be purged away; but with Blood."[19]

Anticipating widespread violence, Brown rehearsed one of the most powerful, and incendiary, arguments made by antislavery radicals in the prewar years: if white Americans did not repent, and reform, they would suffer retributive violence at the hands of black insurgents, or of an angry God acting on behalf of the enslaved. During wartime, however, divine

retribution provided a popular explanation for the extremity and duration of battlefield carnage. This interpretation of the war derived from
the belief, shared by many Protestant denominations, that America had
been chosen to suffer special tribulations that would precede the revelation of God's will on earth.[20] The language of insurrection, which threatened white Americans with fiery death, was readily accommodated by
a nationalist narrative that took extreme suffering to affirm the country's exceptional status. Interpreting wartime carnage as an expression of
divine wrath allowed Northerners to acknowledge that slavery was wrong
while affirming an expansionist vision of the United States as a nation
among nations.

In a millennial context, violence appeared, once again, regenerative:
sanctioned by God, it was the sign, and the source, of better things to
come. If a war to prohibit secession was at times difficult to justify in
light of the revolutionary precedent, a war for emancipation could be
viewed as a holy endeavor. The enlistment of black soldiers, in particular,
harmonized a secular view of violence as a means to self-determination
with the millennial expectation that war would usher in a better age for
humankind. Frederick Douglass described the nation at war as enslaved
by its own past and, on this basis, united the interests of black people
and the federal government. In May 1861 he wrote, "The power given to
crush the Negro now overwhelms the white man. The Republic has put
one end of the chain upon the ankle of the bondman, and the other end
about its own neck. . . . Any attempt now to separate the freedom of the
slave from the victory of the Government over slaveholding rebels and
traitors . . . will be labor lost."[21] Douglass consistently argued that the
nation could not be freed from its own sinful past until slaves were emancipated and allowed to fight. Once black soldiers were given a chance to
liberate themselves, they provided a powerful symbol for the deliverance
of the American people through warfare.

To the extent that the wartime state appeared to be the surrogate for a
punishing God, the spectacle of mass death on the battlefield promised
a radical reordering that would pave the way for equality and harmony.
At the site of execution, however, where the government used the bodies
of outliers—criminals, insurgents, deserters, and traitors—to articulate
its power, an alternative account of the causes and aims of war begins to
emerge for us. On the military scaffold, state violence appears intentional
and effective, and soldiering an effect of coercion analogous to slavery
itself.

In August 1861, shortly after the war had begun, Congress outlawed whipping as a military punishment. In doing so, legislators implicitly acknowledged the inflammatory comparison between slavery and military service. In abolitionist discourse, the scene of corporal punishment, in which slaveholders wielded unrestrained violence over the bodies of slaves, represented the excesses of slavery. Abolitionists participated in a broader critique of corporal punishment that placed sympathy in opposition to state-sanctioned violence. From the late eighteenth century onward, sympathy, rather than force, provided the ideal basis for social order, and the display of state power appeared repugnant to spectators who responded compassionately to the criminal's suffering. Indeed, the history of punishment in the United States and elsewhere is replete with instances, like the execution of John Brown, in which the scaffold becomes the site of militant sympathy and criminality is politicized by the exhibition of state power.

In battle, all soldiers were subject to the threat of state-sponsored violence typically directed at criminals. Ironically, the potentially alienating, even radicalizing, nature of this experience required the expression of a severe and exacting discipline to keep soldiers in line. The Civil War witnessed an unprecedented number of Union army executions— an estimated 267—unequalled by any subsequent war in U.S. history.[22]

Conducted in front of large gatherings of troops, military executions were spectacular public events intended to demonstrate the army's might to soldiers and civilians and, in doing so, ensure obedience. Standing at attention in front of the scaffold, soldiers demonstrated the power of state violence to order and discipline masses of men. In order to intensify the impact of this spectacle, troops were often paraded past the dead soldier and forced to look closely at his corpse after the execution was over. Yet these spectacular executions ran the risk of jeopardizing the soldier's devotion to the army and, by extension, to the nation. Private letters record the repulsion that some soldiers felt witnessing executions, while the public record includes instances of disobedience. On one occasion, for example, two soldiers on a firing squad failed to discharge their weapons and were led away from the execution site in chains.[23]

Legends of regenerative violence obscure not only the devastation of war but also the role that war violence played in disciplining a national public. When we consider soldiers' corpses in relation to the history of corporal punishment, closely associated with slavery in the antebellum United States, they appear to be an effect of the state's intentional violence. This perspective, however, was rarely available in the culture of the Civil War. Narratives of divine retribution described soldiers as surrogates for a punishing God and, in this way, mediated the government's relation to the spectacle of mass death. Viewed in this light, the war dead not only redressed the sin of slavery but also confirmed America's special status as a nation ordained to suffer intensely and, in consequence, lead the world into a glorious future.

As I write this introduction in my office at Oregon State University's Center for the Humanities, a photography exhibit titled "Children of the Gulf War" is on display in the common room downstairs. The photographs show Iraqi children playing, working, attending school. Many of them profile children who are dying of cancer. Noting that "Iraqi hospitals are filled with children suffering from leukemia, cancer and physical deformities," photographer Takashi Morizumi explains that these cancers and birth defects are most likely caused by

> depleted uranium munitions used by the multilateral forces. Depleted uranium is a by-product of the manufacture of nuclear weapons and fuel for nuclear power reactors. . . . Taking advantage of the hardness and density of this material, the defense industry has developed a new type of armor-piercing shell, which is fired at high speed against the target. The impact generates intense heat and severe burning. Artillery penetrators and machine-gun bullets made of depleted uranium were first used in the Gulf War, a total quantity estimated at over three hundred tons. The shell disintegrates into particles that permeate the air and soil of the surrounding area and pollute the water. When this toxic metal penetrates the body or is ingested, the incidence of cancer, leukemia, liver and kidney disorders, tumors and birth defects is high.[24]

In my eyes, Morizumi's strategy—exposing the methods of modern warfare by focusing on the suffering of blameless children—is as effective today as it was when Stowe wrote *Uncle Tom's Cabin*. Taking up cherished justifications for war in light of the bodies of dead soldiers and slaves, I hope not only to offer historical context for how we continue to think about death in war but also to move toward a methodology that reverses the trajectory of abstraction by reconsidering the process of idealization in light of some of war's particulars. The mechanics of war—whether they pertain to bodies, policies, or poetry—are ever changing. They provide the point of entry for adjudicating war's purpose and its results. In isolation, these details may amount to nothing more than a compulsive recitation of incidents that constructs war as a matter of contingency. When viewed in light of those sweeping "truths" that have served to justify one war, and then the next, these particulars help us to rediscover the weave of intention and result too quickly forgotten as wars assume their triumphal narrative shape.

THE BLOOD OF MILLIONS
JOHN BROWN'S BODY, PUBLIC VIOLENCE, AND POLITICAL COMMUNITY

1

Accustomed to the overnight successes, unexpected comebacks, and sudden reversals of celebrity culture, we might still find cause to wonder at the course of John Brown's fame. At the time of his capture in October 1859, Brown was a pariah, a fanatic, a blunderer of enormous proportions. By the summer of 1861 he was a mascot of sorts for the Union army—his death commemorated time and again as soldiers prepared to fight, his name synonymous with bravery, self-sacrifice, and patriotism. No one was more aggrieved by this transformation than John Wilkes Booth. Writing to his brother-in-law in 1864, he lamented, "What was a crime in poor John Brown is now considered (by themselves) as the greatest and only virtue of the whole Republican party. Strange transmigration!"[1]

From Sunday, May 12, 1861, when it was first sung at Fort Warren, "John Brown's Body" quickly became a Union favorite:

John Brown's body lies a-mouldering in the grave,
John Brown's body lies a-mouldering in the grave,
John Brown's body lies a-mouldering in the grave,
His soul is marching on.

CHORUS:
Glory, glory, hallelujah!
Glory, glory, hallelujah!
Glory, glory, hallelujah!
His soul is marching on.

He's gone to be a soldier in the army of the Lord,
He's gone to be a soldier in the army of the Lord,
He's gone to be a soldier in the army of the Lord,
His soul is marching on!

John Brown's knapsack is strapped upon his back,
John Brown's knapsack is strapped upon his back,
John Brown's knapsack is strapped upon his back,
His soul is marching on!

His pet lambs will meet him on the way,
His pet lambs will meet him on the way,
His pet lambs will meet him on the way,
They go marching on!

They will hang Jeff Davis to a sour apple tree,
They will hang Jeff Davis to a sour apple tree,
They will hang Jeff Davis to a sour apple tree,
As they march along!

Now, three rousing cheers for the Union,
Now, three rousing cheers for the Union,
Now, three rousing cheers for the Union,
As we are marching on![2]

Offering a secular rendition of Christ's burial and resurrection, "John Brown's Body" puts religion to work in the service of wartime nationalism. Opening with the graphic "John Brown's body lies a-mouldering in the grave," the song proceeds to describe the transformation of Brown's corpse; he becomes a foot soldier in "the army of the Lord," and finally a martyr. As Brown's body decays, his spirit is reborn and, in turn, donates new life to the army and the nation it serves.

Singing this song, soldiers celebrated the power of Brown's body, as it disappeared, to produce a spirited community that found expression in "three rousing cheers for the Union." And yet, even as the song translated death into martial enthusiasm, reminding soldiers that they died on behalf of a greater cause, it did not allow them to ignore the difficult reality of violent death. Brown's body could not be forgotten long; each time the song was sung, his rotting corpse was brought back into view. When soldiers sang "John Brown's Body," they celebrated not simply Brown's death or its redemptive aftermath, but rather the very process of transformation through which corpses, in all their gruesome and seemingly intractable materiality, are reinterpreted as group spirit. The song schooled soldiers in the abstraction of bodily suffering that allows for the amplification of the body's social meaning.[3]

Keeping the rotting corpse firmly in view, the song speaks to the problem, at once psychological and political, posed by war: how can citizens and soldiers believe that the losses they suffer, individually and collectively, are worthwhile? More dramatically, why do soldiers continue to fight once exposed to the deaths of their comrades and the harrowing experience of combat? Imaginatively reversing the effects of violence, granting both agency and meaning to the process of decay, the song suggests that progress begins with the body's demise. In this way, Brown's example may have helped soldiers envision their own deaths as a source of collective rejuvenation; the song encouraged soldiers to believe that an individual's death might enable the larger community—the people or nation—to endure.

While "John Brown's Body" put Brown's death to work in service of the state, Brown, championing the cause of the enslaved, died the state's enemy. Many versions of the song, like the one cited above, make no mention of slavery, the cause for which Brown chose to martyr himself.[4] Brown's wartime incarnation as a martyred hero does not, however, represent the erasure of his abolitionist past but rather its translation: in its emphasis on physical suffering as the basis of political community, the song remains faithful to the principles, if not the purposes, that structured Brown's abolitionism and led him to radical action at Harpers Ferry. Like other abolitionists, Brown saw slave suffering as a catalyst for identifications that might further resistance to slavery. In the weeks before his execution, he described his impending death as the consequence of his sympathy for slaves, and hoped that his public suffering would prompt others to action. When applied to the problem of wartime nationalism—how to create an affective bond between state and citizen strong enough to compel the citizen's willing self-sacrifice—Brown's own belief that pain produces political community substantiated a vision of the nation rejuvenated by the deaths of soldiers.

Brown's martyrdom, an instance of the radical consequences of compassion, brings to culmination a tradition of abolitionist sympathy; in turn, his death is one of the founding moments in the development of a Northern nationalism based on the affective power of self-sacrifice. In analyzing the relationship between reformist efforts to cultivate compassion and nationalist efforts to rationalize mass violence, I will not contend that one leads inexorably to the other, or that the two are fundamentally opposed. Instead, I hope to use a set of discrete historical events to demonstrate that the production of sympathetic feeling can check or further violent practice. This chapter will examine the construction of Brown's martyrdom—by friends and foes, the press, and Brown himself—in the weeks preceding and following what he liked to call his "public murder." The struggle over the significance of Brown's death was, most broadly, a contest over the political meaning of the violated body—its ability to confer identity on a group and to grant that identity political legitimacy. Abolitionists who supported Brown took their cues from Brown himself: describing the raid on Harpers Ferry as an example of sympathy put into practice, they viewed the violence initiated and suffered by Brown as a model for further antislavery activism. Embracing Brown's resistance to unjust laws, they rededicated their commitment to a "higher law" and renewed their sense of collective purpose. By contrast, state authorities reasserted the power of the law in the face of Brown's incendiary violence and, in doing so, sent a warning to insurrectionaries, North and South: disobedience would not be tolerated. They hoped that the spectacle of execution would sever public identification with Brown and put an end to the inflammatory potential of his example.

This chapter reconsiders the legend of Brown, canonized by "John Brown's Body," in light of the sweeping influence of antislavery rhetoric during the prewar years and, more locally, the logistics of his widely publicized execution. Poised between two of the great crises of the nineteenth-century United States—slavery and the Civil War—Brown's martyrdom suggests the expansive tendency of sympathy, which leads inevitably toward abstraction, and the impotence of the state to halt this process. Indeed, the government failed to discipline the radical sympathies of Northern abolitionists or the insurrectionary aspirations of secessionists; providing a rallying point for the antislavery community, Brown's execution only aggravated Southerners inclined to secede. During the war, however, the state derived its authority from the escalation of violence rather than from the ability to control it. As "John Brown's Body" suggests, the state was ultimately fortified by the logic of sympathy that initially posed a threat to the rule of law: Brown's martyrdom prefigured a wartime nationalism that relied on individual self-sacrifice and took the escalation of violence to be a source of collective identity rather than a threat to the state's integrity.

At the time Booth witnessed Brown's execution, he may have assumed that Brown's career as an agitator had come to an end. Brown himself, however, understood that a traitor put to death by the state might exert untold influence. Accustomed to struggle and bitter disappointment—the deaths of his first wife and ten of his twenty children, failed business ventures, dislocation, and poverty—Brown greeted his capture, imprisonment, and execution with exuberance. Writing from prison, Brown assured his cousin, the Reverend Luther Humphrey, "No part of my life has been more happily spent than that I have spent here." In another letter, he exclaimed, "I certainly think I was never more cheerful in my life." Brown was happy, at least in part, because he saw an opportunity for public influence that had never before been available to him: "I am worth inconceivably more to hang than for any other purpose."[5] Brown recognized that his body, subject to the violence of the state, had become a source of public meaning. During the month between his sentencing and his execution, he seized every opportunity to address a Northern audience from the courtroom, his cell, and finally the scaffold; his words and gestures carried great significance as they circulated widely in the Northern press. Brown was aware that he had the power to move his audience, and he used it masterfully. As Henry David Thoreau described it, "They did not hang him at once, but reserved him to preach to them . . . and so his victory was prolonged and completed. No theatrical manager could have arranged things so wisely to give effect to his behavior and words."[6]

On November 2, 1859, Brown, having been convicted of treason, conspiring with slaves to rebel, and murder in the first degree, was given an opportunity to address the court. In this speech, he went some distance toward shaping the meaning of his death for his contemporaries as well as future historians. Brown embraced his impending execution with the following words: "Now, if it is deemed necessary that I should forfeit my life for the furtherance of the ends of justice, and mingle my blood further with the blood of my children and with the blood of millions in this slave country whose rights are disregarded by wicked, cruel, and unjust enactments, I say, let it be done!"[7] In a sweeping rhetorical gesture made meaningful by his impending death on the scaffold, Brown used the figure of blood to ally his extraordinary fate with the routine abuse of slaves. Blood, imagined here as a sort of universal fluid, unites Brown, his family, and countless slaves.[8] Combining his lifeblood with the "blood of millions," Brown participates in, and radicalizes, a tradition of abolitionist sympathy that dramatizes slave suffering in an effort to mobilize readers. Putting sympathetic epistemology into practice, Brown demonstrates his own capacity to feel the pain of others and to act on their behalf.[9]

Antislavery authors and orators hoped to convert audiences to the cause by conveying the slave's physical and emotional pain: they imagined representations of slave suffering setting in motion a chain of responsive anguish that would culminate in the eradication of slavery itself.

In "The Story of 'Uncle Tom's Cabin'" (1878), Harriet Beecher Stowe describes the composition of her antislavery novel as the result of a mysterious encounter with a brutalized slave. She tells her readers that the "first part of the book ever committed to writing was the death of Uncle Tom." While taking communion at a small church in Brunswick, Maine, Stowe received a vision of Tom's death. She was "perfectly overcome by it, and could scarcely restrain the convulsion of tears and sobbings that shook her frame."[10] This encounter initiates a series of exchanges in which Tom's suffering, conveyed through the medium of fiction, causes others to suffer. After receiving her vision, Stowe rushed home and put the scene down on paper. When she read it aloud to her sons, they too broke down in "convulsions of weeping, one of them saying, through his sobs, 'O mamma, slavery is the most cursed thing in the world!'" (xix). Once published, the novel was so popular that "eight power-presses, running day and night," barely satisfied public demand. As Stowe's unaccountable vision is transmitted in ever-widening circles, the anguish "that had long weighed upon her soul, seemed to pass off from her and into the readers of the book" (xxi–xxii). Describing an encounter between the abused, black male body and the responsive feminine imagination as the source of her abolitionist fiction, Stowe maintains that narrated pain, transmitted through the vulnerable body of the sympathetic listener or reader, will produce a compassionate community.[11]

Such extraordinary confidence in the power of narration to bridge experiential distance helped antislavery writers to cope with their own ignorance. Northern abolitionists stood at a vast remove from the scene of slavery; by and large, they lacked firsthand knowledge of the institution they sought to dismantle. They addressed an audience that, likewise, gained its knowledge of slavery through oral and written testimony. Stowe herself faltered in the face of inexperience. When Tom boarded a steamboat headed South, Stowe missed her weekly installment in the *National Era* and appealed to Frederick Douglass for information about plantation life.[12]

While Stowe's lack of firsthand knowledge caused her some anxiety, one might argue that her inexperience accounts for much of the novel's power. At its most effective, abolitionist writing makes a virtue out of necessity by transforming the condition of geographical dislocation into an epistemological challenge: how can one feel for strangers over great distances? Or, to put it another way, how can one feel the pain of a suffering body when the body itself is absent? In keeping with her inability to deliver up the body of the suffering slave, Stowe renders Tom's death without graphic detail. His deathblow is described in one sentence: "Legree, foaming with rage, smote his victim to the ground." In the next, Stowe tells us that "scenes of blood and cruelty are shocking to our ear and heart. What man has nerve to do, man has not nerve to hear."[13] At Tom's deathbed, Stowe again turns our attention away from his physical suffering and toward the redemptive sorrow of those moved by Tom's example: Sambo, Quimbo, Cassy, and others are converted to Christianity by Tom's death. Rather than allowing us full access to her mystical encounter, Stowe reproduces the absence of firsthand experience that prompts and structures abolitionist writing. If Stowe is constrained by her distance from the scene of slavery, this distance becomes, in turn, a great resource: antislavery writing can be viewed as a sustained meditation on the power of the imagination, and its limitations, in the face of inexperience.

In lieu of the actual body of the suffering slave, the body of the witness, who imitates the slave's pain in the process of identifying with her, often becomes the object of scrutiny in abolitionist texts. In anatomizing the process of readerly identification, Elizabeth Margaret Chandler uses the term *mental metempsychosis*. Metempsychosis, a word that derives from spiritualist practice, denotes the soul's migration, after death, into another body. Chandler applies the concept to the imaginative migrations of the abolitionist reader. If her audience could "imagine themselves for a few moments in his [the slave's] . . . circumstances . . . enter into his feelings . . . transform themselves mentally into his very self," compassion would surely follow. In particular, readers must strive to reenact the physical pain of punishment. Chandler asks her readers to "let the fetter lie with its wearing weight upon their wrists . . . and the successive strokes of the keen thong fall upon their shoulders till the flesh rises in long welts beneath it, and the spouting blood follows every blow."[14] As this passage suggests, in the face of their distance from the scene of slavery and the consequent absence of the slave's abused body, abolitionist authors and readers are compelled by imagined pain: the suffering conjured by the abolitionist author or reader takes place in her own mind. At its most successful, identification loses sight of its object, and sympathy appears to be a closed circle in which the reader's projections give rise to her experience of pain.

Here, as elsewhere, the practice of sympathetic identification presents a certain dilemma: should we understand *mental metempsychosis* as an exercise in solipsism, in which sympathy produces a particularly acute experience of one's own body, or as an imaginative encounter that briefly shatters the very bounds of identity?[15] Shirley Samuels describes the "corporealizing and transcendentalizing double impulse of sentimental discourse."[16] Indeed, it is this double impulse that allows the reader to acknowledge the suffering of others and to absorb it as if it were her own. Yet rather than viewing both impulses as integral to sympathetic epistemology, critics tend to praise a sentimental interest in embodiment while taking a more critical view of the urge to abstraction. Reform-minded sentimentalists demonstrated that certain groups of people were excluded from the privileges of citizenship on the basis of their bodily characteristics. In this way, they provided a corrective to political discourse that viewed democratic citizens as disembodied. This contribution to political thought was compromised, however, by the tendency of the sentimental witness to appropriate the pain of the suffering victim, thus obscuring the particularity of the victim's experience.[17] In this view, an emphasis on the responsive suffering of the spectator or reader evidences a certain ineffectiveness, even brutality, at the heart of sentimental method.[18]

Such evaluations of sentimentality assume that pain is most valuable as a means of stimulating political change when it remains an unassimilable attribute of the person who has suffered it. Perhaps because we live during an era in which mass movements have been galvanized by appeals to experience, it is hard for us to fathom the depth of a sentimental commitment to intersubjectivity. Although critics often view efforts to politicize bodily suffering and efforts to generalize it as fundamentally opposed, sentimentalists regarded the discursive transformation of particular, embodied experience into abstract, collective experience as a means to political change.[19]

This is not to say, however, that such claims were self-fulfilling or their ethical valence clear-cut. While abolitionists wanted to describe suffering in order to eradicate it, they often narrated its proliferation: representing pain as easily and widely communicable, abolitionists envisioned a community bound not by race, gender, or class identity but by pain itself. The spectator's response to pain, imitated in turn by the sentimental reader, initiates a chain reaction in which many people potentially suffer as a result of a single act of violence. While the abstraction of pain can enable a broad audience to engage the problem of suffering, it can also allow people to revel in the dramatic prospect of violence without end. I would identify the tendency to use the abstraction of bodily pain to imagine alternately the elimination of suffering *and* its proliferation as the double impulse that at once characterizes and problematizes abolitionist sentimentality.

In "The World's Homage" (1882), a poem written for Stowe on her seventieth birthday, Oliver Wendell Holmes praised her famous anti-slavery novel by comparing Uncle Tom to John Brown:

> All through the conflict, up and down
> Marched Uncle Tom and Old John Brown,
> One ghost, one form ideal;
> And which was false and which was true,
> And which was mightier of the two,
> The wisest sibyl never knew,
> For both alike were real.[20]

Dwelling on the interchangeability of fact and fancy, fictional character and historical actor, Holmes celebrates the political efficacy of Stowe's fiction by comparing Uncle Tom to the maverick Brown. As Elizabeth Barnes has noted, sentimental writing does not distinguish between real and fictional characters "for the simple reason that, based on the principles of sympathy, other people become real to us through our projected sentiments, not by their objective presence in the world."[21] If sympathy aims to reconstruct social division as affective harmony, the relationship between a real reader and a fictional character and, more broadly, between fictional and real worlds provides an analog to the problem of social difference. Indeed, the process of identifying across the bounds of representation resembles the imaginative work of cultivating feeling for strangers. And yet, while Holmes uses Brown's example to substantiate the political effect of Uncle Tom, and of sentimental fiction more broadly, it is tempting to reverse this relationship and ask if Brown might not derive credibility from Uncle Tom's example. A white man who dies on behalf of slaves, a Northerner who encroaches on Southern territory, Brown suggests the practical consequences of the imaginative self-extension that Stowe's novel demands.[22]

In his courtroom speech, Brown, like Stowe, is concerned with the transformation of victimization into community. But because Brown's pain is not imagined but real, he is able to realize and extend the premises of abolitionist sympathy. While abolitionists analogized actual and imagined suffering in an effort to produce identifications, Brown literalized this analogy by offering his own body to stand in place of the slave's.

Brown explains that his actions at Harpers Ferry, as elsewhere, were inspired by the Golden Rule. He tells his audience that the Bible "teaches me that all things whatsoever I would that men should do to me, I should do even so to them. It teaches me, further, to remember them that are in bonds, as bound with them. I endeavored to act up to that instruction."[23] Brown is, in a sense, the ideal sympathetic reader. Taking to heart the Bible's injunction to remember those who suffer, he demonstrates the power of identification by placing his own body on the scaffold.

Years after his father's death, John Brown Jr. told a story that suggests that the principle of substitution had long united his father's religious and political practice. During an unruly phase in his son's life, John Brown kept an account of how much punishment was due for John Jr.'s various infractions: for disobeying his mother, he owed eight lashes; for telling a lie, eight more. When the time came, John Sr., as anticipated, applied the whip to his son's back. A third of the way through the allotted number of strokes, however, he stopped, handed the whip to his son, took off his shirt, and demanded that his son finish the beating. John Jr. recounts, "I dared not refuse to obey, but at first I did not strike hard. 'Harder!' he said; 'harder, harder!' until he received the balance of the account." Initially mystified, years later John Jr. realizes that his father was offering a "practical illustration" of the doctrine of atonement—that "justice could be satisfied by inflicting penalty upon the back of the innocent instead of the guilty."[24] As in the writing of Stowe and Chandler, the scene of punishment provides an opportunity for actual and imagined substitutions. Trading places with his son, Brown seems less interested in the exercise of compassion than in elaborating a certain structural relation, one of equivalence that is realized through substitution and its result—shared pain.

Brown's admirers frequently praised him for submitting to punishment intended for slaves alone; they celebrated his willingness to die for the rights of others. Speaking in New York shortly after Brown's execution, Wendell Phillips declared, "Heroes of other days died for their own rights. John Brown died for a race in whose blood he had no share."[25] Yet if Phillips believed that Brown was a hero because he was a white man willing to suffer on behalf of slaves, Brown himself saw such substitutions as a means of confounding racial identity altogether. While Phillips uses the language of blood to distinguish between those who die for themselves and those who die for others, in his courtroom speech Brown refuses this distinction. Blood shed, first by slaves and then by Brown himself, is reinterpreted as one blood, a common fluid that circulates between Brown, his children, and enslaved millions. An analog to Stowe's "eight power-presses," Brown's blood provides the medium that binds a far-flung imagined community.

By envisioning the communication of pain as a means of achieving social transformation, many abolitionist writers, both black and white, drive toward Brown's apocalyptic figure of common blood. And yet their rhetoric never abandons racial distinctions. An emphasis on the slave's corporeal suffering tends to essentialize racial difference: physical pain becomes the province of slaves, and suffering, by extension, a property of blackness. The analogy between physical and emotional pain promises that suffering can be shared across an experiential divide while maintaining a racialized distinction between forms of suffering. Positing a common blood that transcends racial boundaries, Brown dismisses the literal form of the body, white or black, in favor of an emphasis on bodily substance, which, as it flows, inheres in no particular body. Blood signifies a common medium extracted, or abstracted, from the staggering material differences between the enslaved and the unenslaved. Taken to its logical extreme, the figure of mingled blood detaches pain from any concrete bodily or racial referent. Because he is willing to suffer physical rather than emotional pain, the martyr undermines the analogy between bodily and emotional suffering that at once unites and distinguishes victim and spectator in an abolitionist context. In doing so, he realizes the most extraordinary and ominous implications of sympathetic thought— that suffering inflicted on one person, or one group of people, will inevitably spread as violence overwhelms distinctions of circumstance and identity.

When Lydia Maria Child learned that John Brown had been captured and wounded, she responded with characteristic practicality. She wrote to Virginia Governor Henry Wise to ask for permission to visit Brown in prison. In her letter, she explains that while she does not approve of Brown's raid, she and "thousands of others" cannot help but "feel a natural impulse of sympathy for the brave and suffering man." However misguided his actions, Brown now needs "a mother or sister to dress his wounds, and speak soothingly to him." Praising Wise as a "man of chivalrous sentiments," she asks, "Will you allow me to perform that mission of humanity?"[26]

Wise's reply to Child was nothing if not chivalrous. As Virginia and Massachusetts are "involved in no civil war," and as both abide by a constitution that grants the same "privileges and immunities" to all citizens as they travel between states, Wise is "bound to protect" Child if she wishes to visit Virginia for any purpose. "You have the right to visit Charlestown," Wise assures her, "and your mission, being merciful and humane, will not only be allowed, but respected, if not welcomed." Yet Wise's studied deference quickly gives way. He continues, "I could not permit an insult even to woman in her walk of charity among us, though it be to one who whetted knives of butchery for our mothers, sisters, daughters, and babes." Child presents her desire to nurse Brown as a natural and uncalculated expression of sympathy. Wise turns the tables by attacking such feminine feeling as the source of sectional strife. While Virginians, ever cordial, know how to treat a lady visitor, Child must make no mistake—they "have no sympathy with your sentiments of sympathy with Brown." To the contrary, Brown's raid "was a natural consequence of your sympathy, and the errors of that sympathy ought to make you doubt its virtue from the effect on his conduct."[27]

While Wise's charge might appear, at first, outlandish, his hardheaded response to Child's letter asks us to regard Brown's radicalism, and the consequent escalation of sectional hatred, as one manifestation of sympathy as it was popularized by antislavery activists. Wise asserts that the violence that characterized the struggle over slavery during the 1850s was the product of a reformist discourse that took compassion as its motive force. Calling claims to an organic and spontaneous outpouring of emotion into question, he demands that we consider the strategic uses of sympathy. As sectional hostilities mounted and legal measures failed to produce resolution, Northerners and Southerners feared that violence was inevitable. Southerners imagined that Brown and his men were backed by a Northern mob willing to take the law into its own hands. Antislavery Northerners obliged this fear by celebrating Brown's transgressions, and pledging their dedication to a "higher law." The status of *sympathy*—a key term in this conflict—was called into question time and again: was it a transformative power associated with individual and collective renewal, or was it a byword for partisan aggression that stood in opposition to the law?

Child's response to Brown's raid on Harpers Ferry was intense. Throughout the fall of 1859, she was preoccupied with the Brown affair. She confessed to friends, "I can think and talk of nothing but Capt John Brown." Writing to her niece, Child announced, "Recent events have renewed my youth and strength. I am full of electricity."[28] Indeed, Brown's action revived Child's waning abolitionist energy, inaugurating a period of intense political activity.[29] Her reaction was not uncharacteristic. While Northerners largely disapproved of Brown's raid, antislavery radicals—authors, clergymen, activists—were inspired by his actions. Thoreau, for example, described being "so absorbed in him as to be surprised whenever I detected the routine of the natural world surviving still."[30]

Brown's raid, trial, and execution energized the abolitionist community. Supporters were happy to find themselves roused from their daily routines by a vicarious experience of Brown's millennial commitment. In addition, Brown's trial and execution provided the impetus for a flurry of political organizing. From the time of Brown's arrest at Harpers Ferry until some weeks after he was executed, public meetings were held in many Northern cities to express solidarity with Brown and to commemorate his martyrdom. These meetings gave the era's most illustrious thinkers and activists an opportunity to renew their assault on slavery. They also provided an occasion for fund-raising.[31] Those attending were often charged a fee at the door and once inside had a chance to buy Brown paraphernalia—photos of Brown or copies of his courtroom speech featuring a facsimile of his signature on the back. As well as raising money for Brown's family, these meetings disseminated commemorative objects that materialized, and thus fostered, the community's attachment to Brown.

The speeches delivered at these meetings often celebrated Brown's raid by describing its restoring effect on a society stupefied by commerce and legalism. Speakers routinely defended Brown's actions by appealing to a "higher law." By acting his conscience in defiance of the law, they argued, Brown renewed the legacy of the founders or—the more frequent claim—that of the austere and devout Puritans, who, in the public imagination, so resembled Brown. In either case, Brown's violence regenerated society by affirming a commitment to original principles that had been degraded by the legal compromises of the 1850s. Thoreau, one of Brown's most ardent supporters, offered an extravagant rendition of these ideas in "A Plea for Captain John Brown." Less than two weeks after Brown's capture, Thoreau convened a public meeting in Concord where he delivered a passionate defense of Brown's raid. Written hastily on the basis of his journal entries, Thoreau's speech combines unbridled praise for Brown's character with a vituperative indictment of contemporary life. Brown's bravery throws the mediocrity of the common citizen into relief; he towers above a people plagued by an "all but universal woodenness of both head and heart."[32] Free of self-interest and undaunted by the prospect of bodily suffering, Brown has no equal.

And yet, even as Thoreau celebrated Brown's unrivaled individual powers, he imagined that in death Brown would communicate his rare sensibility to the public at large. While others, like Child, hoped Brown would be spared, Thoreau feared to "hear of his deliverance, doubting if a prolonged life, if any life, can do as much good as his death."[33] In his "Plea," Thoreau describes the power of Brown's death to rejuvenate public life as an organic process, proclaiming that "in the moral world, when good seed is planted, good fruit is inevitable . . . when you plant, or bury, a hero in his field, a crop of heroes is sure to spring up." He portrays the North as a single body through which Brown's influence, metaphorized as blood, might flow. Echoing Brown's own insistence on blood as a medium of collective meaning, Thoreau proclaims that Brown's "acts and words" have "quickened the feeble pulse of the North, and infused . . . generous blood into her veins and heart."[34] Figuring Brown's body as a source of collective well-being, Thoreau, like many of Brown's defenders, imagines the martyr's death as a life force.

If Brown imagined his own representative body infused by the blood of slaves, his followers imagined Brown's body reinvigorating the antislavery community and inspiring Northerners at large. Brown's supporters proclaimed the martyr's power to generate community in opposition to the law. In doing so, they embraced the idea that insurrectionary violence, the natural outcome of a deeply felt sympathy, might renew American political life. While organic images of growth and circulation provided figures for a nascent Northern nationalism, Southern regional community formed in defense of the law. If Brown's raid prompted increased public demonstration in Northern states, it provoked an unprecedented militarization in the South. In the wake of Brown's raid, Wise was confronted with a number of difficult decisions. At every juncture he chose to escalate rather than pacify sectional animosity: he decided to have Brown tried by a Virginia court rather than turning him over to federal authorities; he repeatedly mobilized the militia during the weeks preceding Brown's execution, thus contributing to an atmosphere of suspicion and hysteria; and he refused to commute Brown's death sentence.[35]

During the weeks before Brown's execution, Wise received countless letters from both Southerners and Northerners urging him not to hang John Brown. They warned that, by executing Brown, Wise would ensure his martyrdom and, consequently, galvanize the antislavery community. This point of view enraged Wise, who argued that Brown's raid should be regarded as the result rather than the cause of Northern solidarity. In a speech to the Virginia legislature two days after Brown's death, Wise defended his decision to execute Brown. Wise asked, "Will execution of the legal sentence of a humane law make martyrs of such criminals? Do sectional and social masses hallow these crimes? Do whole communities sympathize with the outlaws, instead of sympathizing with the outraged society of a sister sovereignty? If so, then the sympathy is as felonious as the criminals, and is far more dangerous than was the invasion. The threat of martyrdom is a threat against our peace, and demands execution to defy such sympathy and such saints of martyrdom . . . Sympathy was in insurrection, and had to be subdued more sternly than was John Brown."[36] In this fierce attack on Northern sympathy, Wise argues that Brown's raid was not, as Republicans asserted, the work of an extremist, but rather an expression of widespread regional hostility.[37] He insists that the raiders were not ruffians or bandits acting alone but representatives of "an extraordinary and actual invasion, by a sectional organization."[38] In his view, the sympathy expressed by Northerners in response to Brown's raid was one instance of the regional consensus that made the raid possible in the first place. While Child and Thoreau found themselves transformed by Brown's unprecedented heroism, Wise, unwilling to accept this model of political influence, maintained that the sensibility of a community might generate seemingly extraordinary acts of violence.

Like Brown's supporters, Wise set sympathy in opposition to the law; unlike them he held that the law must be reasserted with force. Orchestrating the circumstances of Brown's execution, Wise faced an enormous challenge. He not only had to assert the rule of law in an effort to discourage would-be insurrectionaries, but also had to defuse the belief — a cornerstone of sympathetic thought and representation — that a single suffering body might radicalize and animate a vast community. On the one hand, Wise had to deter the actions of an anti-Brown lynch mob that would tar Virginia with the brush of vigilante violence. On the other, he needed to guard against the possibility that Brown's execution would prompt sympathy in a community of spectators. The power of the martyred body to produce strong emotions and, consequently, to incite an unruly community, had to be suppressed: in the process of organizing Brown's execution, Wise did his best to ensure that Brown's death would fortify state authority.

Emotion ran high in Charlestown as Brown's execution approached. Rumor had it that abolitionists were preparing to attack the town and break Brown out of jail. All the same, the mood was festive. Drums beat and music played as soldiers poured into town. The graveyard doubled as a campground where soldiers played cards and ate their meals on headstones. Locals who gathered outside the Baptist church to watch a carpenter build Brown's scaffold hoped to obtain a splinter of wood as a souvenir.[39] John Wilkes Booth was so eager to witness Brown's execution that he borrowed a uniform and talked his friends in the Virginia militia into letting him join them. Passing as a soldier, Booth watched Brown hang.[40]

A hundred years earlier, the day's festivities would have extended to the foot of the scaffold. By midcentury, however, executions were, by and large, conducted privately. While executions once provided an occasion for collective admonition and instruction, people now feared that public punishment would promote unrest and undermine the power of the law.[41] Although Brown's execution was conducted publicly, every effort was made to keep witnesses at a distance. In an attempt to ensure against public violence, Wise stopped just short of imposing martial law in Charlestown. He circulated a proclamation cautioning citizens to remain at home and guard their property. The army took over the Winchester and Potomac railroads, refusing passage to civilians and arresting "strangers" who could not account for themselves. Further militarizing the scene of Brown's execution, Wise deployed 1,500 troops around the scaffold. These preparations ensured that unruly crowds would not gather at the site. A crowd of vengeful residents was hardly more attractive to authorities than a crowd of unruly sympathizers. Virginia represented the law in the face of Brown's lawless aggression and, more significantly, the irreverence and hostility of antislavery Northerners. To allow for any expression of violence from civilians would suggest Brown's power to disrupt civic order and recall the disreputable vigilante customs that had given antiabolitionism a bad name. In his eyewitness account of Brown's execution, David Hunter Strother, the Southern illustrator more commonly known by his pseudonym Porte Crayon, emphasized the difference between the frenetic wrath of a mob and the austere composure of the law in action: "No man capable of reflection could have witnessed that scene without being deeply impressed with the truth that then and there was exhibited, not the vengeance of an outraged people, but the awful majesty of the law."[42]

Guarding against public disorder, Wise also hoped to deny Brown access to the press and, through the press, the Northern public. Reversing a lax policy that had allowed Brown's words and deeds to flow freely to the Northern press, Wise tried to make sure that Northern newspapers

FIGURE I.I. *Alfred Berghaus, "Carrying Prisoners from the Armory to the Railroad Station,"* Frank Leslie's Illustrated Newspaper, *November 12, 1859. West Virginia State Archives, Boyd B. Stutler Collection.*

would not convey Brown's heroism in death. It was not only the spectacle of Brown's execution Wise hoped to suppress, but also the power of his public speech. Although Wise claimed he did not want witnesses caught in the crossfire in the event of a rescue attempt, members of the Northern press believed that witnesses were kept away from the scaffold so that no one would hear what Brown might say in the moments before his death. Noting that only military men would be permitted "within hearing of what Brown may say," a reporter speculated, "why this jealous caution? Can it be that it is feared this old man's sturdy truths and simple eloquence will stir a fever in the blood of all who listen, that shall break down the barriers of prejudice, and shatter their feeble principles like glass?"[43] While Brown promised that he would not speak from the scaffold, Wise could not be sure; with the influence of Brown's courtroom speech still fresh in mind, Wise was determined to avoid a repeat performance.

FIGURE I.2. *W. S. L. Jewett, "Trial of Ossawattamie* [sic] *Brown,"*
Frank Leslie's Illustrated Newspaper, *November 12, 1859.*
West Virginia State Archives, Boyd B. Stutler Collection.

Sentenced to die, Brown attained a certain authority. From the day
of his sentencing until the moment of his execution, the condemned
man speaks from the midst of a violent act suspended and attenuated;
the victim of certain violence that is yet to be performed, the prisoner
awaiting execution can narrate anticipated suffering. Indeed, Brown did
all he could to dramatize his pain. Throughout his trial he lay on a cot
in the middle of the courtroom. At times he closed his eyes or let out
a pained groan. Visual representations of Brown that circulated in the
illustrated press often show him lying down, emphasizing his weak and
injured body. These illustrations construct the weeks preceding Brown's
execution as an extended and eventful deathbed scene (see figs. I.I, I.2).

As if to suppress any emotions that the spectacle of Brown's suffering might provoke, Wise deployed a crowd of armed spectators at the
scene of Brown's death; these soldiers, standing "mute and motionless,"
expressed the power of the state.[44] In the end, however, Wise's order for-

bidding journalists to get close to the scaffold was "partially rescinded," and a handful of reporters were allowed a position near the major general's staff.[45] It is difficult to understand why, at the last moment, they were allowed on the scene. One suspects that even though authorities wanted to deny Northern readers access to the pathos of Brown's execution, they also wanted to use newspaper publicity to display Virginia's military power. Such a display would impress Northerners with the military might of a Southern state while also representing federal authority in the face of treason. The massive military spectacle at the foot of the scaffold might convince spectators near and far that Virginia could bring force and efficiency to its defense of the law. Eyewitness Major Preston testified to the awesome spectacle of state violence: "The field of execution was a rising ground that commanded the out-stretching valley from mountain to mountain, and their still grandeur gave sublimity to the outline . . . Before us was the greatest array of disciplined forces ever seen in Virginia, infantry, cavalry, and artillery combined, composed of the old Commonwealth's choicest sons, and commanded by her best officers, and the great canopy of the sky, overarching all, came to add its sublimity."[46] Ideally then, a huge military presence would at once impress spectators with Virginia's might *and* serve as a buffer to keep spectators from getting too close to the scene of execution.[47]

Spectators could, however, watch Brown's execution from afar. One journalist noted that the field of execution, which he saw from his window, was open to public view. He observed, "Not a tree, save one solitary antiquated thorn tree in the centre, is there to intercept the view so that many of the residents of Charlestown can enjoy the prospect of John Brown's strangulation without leaving their homes."[48] While witnesses were kept from getting too close, Brown's execution remained an emphatically public event. Accordingly, "The Death of John Brown" (fig. 1.3), published in *Frank Leslie's Illustrated Newspaper* on December 10, depicts the execution from a distance. We view the scaffold from the far end of the field, looking across hundreds of soldiers standing in formation. The foreground is occupied by two groups of civilians who stand chatting, seemingly uninterested in the proceedings. They stand just behind a line of cavalry soldiers. Only a few of these men appear to be interested in Brown's hanging. Others glance off to the side, distracted by something happening nearby, or engage in casual conversation. At some distance from these observers—whose posture and expression we are able to examine in some detail—we see troops lined up around the scaffold, their disciplined gaze trained on the victim. These soldiers appear

FIGURE I.3. *"The Death of John Brown,"* Frank Leslie's Illustrated Newspaper, *December 10, 1859. Neg. #29062, Collection of The New-York Historical Society.*

to us in miniature—we note their rigid posture as they stand at attention, but cannot discern their expressions. The interested viewer must traverse a field of spectatorial models before arriving at the body in question. When our gaze reaches Brown himself, we may be somewhat disappointed: his body is an undifferentiated black splotch at the far side of this military display. Although the executioner is engaged in some action, we cannot tell whether he is letting Brown's body fall, or raising it up again. The features of Brown's body, and of the event itself, are subordinated to an examination of the crowd that gathers at the scaffold.

Wise imagines the community of Northern sympathizers as yet another violent mob that must be kept at a distance from the prisoner. What he does not understand is that the space between Brown's body and the spectating community may incite, rather than suppress, a potentially inflammatory sympathy. While "The Death of John Brown" turns its attention away from Brown's corpse and toward the display of military power, this distance may urge the viewer to work harder to imagine Brown's death. As I have argued, sentimental representations of suffering rely on the distance between victim and viewer to provoke the viewer's imaginative exertions. Far from diluting the effect of Brown's execution, the military barrier presents a familiar challenge to those schooled in the conventions of sentimental reading: how to envision the suffering body that is not in full view.

The vast space between scaffold and spectator allows for the abstraction of the body that is the essence of martyrdom. Melville's poem "The Portent" (1859) anatomizes the process through which the absent body acquires meaning. Nowhere else is the elision of Brown's corpse expressed with more formal precision and linked more explicitly to the breadth of its political meaning. Melville begins with a lurid evocation of Brown's body:

> Hanging from the beam,
> Slowly swaying (such the law),
> Gaunt the shadow on your green,
> Shenandoah!"[49]

There is, however, no subject in these opening lines, no noun or pronoun to realize the body's presence in language. Instead of "the corpse" or "his body," we are offered "the shadow." Brown's body is available only in the darkness cast on the land ("Shenandoah!") by its passing. In the second stanza Brown's face is again "Hidden in the cap" and analogized to Virginia's "veiled" future. In the absence of the literal body, the meaning of Brown's corpse grows. It comes to signify a future of apocalyptic violence. In retrospect, the military spectacle intended to control Brown's power seems instead to embody it; standing in for Brown's body, this group of soldiers—yet another community brought into being by Brown's actions—testifies, unwittingly, to his influence.

≈ On December 2, one month after delivering his courtroom speech, Brown was escorted to the scaffold where, surrounded by 1,500 cavalry and militia, he was executed. According to *Harper's Weekly*, by the time Brown reached the field, "the military had already full possession. Pickets were established, and citizens kept back, at the point of bayonet, from taking any position but that assigned to them."[50] Brown expressed his dismay that citizens were not allowed near the scaffold. But he was not about to miss his last opportunity to speak to the public he had recently cultivated. Outsmarting the governor was probably the last thing on Brown's mind, but once again he managed to dwarf Wise's appeal to law and order. Leaving prison, he handed a scrap of paper to one of his guards. It read: "I John Brown am now quite certain that the crimes of this guilty, land: will never be purged away; but with Blood. I had as I now think: vainly flattered myself that without verry [sic] much bloodshed; it might be done."[51]

On the morning of his execution Brown spoke not in imitation of Christ's selfless love but with the unrelenting voice of his own Calvinist God: in his last public utterance, blood was not the medium of sympathy but of retribution. On the scaffold, Brown represented both a suffering slave population and a guilty white nation. Because he was a white man, the act of self-sacrifice doubled as an act of penance; to suffer in concert with slaves was also to pay a historical debt for the injuries whites had inflicted on slaves.

Pointing toward the massive violence of the Civil War, Brown's last statement has been read as prophetic. When read alongside his court-room address, it suggests the transformation that the rhetoric of suffering underwent during the war years. As the bodies mounted, a theological emphasis on Christ's love as a model for human compassion failed to account for the crisis. Those responsible for narrating the war—from politicians to poets—conjured a punitive God who exacts obedience in the form of human suffering.

Whereas Brown's courtroom speech imagines the eradication of suffering, his final statement predicts its nationalization. As I have argued, however, these two renderings of blood sacrifice are not as different as they might at first appear. Indeed, when Brown proclaims that bloodshed will "purge" the nation's guilt, he extends the implications of his court-room speech, which describes blood as the medium of common pain. Sympathetic identification entails the imagined dissemination of violence, as represented pain is communicated to an unimplicated reader. Valorizing substitutions in which those who have not suffered stand in for those who have, the practice of sympathy lays the cultural groundwork for a nationalist vision of martyrdom as the basis for collective unity.[52] In both contexts, pain, transformed from a singular into a universal condition, provides a source of common identity.

In a sermon commemorating Brown's death, Fales Henry Newhall used blood to represent the transformation of slave suffering into national suffering: "For years and generations God has been bottling these tears [of slaves], and if he returns them to us in showers of blood, who will dare to murmur at his justice? The tears and the blood of the strong and of the weak, of the white and of the black, are alike to Him 'who hath made of one blood all nations of men.'"[53] Here blood at once punishes the errant community and substantiates a biblical rendering of national identity in which all are "alike" in God's view. Brown expressed a similar view of the relationship between violence, equality, and national identity when he explained to Franklin Sanborn that the Golden Rule and the Declaration of Independence, identical in their thoroughgoing commitment to equality, augured apocalyptic destruction. "That is the doctrine, sir," he announced, referring to sacred and secular laws in a single breath, "and rather than have that fail in the world, or in these States, 't would be better for a whole generation to die a violent death."[54] Violence, in Newhall's view and in Brown's own, realizes a God-given homogeneity that is, in turn, the source of national identity. Retributive violence not only visits bloodshed on a guilty community, thus evening the historical score, but it also redistributes and equalizes pain, suggesting the possibility of commonality achieved not, for example, through property ownership, but through violence applied evenly, over time, to blacks and whites.

On the occasion of Abraham Lincoln's death, Ralph Waldo Emerson compared Brown's courtroom speech to the Gettysburg Address.[55] Indeed, both are powerful meditations on the power of the martyred body, stripped of its particular identity, to generate political community. At Gettysburg, Lincoln asked living patriots to rededicate themselves to the unfinished business of war by following the example of the anonymous dead who "gave their lives so that the nation might live."[56] While Lincoln struck the perfect note at Gettysburg, he had been thinking about the relationship between physical suffering and political community for a long time. In his Address to the Young Men's Lyceum of Springfield, delivered in 1838, Lincoln imagined that the spectacular suffering of wounded soldiers might contribute to national stability. Worried over the prospect of civic unrest in post-Revolutionary America, Lincoln argued for obedience to the law. And yet his shrill insistence on the virtue of the law and his sensational renderings of the dangers that assail it suggest Lincoln's uneasiness about the law's power to maintain stability. Toward the end of the speech, he turns to the wounded bodies of Revolutionary War veterans, describing their power to unify a national public. "At the close of that struggle," Lincoln writes, "nearly every adult male had been a participator in some of its scenes. The consequence was, that of those scenes, in the form of a husband, a father, a son or a brother, a living history was to be found in every family—a history bearing the indubitable testimonies of its own authenticity, in the limbs mangled, in the scars of wounds received, in the midst of the very scenes related." Lincoln imagines that during the Revolutionary era the bodies of wounded war veterans rededicated citizens to founding principles. Unlike the abstruse text of the law, or the arcane history book, these illustrative bodies offered a history that could be "read and understood alike by all, the wise and the ignorant, the learned and the unlearned." Lincoln is concerned, however, over what will happen when these bodies disappear and "can be read no more forever." Comparing the old soldiers to giant oaks leveled by a hurricane, Lincoln laments that while one now finds, "here and there, a lonely trunk," soon they all will "sink, and be no more."[57] Extolling the power of the soldier's wounded body to attach citizens to the state, Lincoln mourns the disappearance of that body.

By the time that Lincoln arrived in Gettysburg, however, he understood that the features of the body—dead or wounded—had little to do with its capacity to motivate an audience. Lincoln's brief speech makes no mention of the particulars of the battle or the actions and identities of individual soldiers. Years earlier, Lincoln had longed for the distinctive bodies of wounded soldiers whose scars would tell the story of war to the uninitiated. Invested in the form of the wounded body, Lincoln assumed that when the body disappeared its communicative powers were lost. At Gettysburg, the identity of the dead body and the particulars of its demise have no place. What remains important, however, is the ability of the dead to sustain community. The brevity of Lincoln's address suggests humility: what is there to say, he implies, in the face of such profound loss? Observing that "in a larger sense, we can not dedicate—we can not consecrate—we can not hallow—this ground," Lincoln describes a nation of mourners similarly humbled by the spectacle of mass death. While Lincoln portrays himself and his fellows as nearly immobilized by the tragedy of war, he grants tremendous agency to those buried at Gettysburg. Having declared his inability to commemorate the dead adequately, Lincoln asks those gathered to take "from these honored dead . . . increased devotion." This devotion, directed to the Union cause, ensures that the nation will have "a new birth of freedom."[58] In the absence of any individualizing features, the Gettysburg dead exert great influence. As in "John Brown's Body," which enacts the power of the martyred body to inspire a living army, these unidentified corpses nourish the will of the community.

During the war years, Lincoln reconceptualizes *citizenship* as a form of dependence based not on the individual's claim to rights but on the "heroism of self-subordination."[59] Abstracting the materiality of violent death and redefining *national citizenship* as an exercise in self-surrender, Lincoln not only enables identifications between the living and the dead indispensable to the war's continuation, but also disavows the state's responsibility for wartime losses. The power of the dead to inspire the living effectively obscures the power of the state to inflict violence on its citizens: in the Gettysburg Address, the nation appears to be (re)generated by the sacrifices it, in truth, demands. Civil War scholars have often subjected the war itself to a similar abstraction, viewing wartime violence as the source of a revitalized national identity. Robert Penn Warren, for example, asserted that the Civil War created the nation as we know it. "Before the Civil War," he writes, "we had no history in the deepest and most inward sense." The "dream of freedom" articulated by both the Declaration of Independence and the Constitution remained unrealized; the founding fathers had failed to "create a nation except on paper." Violence was needed to transform these abstractions, which existed only in language, into "'felt' history—history lived in the national imagination." Only through the direct and costly experience of war did America gain a "real" past and, consequently, a "real" identity: the vision of the founders "became a reality, and we became a nation, only with the Civil War."[60] If war's violence gave body to founding abstractions, it in turn transformed the materiality of historical event into an edifying ideal. The Civil War offers ample evidence of "rancor, self-righteousness, spite, pride . . . and complacency," but out of the "complex and confused motives of men and the blind ruck of event," the ideal of union emerged (108). Although this ideal remained unrealized, it, in Warren's view, continued to orient and inspire the way Americans thought about themselves and their nation. Violence converts historical event, in all its messy complexity and contradiction, into consensus regarding the possibility, if not the reality, of an American community.[61]

By imagining dead bodies transformed into collective spirit, both "John Brown's Body" and the Gettysburg Address make the counterintuitive, if familiar, claim that violence gives life, creating community rather than destroying it. During the Civil War, an organic model of civic unity, governed by the principles of transformation and growth, helped to convince the public that self-sacrifice was a source of collective renewal. I have retold the story of Brown's death, situated between a period of intense struggle over slavery and the war itself, in an effort to historicize and interrogate the belief that suffering creates community. Rather than suggesting, as Warren does, that mass death generates new ideas, I have tried to show how certain ideas and rhetorical conventions, popular before the war began, helped to make violence possible. The notion that the deaths of thousands of soldiers can generate national identity is indebted, in part, to the work of abolitionists, including Brown himself, who tried to figure out how to transform pain into political agency. Brown employed the conventions of sympathy, used by abolitionists to represent the violence done to slaves, to describe his own death. Both abolitionists and soldiers, in turn, took up his martyrdom as the source of their political commitment and camaraderie. Yet the consequences of the appropriation and abstraction of slave suffering were by no means uniform; if sympathy reliably intimates the power of individual suffering to generate group identity, its applications vary widely. In Brown's hands, the substitution of white bodies for black was the cornerstone of white militancy—a commitment to ending slavery through violence. By contrast, in the context of a wartime rhetoric of self-sacrifice and redemption, the absence of black bodies suggests the tendency of Civil War culture to suppress the importance of slavery while taking the suffering of slaves as a model for the suffering of soldiers.

As the enduring popularity of "John Brown's Body" suggests, Governor Wise failed to subdue Brown; in the months following his execution, Brown's public stature continued to grow. Indeed, in 1861 Wise himself urged fellow Southerners to "take a lesson from John Brown" and resist a Northern invasion with force.[62] While Brown's execution failed to fortify the rule of law in the face of insurrection, his death sustained the state during war. "John Brown's Body" is one expression of a wartime nationalism that derives not from the law's ability to maintain order or implement justice but from the willingness of citizens to sacrifice themselves in the name of the state. Abolitionists disseminated the pain of slaves in an effort to build a community that would put an end to slavery. But as the war approached and the cause of antislavery dovetailed with a growing sectional antagonism, violence began to appear to abolitionists and others as a solution to the conflicts at hand. In the context of war, the insistent abstraction of violence, performed by sympathy and nationalism alike, goes hand in hand with its actual proliferation: the martyred bodies of slaves and soldiers fuel an apocalyptic nationalism that takes violence as the basis for collectivity rather than imagining collectivity as a means of putting suffering to rest.

THE BLOOD OF BLACK MEN
RETHINKING RACIAL SCIENCE

2

When 3,000 mourners gathered in an Oberlin church to observe the death of John Copeland, they looked on an empty casket. Friends listened not to celebratory tales of triumphant martyrdom but to Oberlin professor James Monroe's account of his fruitless attempt to obtain Copeland's body. Copeland's parents had begged Monroe to travel to Virginia to retrieve their son's corpse; in addition, his father wrote to Virginia governor Henry Wise to request that the body be sent back to Ohio. Despite these appeals, Copeland's body, like that of his comrade Shields Green, was disinterred by medical students and taken to the Winchester Medical College for dissection. On the day of their execution, the *New York Daily Tribune* reported matter-of-factly: "They will be interred tomorrow on the spot where the gallows stand, but there is a party of medical students here from Winchester who will doubtless not allow them to remain there long."

The burial of Brown's corpse, commemorated by "John Brown's Body," allowed mourners to participate in the process of abstraction that, as I have argued, renders violence meaningful. If martyrdom entailed the gradual abstraction of the dead body as it came to signify shared emotion and experience, penal dissection undermined the rituals and beliefs that gave death its spiritual and social significance. Denied a grave from which to be resurrected, John Copeland and Shields Green were shut out of religious narratives of regeneration that imagined the body, buried in the soil, rising again, as well as secular narratives that took the corpse's decay as a figure for collective renewal. Likewise, friends and family who mourned Copeland's death were unable to tend his corpse and, in doing so, express grief and cultivate memory in conventional ways.

A practice that reaches back to early modern Europe, penal dissection extends the course of retribution to the criminal's afterlife.[1] During the nineteenth century, as anatomy became increasingly important to the study of medicine, dissection removed the body from commemorative settings in order to establish it as a source of useful knowledge. In the context of anatomy, dissection transformed the dead body, an object of sympathy and identification, into an instrument of professional expertise. Not surprisingly, those least empowered and without the protection of family and community were most often the victims of dissection: the bodies of criminals, the poor, people of color, and the homeless were routinely subjected to the anatomist's knife.

Robert Christies, a medical student at the Winchester Medical College during the 1850s, described the terror with which African American inhabitants of Winchester regarded "doctor students" like himself. Boasting of his midnight raids on the graves of his black neighbors, Christies wrote, "They could not understand, in their simple way of thinking, how a part of the body here, and a part there; how the flesh and skin after being disrespectfully used, and thrown into a sink, and promiscuously mixed up with like parts of others with whom they were not acquainted, or on speaking terms—the arm bones in some doctor's office, the leg in some other doctor's, and, the skull in still another's, and it sometimes used by unmerciful students as a candle-stick, with a candle in the foramen magnum occipitis; how all these heterogeneous and scattered parts, all mixed up indiscriminately could be got together without making mistakes."[2] Christies takes a mean delight in exposing the "simple" superstitions of his victims: black inhabitants of Winchester wondered how God would recognize the believer if her body did not appear intact on Judgment Day. Mocking these fears, Christies dramatizes the anatomist's power to deny the social nature of the corpse; reduced to its constituent parts, the dissected body appears to be dead matter that, in the absence of an animating identity, can be put to varied uses.

In this chapter, I will argue that dissection is a significant, if underexamined, form of racial violence used during the antebellum period to terrorize African and Native Americans and justify their continued subjugation. If dissection helped to promote a utilitarian attitude toward the dead it also contributed to the growth of scientific racism, which came into its own during this period. Racial scientists dissected the bodies of African and Native Americans in an effort to establish the inferiority of nonwhite people. Taking careful measurements of skeletons, they inferred the intellectual and moral deficiencies of various ethnic groups.

In the case of Copeland and Green, the anatomist's knife suppressed the spectacle of black martyrdom; more broadly, ethnologists scrutinized the remains of the dead in an effort to invent a black subject incapable of intelligent, sustained resistance.

During the early nineteenth century, the bodies of African and Native American insurrectionaries were routinely subjected to postmortem dissection. After Denmark Vesey and twenty-two of his followers were executed in South Carolina in 1822, their bodies were dissected; Seminole insurgent Osceola was dissected after his death in 1838; thirty-eight Sioux Indians executed in Mankato, Minnesota, in 1862 (the largest mass execution in U.S. history) were unearthed and dissected by local doctors; and it seems likely that Nat Turner came under the anatomist's knife. While most anatomical specimens were roughly handled and carelessly discarded, the body parts of famed insurrectionaries became prized possessions—studied and admired as they were passed from one generation to the next. Distinguished by his bravery and mental powers, the insurrectionary presented a particular challenge to essentialist accounts of racial difference. By enacting violence that could not be deduced from physical attributes or behavior, insurgents gave the lie to theories of racial inferiority.

Turning the corpse into an object of study, dissection staged the triumph of science over the insurgent: the urge to take possession, inherent in the diagnostic gaze, was rendered explicit as doctors became collectors who proudly displayed the remains of their dead. At the scene of punishment, however, insurrectionaries gave voice to their ongoing inscrutability and power. This chapter will consider a handful of texts—Herman Melville's "Benito Cereno," David Walker's *Appeal to the Coloured Citizens of the World*, *The Confessions of Nat Turner*, and Copeland's own prison letters—that portray the insurgent mind in the face of death. While the purposes of these texts vary greatly, all of them view insurrection in relation to knowledge and all claim a radically expanded interiority for the insurgent subject.

Abolitionist writers often represented the physical and emotional pain of slaves in order to produce compassion and, by extension, resistance to slavery. The whipping post and the auction block provided representative sites of violence: corporal punishment demonstrated the bodily pain inflicted on slaves, and the separation of family members provided its emotional equivalent. Racial scientists, by contrast, violated the dead rather than the living, thus causing pain that was psychic, or symbolic, and highly abstract. Rather than separating individual family members, ethnologists divided humankind by defining ethnic groups as different species. The literature of insurrection responds to the far-reaching ambitions of racial science—to use the racialized corpse to establish a hierarchy of species—by laying claim not to the enslaved body but to disembodied knowledge. Writers who took insurrection, rather than reform, as the means of abolishing slavery critiqued the objectification of black bodies and claimed the critical gaze for the black subject. Inverting the relationship between the scientist and the object of study, these texts mount an aggressive critique of ethnological inquiry. In doing so, they pave the way for narratives of racial apocalypse that describe the insurgent mind as a conduit for God's agency, and insurrection as the instrument of divine retribution.

⬥ On the morning of his execution, Copeland wrote a letter of consolation to his family. One imagines that, like Brown, Copeland felt the urge to explain himself, and perhaps secure his own legacy. His letters, again like Brown's, circulated in the antislavery press and were intended for a private audience—Copeland's own family—as well as an abolitionist public. Addressed to his father and mother, three brothers, and two sisters, this letter describes Copeland's equanimity in the face of death. He assures his loved ones that "God in his mercy has spoken peace to my soul" and promises that the pain of death will be easily transcended when they are reunited in heaven. He anticipates meeting his brother and sister, already deceased, before his letter has reached its destination, and urges surviving family members to prepare themselves so that "though we meet no more on earth, we shall meet in Heaven, where we shall not be parted by the demands of the cruel and unjust monster Slavery."[3] Emphasizing the "ties of blood and relationship" that Copeland views as "the strongest that God ever instituted," this letter champions the redemptive power of familial love in the face of state execution.

Copeland tries to offer his family an exemplary death in which he calmly accepts his fate, assures them that his spiritual house is in order, and anticipates their happy reunion in the afterlife.[4] He portrays death and life as continuous, and expresses his confidence that family ties will survive the transition. Employing the familiar sentimental trope of a family divided by slave powers, he looks forward to meeting with his loved ones after death. Despite these comforting words, his family was tormented by the possibility that Copeland's body would be dissected. According to James Monroe, who agreed to travel to Virginia to retrieve Copeland's corpse, Copeland's death on the scaffold placed him in the company of "great and good men," like Brown himself, and was thus "a tolerable affliction" to his parents. The prospect of dissection, to the contrary, inflicted more "torture . . . than the brain and heart could endure."[5]

In order to fully understand the violence suffered by Copeland and, by extension, his parents, siblings, and friends, we must consider the dissection of his corpse in the context of nineteenth-century death customs. In the antebellum United States, a Christian narrative of burial and resurrection went hand in hand with a broader commitment to the continuity between this life and the next: people imagined the afterlife as a parallel sphere where the dead retained their identity. Beautifying the corpse, and then gazing on it, mourners fixed the identity of the dead in the mind's eye; producing a range of memorial objects to recall the dead, they fostered an ongoing sense of kinship. Using the corpse itself as an expressive medium, mourners demonstrated the continuity between life and death, asserting an undying love that flew in the face of the body's demise.

During the first half of the nineteenth century, greater geographical mobility led to the wider incidence of contagious disease. As a result, between 1790 and 1860 life expectancy declined dramatically from fifty-six to forty-eight years.[6] Perhaps in response to these difficult conditions, during this same period people viewed death as an opportunity to exercise spiritual agency. At the moment of death, spiritual identity was fixed for all time; religious instruction asked individuals to meditate on death and, in doing so, prepare to die well.[7] Ideally, the dying person, triumphing over pain and fear, would express her willingness to die. In this way, she embraced God's will and demonstrated spiritual resilience. Family, friends, and religious counselors gathered around the deathbed to offer reassurance and to witness the dying person's spiritual condition at the moment of death. Adequate proof that she was heaven bound gave consolation to those left behind.[8]

The death scene was one of heightened awareness in which the dying offered appropriate signs that witnesses observed carefully. Efforts to beautify the corpse in order to produce lasting images expressed a similar urge on the part of survivors to control the bodily disposition of the departed soul. After death, family members, usually women, washed, groomed, and dressed the corpse in preparation for an open-casket funeral. Friends and relatives kept watch over the corpse around the clock for between one and three days.[9] Wealthier families might commission a postmortem portrait, and, by the 1850s, corpses were often photographed. Like the deathbed scene, the convention of the "last look" shaped the experience of loss. Just as the spiritual condition of the dying person was fixed at the moment of death, her identity was fixed in the mind of the mourner, who looked not once but any number of times on the dead body. The vigil, open-casket funeral, photograph, and portrait all helped survivors cultivate an image of the dead that resembled the once-living person as nearly as possible.

At the same time, mourners offered up the spectacle of their own grief to the gaze of their larger community. Mourning clothing and stationery, black crepe, funeral wreaths, and postmortem daguerreotypes provided signs of recent loss. Increasingly, these displays involved the purchase of mass-marketed, standardized goods. Efforts to beautify the corpse and its domestic surroundings were part and parcel of the commodification of mourning and signified a cultural authority not readily disentangled from class privilege. Poems, photographs, black-clad parlors, and corpses themselves offered proof of the mourner's spiritual and monetary resources. Far from expressing the humility of the survivor in the face of death's immensity, these displays demonstrated her ability not only to cope with disease, mortality, and loss but also to create beauty from these painful circumstances.

Mourners did not ignore the corpse or deny the difficult aspects of dying and its aftermath. To the contrary, they used the corpse to demonstrate the power of affection, and artistry, to create continuity out of crisis. The corpse—cold, stiff, pallid—signaled the difference between dead and living bodies. Attempting to beautify and reanimate it, mourners softened the effects of death on the body and gave form to the belief that there was little change in death.[10] The home was not, however, the only place where attitudes toward the dead took shape. In the medical school classroom, the anatomical museum, and the illustrated volumes of ethnologists, the dissected cadaver was objectified not in the service of memory but in that of science.[11] If, as Foucault has argued, public torture was "an art of unbearable sensations" intended to protract and elaborate the experience of pain to the very limit of human endurance, dissection pursued the body past the realm of sensation: the anatomist violated the body without eliciting any response at all, proving it to be vacant and lifeless.[12] Dissection dramatized the body's inability to feel pain and thus to remain connected, however tenuously, to the world of the living. While domestic death rituals employed the corpse's materiality as an expressive medium intended to manifest the relatedness between the living and the dead, dissection denied the social nature of the corpse.

During the second half of the eighteenth century, with the establishment of the first medical colleges and the advent of public courses and lectures in anatomy, the demand for corpses increased dramatically. As scientists began to abandon broadly applicable theories of the body's structure and function in favor of empirical data, they turned their attention to close observation of the particular body and its individual disturbances. As the study of pathology grew, autopsy became a crucial part of medical training.[13] In the past, anatomy students had mastered an abstract, descriptive account of the body's structure. The new practical anatomy emphasized direct experience of the body and the application of anatomical knowledge. Anatomy professors insisted that dissection was the "great essential" of anatomical study; without repeated hands-on experience with cadavers, students would be inadequately prepared to ply their trade.[14]

Throughout the nineteenth century, however, Northern and Southern medical colleges faced a critical shortage of dead bodies. As a result of fierce competition among medical schools, an institution's reputation, and thus its ability to attract medical students, depended on the availability of teaching specimens. While medical colleges used the promise of free medical care to attract black and poor white patients, obtaining cadavers for dissection proved a greater challenge. In response to this crisis, doctors and administrators employed grave robbers, or drafted young medical students, to steal bodies from morgues and cemeteries. Grave robbers—often referred to as "resurrectionists"—violated the burial grounds of the least powerful, raiding black cemeteries and "potter's fields" where the indigent were laid to rest.[15]

Dissection, increasingly important to the practice of medicine, was deplored by the public at large. Indeed, the controversy over dissection provided a flash point for competing attitudes toward dead bodies: were they sacred objects that must be properly commemorated, or were they the source of valuable scientific expertise? There is no underestimating the heat generated by these opposing views. The New York Doctors' Riot of 1788 was the first in a series of riots, occurring throughout the nineteenth century, in which citizens protested the unregulated abuse of the dead. Months before the Doctors' Riot, free blacks petitioned the city to stop medical students from raiding African American burial grounds. They proposed an alternative source of cadavers, suggesting that felons be sentenced to postmortem dissection. In the wake of the riots, the New York state legislature took up this suggestion, declaring grave robbing a criminal offense and authorizing the courts to turn the bodies of criminals executed for murder, arson, or burglary over to surgeons for dissection.[16] In 1790, a similar statute was passed by Congress, giving federal judges the power to add dissection to the sentence of a convicted murderer.[17]

By institutionalizing the longstanding practice of dissecting criminal corpses, the state tried at once to appease public outrage over grave robbing and to supply cadavers for scientific study. There were not enough of these bodies, however, to redress the shortage, and states began to pass anatomy acts that turned all unclaimed bodies over to medical practitioners. Anatomy legislation identified people without homes or families as the appropriate candidates for dissection.[18] In 1831, Massachusetts became the first state to sponsor an anatomy act, and a number of states quickly followed suit. Many states, however, repealed their anatomy laws almost as soon as they went into effect. If the work of grave robbers was objectionable, legally sanctioned dissection was no less abhorrent to a public fundamentally opposed to such experimentation.[19]

The halting development of anatomy legislation throughout the course of the nineteenth century expressed both the state's increasing identification with the interests of medical science and the public's continued resistance to the medicalization of the dead.[20] While failing to fully redress the problem of grave robbing, new legislation that offered up unclaimed bodies for scientific research signaled the government's growing interest in the dead: as cadavers became more valuable, the state became increasingly involved in legislating their use. At midcentury, however, competition over the ownership and appropriate use of the corpse continued to rage. Doctors and legislators advocated a utilitarian view of the dead, using the notion of the "public good" to justify and promote anatomy, while a disapproving public remained committed to the integrity of the dead body.[21]

It was only after the Civil War that a significant number of states passed anatomy acts that remained in place, and by the beginning of the twentieth century the practice of grave robbing had abated.[22] The legal remedy to the problem of grave robbing at last took hold: people who had no family to bury them came to be accepted as the appropriate subjects of anatomical study. The advent of the category "unclaimed" would, in the end, provide a population of corpses large enough to satisfy the needs of medical schools while also obscuring the fact that these bodies belonged disproportionately to black and poor people. State legislation formulated a particular kind of dead body, defined by the absence of family ties, that need not be given the care or attention typically afforded the corpse. While domestic death rituals gave enduring form to the particular identity of the dead individual, the scientific establishment, in concert with the law, worked to erase the signs of social identity that politicized the production of anatomical knowledge.

≈ If dissection helped to promote a utilitarian attitude toward the dead, it also contributed to the growth of scientific racism, which came into its own during this period.[23] While anatomists stripped the dead of identity and social context, ethnologists recontextualized the dead by using skeletons to establish racial types. Racial scientists dismembered and analyzed the bodies of nonwhite people in order to legitimate pseudoscientific theories of racial difference and justify both slavery and the dispossession of Indian tribes.[24]

At their most extreme, racial scientists asserted the doctrine of polygenesis, which held that God had created humans not once, but a number of times.[25] If racial difference was the result of separate creations it stood to reason that inequality was God's intention. Thus racial scientists tentatively resolved the contradiction that had plagued American political life since the Revolution: how to reconcile the assertion that "all men are created equal" with the practice of enslavement? Their answer: blacks were not human, and, therefore, the Declaration of Independence did not apply to them. The rise of racial science established inequality as a fact of nature, divinely sanctioned and, by definition, beyond the reach of political remedy.

As early as 1787, Thomas Jefferson called on scientists to study the black body in order to definitively establish the inferiority of black people. In Query 14 of *Notes on the State of Virginia*, Jefferson details the physical, intellectual, and emotional inferiority of blacks at great length. He summarizes his thoughts on racial difference, however, with a note of caution when he concludes, "The opinion, that they are inferior in the faculties of reason and imagination, must be hazarded with great diffidence." He goes on to explain, "To justify a general conclusion, requires many observations, even where the subject may be submitted to the Anatomical knife, to Optical glasses, to analysis by fire or by solvents. How much more then where it is a faculty, not a substance, we are examining; where it eludes the research of all the senses; where the conditions of its existence are various and variously combined; where the effects of those which are present or absent bid defiance to calculation; let me add too, as a circumstance of great tenderness, where our conclusion would degrade a whole race of men from the rank in the scale of beings which their Creator may perhaps have given them."[26] The distinction between substances, which can be easily observed, and faculties, which are far more "elusive," does not, however, lead Jefferson to forgo empirical observation. Indeed, Jefferson worries that in regard to questions of race it has not been pursued vigorously enough: "To our reproach it must be said, that though for a century and a half we have had under our eyes the races of black and of red men, they have never yet been viewed by us as subjects of natural history" (143). In the hope of being able to assert the inferiority of blacks with more confidence, Jefferson calls for the assiduous application of scientific method to the subject of race.[27]

If a sense of uncertainty dogs Jefferson's assertions, the anatomical knife, historically viewed, provided the empirical evidence he craved. Samuel George Morton, the "father" of ethnology in the United States, built his career on the meticulous measurement of the skulls of different ethnic groups. *Crania Americana*, published in 1839, described and compared the skulls of native tribes of the Americas in an effort to demonstrate the inferiority of American Indians.[28] In order to obtain these specimens, Morton put out a call to physicians practicing in the West to send him all the Indian skulls they could find. Collectors were hired to search tribal burial grounds of Native Americans who had died in recent epidemics.[29] Morton filled these skulls with white pepper seed and lead shot in order to determine their internal capacity. On the basis of his conclusions about cranial size and structure, he argued that Indians were a separate and inferior race.

Discerning the features of the dead body was not, however, an end in itself. Measuring the human skull with precision, Morton did not hesitate to infer the dimensions of human character, or what Jefferson refers to as "faculties." Indeed, the men who pioneered American ethnology sought not only to define the physical attributes of racial types but also to use the body's features to gauge intellectual faculties, emotional traits, and behavior. They had designs not only on the dimensions of the racialized body but also on properties of mind. Their interest in delineating faculties as well as substances found expression in their fascination with the human skull, which at once revealed and symbolized subjectivity.[30] Devoting great attention to the human head, the "new school" of American ethnology scrutinized and measured the skull in an effort to determine the character of the racialized subject in all its breadth.

Anatomists exploited the bodies of the powerless as they worked to produce a serviceable corpse devoid of identity. Ethnologists, by contrast, aimed to establish, rather than ignore, the identity of the dissected body. If, in the context of anatomy, dissection shattered identity, in the

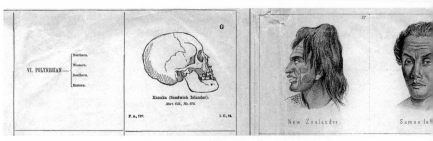

FIGURE 2.1. *From the "Ethnographic Tableau" in Josiah Nott and*
George R. Gliddon's Indigenous Races of the Earth *(1857).*
Special Collections, University of Virginia.

context of ethnology it reinstated character, reanimating the skeleton as
a racial type. The illustrations that fill the important ethnological texts
of the nineteenth century suggest an urge to reconstruct the features
of the anatomical specimen, thus endowing dead bodies with character.
Josiah Nott and George Gliddon's *Types of Mankind* (1854) and *Indige-*
nous Races of the Earth (1857), like Morton's volume, are adorned by
detailed drawings of the skulls that they used in their work. As Samuel
Otter observes, these illustrations imply a strange investment in the impenetrable beauty, the very thingness, of the skeleton.[31] Will the skull,
expressionless and mute, give up the secrets it seems to simultaneously
promise and withhold?

As if to underscore the difficulty of extracting evidence of character
from dead bones, skulls are often juxtaposed to illustrations of the living
ethnographic subject. For example, *Indigenous Races of the Earth* features an "Ethnographic Tableau," subtitled "Specimens of Various Races
of Mankind." On the left, we find black-and-white drawings of a particular kind of skull—"Eskimo," "German," "Blackfoot Indian," "Australian,"
and so on. To the right of a given skull appear six color portraits of the
heads of men from related ethnic groups. The skull of the "Sandwich
Islander" is accompanied by portraits of a "Samoa-Islander," a "Tikopia-
Islander," a "Vanikoro-Islander," and other South Pacific islanders (fig.
2.1). While organized by type, these six portraits bear no resemblance to
one another. Each has a distinctive facial expression, and carefully rendered costumes and hairstyles convey cultural specificity. Although these
are offered up as portraits of generic types, it is impossible not to look at
them and see portraits of expressive individuals.

Reminding readers that the skulls ethnologists study once belonged
to living men, these illustrations foreground, rather than repress, the

violence inflicted on the ethnological subject. Although these portraits posit an essence or identity that will not readily conform to the tools of pseudoscientific investigation, the text contends that ethnic groups have particular features—both physical and intellectual—that can be quantified and are determining. In this context, the vivacity and idiosyncrasy of these illustrations intimate the persistence and skill required to overcome, and finally capture, the qualities of self that would seem to defy categorization. Portraits that reanimate the dead subject dramatize not only the physical violence perpetrated on the dead but also the conceptual violence of reducing them to types.

By enacting resistance that could not be deduced from the body's features, insurrectionaries threatened to topple the central tenets of racial science. If internal qualities are expressed by the human frame, how can the insurgent go undetected? And if African and Native Americans are intellectually inferior, how can they effectively plot to kill? These questions may go some distance toward accounting for the record of strange encounters between medical men and the corpses of African and Native American insurgents. Copeland's body, valued by his family and community, was also prized by the Winchester medical students who were willing to go to great lengths to keep it. Shortly after arriving in Winchester, Monroe met with the faculty of the college. They agreed, unanimously, to return Copeland's body to his parents; the corpse would be delivered to Monroe by nine o'clock the following morning. Early the next morning, however, a group of medical students called on Monroe at his hotel. They informed him that the faculty had no right to turn over Copeland's body because the corpse belonged to them: they had broken into the dissecting rooms of the college the night before and, once again, stolen Copeland's body. Their spokesperson explained, "Me and my chums nearly had to fight to get him. The Richmond medical students came to Charlestown determined to have him. I stood over the grave with a revolver in my hand while my chums dug him up. Now, sah, after risking our lives in this way, for the Faculty to attempt to take him from us, is mo' 'an we can b'ar."[32] After reconvening with the faculty, who believed that under the circumstances further efforts to recover the body would throw "the whole country about us" into "a state of excitement," Monroe decided to give up and return home (172).

Copeland's body was, like all corpses, a valuable commodity in the eyes of these medical students. But the high drama surrounding their defense of this corpse suggests that because this body belonged to an African American insurgent, a member of John Brown's notorious band, it was especially valuable. Indeed, while most dissected corpses were carelessly discarded, the body parts of insurrectionaries became prized possessions, carefully tended and passed from one generation to the next. For example, in the wake of the Mankato executions, Dr. William Worral Mayo claimed the body of one of the executed insurgents. He kept the skeleton in his office and used it to teach anatomy to his two sons who went on to found the world-famous Mayo Clinic.[33] Dr. Frederick Weedon, who befriended Osceola while he was imprisoned in Charleston, took possession of Osceola's head after Osceola died. He displayed it in the window of his pharmacy and used it, on occasion, to frighten his disobedient sons into submission. Some years later, Weedon gave Osceola's head to his son-in-law Dr. Daniel Winchester Whitehurst who, in turn, delivered it to his mentor, Dr. Valentine Mott, as an expression of his regard.[34] In each instance, the alliance between one generation and the next, structured by the transmission of useful and empowering knowledge, was mediated by the body of the mutilated insurgent. The remnants of the insurrectionary's body helped to define pedagogical relationships, conflicted and cordial, between sons and fathers, students and mentors.

As if execution were not punishment enough, medical men continued to violate these insurgents long after they were dead. The homosocial trade in body parts helps us to see dissection as part of a disciplinary system that invests the corpse with an inviolate sensibility, thus establishing it as an object of ongoing interest. Viewed as the repository of a mysterious or incompletely fathomed form of power, the insurrectionary body retains value. While experimentation on the bodies of the disenfranchised contributed to a view of dead people—poor, native, black, homeless—as expendable, it also contributed to a view of African American and Native American men—living and dead—as powerful, frightening, and deserving punishment.

"Benito Cereno" (1856), Melville's fictional account of the rebellion on board the *Tryal* in 1800, describes the insurgent's keen intellect, and his ability to conceal it, as the means to insurrection. Casting Captain Amasa Delano, the story's narrator, as a failed ethnologist of sorts, Melville identifies perception itself as the chief casualty of racial discord. The story begins with Delano gazing onto the expanse of gray sea, birds, and sky. Contemplating the "peculiar" morning—"mute and calm; everything gray" —Delano spots a ship, floating aimlessly, that ominously "showed no colors."[35] Boarding the *San Dominic*, Delano is confronted by a strange and threatening scene: an ailing, incoherent Benito Cereno presides over a shipboard world of social disorder and bizarre ritual. The story traces Delano's failed efforts to understand what is happening on the ship, especially his inability to divine the character of the ship's captain, Benito Cereno, and his attendant, the slave Babo. The reader's point of view is constrained by Delano's own; she sees and understands no more than he does. It is only when Babo attempts to kill Delano that the truth is revealed: once Babo is caught and the insurrection is put down, we receive an extended account, drawn from legal depositions, of what happened on the San Dominic before Delano's arrival and during his time on board. It fills in all that we need to know to make sense of what we have seen but failed to comprehend throughout and, placing impenetrability and revelation in stark contrast, transforms our experience of reading the story.

Contrasting Delano's stupidity with Babo's intelligence, Melville observes that Babo's "brain, not body, had schemed and led the revolt" (116). The story's final paragraph, which graphically describes the violence done to Babo's corpse, renews the threat of his powerful intellect. Melville writes, "The body was burned to ashes; but for many days, the head, that hive of subtlety, fixed on a pole in the plaza, met, unabashed, the gazes of the whites, and across the Plaza looked towards St. Bartholomew's church, in whose vaults slept then, as now, the recovered bones of Aranda, and across the Rimac bridge looked towards the monastery, on Mount Agonia without; where, three months after being dismissed by the court, Benito Cereno, borne on the bier, did, indeed, follow his leader" (116-17). As Maggie Sale observes, Melville "constructs an image dominated by the unknown power of Babo's mind, an intelligence far greater than accounted for by any racialist discourses."[36] Melville reproduces the scene of "cranial contemplation" in which the racial scientist gazes on the skull of his subject; when Babo stares back, defiantly, it appears that he has not only survived the act of punishment but also thwarted the observer's desire to understand him.

Immediately, however, we find ourselves looking not at Babo's head but through his eyes as his gaze expands across space and time and he becomes a witness to the ritual commemoration of Benito Cereno's impending death. In a weird revision of death custom, Babo takes a last look at the body of his victim, and we look along with him. Aligning the reader's gaze with Babo's own in the final sentences of the story, Melville seems to temper, if not completely invalidate, the experience of revelation, thus returning us to the opacity staged by the story's opening. Even as Babo's interiority remains inaccessible, the reader must recognize that Babo surely regards what has happened differently than Delano, Benito Cereno, or the reader herself. For the first time, the reader is invited to reconsider the story from Babo's perspective: how does Benito Cereno's death appear to him? Because his perspective remains opaque—he is, after all, dead—to identify briefly with Babo's gaze is not to feel sympathy but to encounter a form of difference (defined multiply as the difference between the enslaved and the unenslaved, victim and spectator, living and dead) that cannot be quantified or known.

Is Babo the object of our gaze or its point of origin? Viewed as the object of our gaze, Babo's skull reproduces the fantasy of recalcitrant interiority that motivates diagnostic violence. At the same time, however, the impenetrable authority of Babo's stare directs us toward a literature of insurrection that takes the gaze of the condemned insurgent as a source of omniscience, inscrutability, and power.

≋ During the antebellum period African American writers who spoke out against slavery had to grapple with increasingly popular theories of innate racial difference that sought to justify slavery by way of a divinely sanctioned natural order. In a direct assault on theories of black inferiority, David Walker turns to the writings of founding "father" Thomas Jefferson. In his *Appeal to the Coloured Citizens of the World* (1829), Walker exploits the contradictions in Jefferson's writing—the author of the Declaration of Independence was an early advocate of racial science—in an effort to debunk scientific racism and, more broadly, critique efforts to "know" the black subject. Displacing the authority of the white investigator, he makes way for his own visionary subjectivity that, definitively beyond the grasp of empirical method, sees and interprets the ways of God.

At its most extreme, Walker's *Appeal* advocates violent resistance to slavery. Yet his appeal to violence goes hand in hand with a deep investment in the radicalizing power of knowledge: observation, book learning, divine inspiration—all provide resources for Walker as he works to educate a black readership. Walker believed that violence would further black liberation only if it grew from a careful analysis of the oppression of African Americans, past and present. Like Frederick Douglass, he saw resistance following from self-education. Throughout the *Appeal*, he stresses his capacity, and the capacity he hopes to "awaken" in his readership, for "inquiry and investigation."[37]

Staging a heated dialogue with founding father Thomas Jefferson over the subject of racial difference, Walker takes Jefferson's *Notes on the State of Virginia* as the object of his critical scrutiny. He employs the tools of rationalist inquiry, so often associated with Jefferson himself, in order to debunk the claims to objectivity made by proponents of racial science. In this way, he exhibits his intellectual powers and instructs his readers in critical method. Returning repeatedly to Jefferson's text, Walker incorporates it into his own. He asks "How could Mr. Jefferson but say, 'I advance it therefore as a suspicion only, that the blacks, whether originally a distinct race, or made distinct by time and circumstances, are *inferior* to the whites in the endowments both of body and mind?'" (26). He goes on to quote Jefferson at length, pausing to interject his own commentary. "This very verse," he writes "has in truth injured us more, and has been as great a barrier to our emancipation as any thing that has ever been advanced against us" (27). Assimilating passages from *Notes on the State of Virginia*, Walker interrogates Jefferson's account of racial difference and compels his readers to do the same.

Having given an extended critique of Jefferson's discussion of racial difference in *Notes on the State of Virginia*, Walker concludes his treatise with an appeal to the Declaration of Independence. After quoting the Declaration at length, he asks his audience: "Do you understand your own language?" (75). Reversing the trajectory of Jefferson's own thinking, Walker asks his audience to reread this founding document with Jefferson's assertion of black inferiority in mind. If racial science strips the body of its context in order to reconstruct it as a racial type, Walker performs a similar feat on the nation's most cherished founding document: lifting Jefferson's language from its familiar setting, Walker forces us to read the Declaration of Independence in a new light. In doing so, he dramatizes the importance of context in determining truth and suggests that a shift in perspective, which denaturalizes founding texts, is vital to emancipatory discourse.[38]

Foregrounding Jefferson's remarks on race, Walker insists that these are the very substance of Jefferson's legacy. In this context, the Declaration of Independence appears, at best, anomalous, at worst a form of equivocation. Dismantling Jefferson's reputation, Walker not only asserts his own analytic powers but also foregrounds the problem of perspective that scientific accounts of species difference strive to suppress. That is, if Jefferson's text, and his legacy more broadly, is effectively subverted when Walker reads it, Jefferson's own hopes of deciphering the aptitudes of black subjects appear ill fated. Thus the *Appeal* celebrates the emancipatory power of analysis while discrediting scientific claims to objectivity.

In response to the rise of racial essentialism, abolitionist authors frequently appealed to the revolutionary doctrine that "all men are created equal." This appeal to revolutionary precedent structured a political genealogy in which radical black men carried on the founding tradition: just as the founders fought and died to free themselves from British rule, black men would rise up to free themselves from slavery. In *To Wake the Nations*, Eric Sundquist argues that during the antebellum period antislavery writers appealed to the revolutionary example in order to claim "the same moral authority for their own freedom that had served as the foundation of the United States itself."[39] In doing so, they regenerated a lapsed commitment to equality and justice. Rather than reviving a common ideal toward which the nation can continue to strive, however, Walker exposes the founding tradition as, from the first, bankrupt. He hopes, in turn, to found a black revolutionary tradition in response to white racism. While lambasting Jefferson for refusing blacks membership in the "human family," Walker suggests that a tradition of black manhood, one that binds black fathers and sons, might be formed in reaction to Jefferson's discursive violence. Walker encourages "each of [his] brethren, who has the spirit of a man, to buy a copy of Mr. Jefferson's 'Notes on Virginia,' and put it in the hand of his son" (14). Arguing that the nation was founded not on the ideal of equality but by the labor of slaves, Walker hopes to establish an alternative genealogy in which black fathers educate their sons, inculcating the knowledge and solidarity that will make black liberation possible.

Doing his part to advance the prospect of self-education, Walker made every effort to guarantee that his *Appeal* would be read by Southern blacks. Stitching copies of the pamphlet into the clothing of black sailors headed to the South, and contacting Southerners he hoped would be willing to distribute them, Walker made good on his vision of a black community radicalized through reading. When the *Appeal* began to appear in Southern ports within weeks of its publication, it provoked an extraordinary reaction that left no doubt as to the incendiary nature of the work and Walker's efforts to circulate it. Banned in a number of Southern states, it led to the enactment of antiliteracy legislation in Louisiana, Georgia, and North Carolina. More broadly, historians contend that it contributed to the radicalization of antislavery rhetoric in the North and to the emergence of proslavery nationalism in the South.[40]

Even as Walker advocated critical reading and analysis as a means to political agency, he described himself as a visionary who attained prophetic knowledge through submission to God's will. While, on the one hand, Walker described the *Appeal* as the result of his extensive travels and wide observation, he claimed, on the other hand, that it was written in response to "strict commandments of the Lord" (71). Dismantling the racial scientist's claim to empirical knowledge, Walker claimed the powers of prophecy for himself. Justifying insurrection through a secular appeal to equality, Walker in turn threads his own revolutionary agency, and the agency of his readers, through an account of God's will in which justice is paramount, and violence instrumental. Throughout the text, Walker rallies God's vengeance as his central, and strongest, argument for emancipation. The *Appeal* implores white Americans to reconsider the policy of enslavement in order to avert God's apocalyptic wrath: "O Americans! Americans!! I call God—I call angels—I call men, to witness, that your DESTRUCTION *is at hand*, and will be speedily consummated unless you REPENT" (43).

In the course of the *Appeal*, God's wrath takes various forms. Slave insurrection may provide the vehicle for divine judgment; Walker threatens an "unconquerable disposition in the breasts of the blacks, which, when it is fully awakened and put in motion, will be subdued, only with the destruction of the animal existence" (25). Or, a "just and holy" God may visit civil war on the slaveholding nation causing "the very children of the oppressors to rise up against them, and oftimes put them to death" (3). Or, black men may suffer in the cause of retribution. In one extraordinary passage, Walker imagines the immolation of black men as the expression of divine will. Contemplating the complicity of black people in their own enslavement, Walker welcomes the destruction that will prove their essential nobility. He writes,

I aver, that when I look over these United States of America, and the world, and see the ignorant deceptions and consequent wretchedness of my brethren, I am brought oftimes solemnly to a stand, and in the midst of my reflections I exclaim to my God, 'Lord didst thou make us to be slaves to our brethren, the whites?' But when I reflect that God is just, and that millions of my wretched brethren would meet death with glory—yea, more, would plunge into the very mouths of cannons and be torn into particles as minute as the atoms which compose the elements of the earth, in preference to a mean submission to the lash of tyrants, I am with streaming eyes, compelled to shrink back into nothingness before my Maker, and exclaim again, thy will be done, O Lord God Almighty. (28)

In this passage, God's will is manifested by the willingness of black men to die rather than submit to unjust punishment. In the *Appeal*, violence inflicted by black men on whites finds its counterpart in the self-sacrifice of black men in the cause of abolition; the capacity of black men for violent revenge is matched by their hunger for self-destruction.

Describing war as a form of divine retribution, Walker anticipates one of the important ways that the Civil War will be interpreted and remembered. Likewise, his description of black men who prove themselves worthy of freedom when they "meet death with glory" predicts the way that black soldiering will be promoted during the war. As Houston Baker has argued, Walker's *Appeal* takes its place in a tradition of radical black writing that embraces the coming apocalypse in the belief that the "dignity, status, and freedom" of black people are "dependent upon the descent of an apocalypse on a corrupt and oppressive white world."[41] In this view, destruction is a means to liberation. Walker includes black men in the scene of retributive violence and finds himself humbled and exalted by the spectacle. Witnessing (in his mind's eye) the destruction of his black "brethren," Walker weeps, testifying not to the power of human sympathy but to his own submission to God's will. In a melodramatic display of self-effacement, Walker "shrink[s] back into nothingness."

Recognizing, indeed dramatizing, the incendiary nature of his text, Walker anticipates being murdered for what he has written. "If any wish to . . . murder me for the truth," he writes, "know ye, that I am in the hand of God, and at your disposal. I count my life not dear unto me, but I am ready to be offered at any moment. For what is the use of living, when in fact I am dead" (71–72). Describing himself as already dead, Walker not only uses death as a figure for the degradation of black people in a racist society but also claims the power of the dead for himself. As I have argued, black bodies were abused in death as in life: the practice of anatomy, and legislation meant to enable it, contributed to the processes of racial segregation and disempowerment. At the same time, however, the abused dead retained a particular power in the minds of the living. The voice that sounded from beyond the grave provided a resource for antislavery writers who wanted to contest the violence inflicted on black people. The language of a man facing certain death, like that of a ghost that walks unseen among the living, derived its authority from the belief that the dead, far from invisible and impotent, possessed knowledge (most notably of death itself) and exerted influence. When Walker describes himself as already dead, he lays claim to that authority and uses it to contest the objectification of black people.[42]

In 1830, after the third edition of the *Appeal* had been published, rumors circulated that a price had been placed on Walker's head. When he died suddenly on the morning of June 28 many concluded that he had been poisoned.[43] Given the nature of Walker's address, his sudden and mysterious death may not surprise us; certainly, it would not have surprised him. Expecting to be killed in punishment for his incendiary tract, Walker described himself as a martyr who would suffer for holding fast to his beliefs. Speaking as though he was already dead allowed Walker to portray himself as the recipient of special insight that derived not from the world of objects but from the unseen realm of the spirit. He used the language of prophecy, like the performative exercise of critical agency, to contest a racial essentialism in which the black body offers up knowledge rather than wielding it. While Walker's *Appeal* participates in a critique of objectivity that runs through African American writing of the period, it also, at moments, foretells violence that will allow for a radical reordering of things. In doing so, it points toward what may be the era's most vivid and disturbing rendering of racial apocalypse: *The Confessions of Nat Turner*.[44]

≈ *The Confessions of Nat Turner* (1831) profiles the mind of an insurgent in the wake of his killing spree. Published by Thomas Gray, Turner's interlocutor, shortly after Turner's execution, *Confessions* stands at the intersection of ethnological and insurrectionary writing: jointly authored by Turner and Gray, the text records the efforts of a white investigator to comprehend the mind of a black subject while also demonstrating that insurgent subjectivity cannot be penetrated. As scholars have observed, *Confessions* dwells on Turner's religious preoccupations, implying that his rebellion was the work of a madman rather than an appropriate response to enslavement.[45] And yet, if Turner's fanaticism serves an explanatory function for Gray as he tries to pathologize Turner's uprising, it also allows Turner to lay claim to divine authority. Boasting a form of knowledge that cannot be verified—knowledge of God's will—Turner places himself beyond the reach of careful observation. When Gray asks Turner, "Do you not find yourself mistaken now?" Turner replies with a question of his own: "Was not Christ crucified?" (48). The act of interrogation, in which an agent of the state extracts evidence through questioning backed by the threat of violence, breaks down in the face of Turner's mad self-confidence as he, like fanatic John Brown, compares his self-assurance to Christ's own.

Turner's refusal to repent, one indication of his fanaticism, cuts against the grain of the confession genre. Confessions typically offer a display of remorse on the eve of execution. In doing so, they reconcile the criminal with his community, proving that spiritual reform—one intention of punishment—has been accomplished. By contrast, Turner's remorseless recital of the violence he and his cohort committed served to justify a widespread retributive violence: *Confessions* must be read as one tool in a broader effort to punish and discipline blacks in the wake of the Southampton insurrection. In his preface, Gray hopes that the text will demonstrate the importance of laws intended to avert insurrection and "induce all those entrusted with their execution, as well as our citizens generally, to see that they are strictly and rigidly enforced" (41). Ideally, laws that keep blacks from reading, sharing information, and gathering together will nip insurgencies in the bud. But the problem remains: how to identify the insurgent when, like Nat Turner, he offers no sign of his impending violence?

Gray begins his preface by addressing the disturbing discrepancy between external appearances and internal realities that characterized the prelude to the Southampton insurrection. At the time of the uprising "every thing upon the surface of society wore a calm and peaceful aspect . . . not one note of preparation was heard to warn the devoted inhabitants of woe and death." And yet, at this very moment, "a gloomy fanatic was revolving in the recesses of his own dark, bewildered, and overwrought mind, schemes of indiscriminate massacre to the whites" (41). Gray promises to reveal the machinations of the insurrectionary mind to a frightened public that struggles to comprehend the "motives" behind the insurgency. He pitches *Confessions* not as the story of the violence committed by Turner and his followers but as the story of the development of a mind capable of conjuring such destruction: "How it first became bewildered and confounded, and finally corrupted and led to the conception and perpetration of the most atrocious and heart-rending deeds" (41).

The urge to isolate and examine Turner's mind must be read not only in relation to an ethnological fascination with the skull of the racial subject but also in relation to the violence inflicted on insurgents in the wake of the Southampton insurrection. Whites were quick to take revenge on blacks suspected of participating in the uprising. In a number of instances, the bodies of victims were decapitated, and their heads placed on poles. These heads were meant to warn black people against rebellion of any sort. They also worked to demonstrate power by fixing the body in place, offering spectacular evidence of its inability to transcend the site of retribution.[46] The intersection of Barrow Road and the Jerusalem–Cross Keys Highway, where one severed head was placed in the aftermath of the insurrection, became known as Blackhead Signpost. After the head was removed, the post was painted black and left standing as a "permanent warning to disaffected blacks."[47]

While it gave evidence of the brutal and effective effort to put the insurrection down, Blackhead Signpost also implied an enduring and unresolved fascination with Nat Turner's "glaring subjectivity." Sundquist has suggested that while the severed black head, a stand-in for Turner's own, signified the defeat of Turner's revolt, it also "stood for the 'silent satisfaction' with which he (and presumably many other slaves) had witnessed the like dismemberment of the masters."[48] Even as the bodies of Turner and his cohort were subjected to a form of punishment intended to humiliate the dead and curtail their power, the severed head spoke to the possibility that the insurgent's subjectivity was irrevocably expanded in the act of violence.

Indeed, any reading of *Confessions* is plagued by Turner's ability to deflect the motives ascribed to him: he responds to the inquiring gaze with his own knowing stare, as he looks down at the corpses that lie at his feet or up toward the sky for signs of God. Rather than attribute this resistance to Turner himself (though I would not rule this out), I would like to consider how the peculiar circumstances of this text's composition enable the articulation of a subject who evades diagnosis. The ethnological premise of Gray's preface—to offer a precise and trustworthy account of the peculiarities of the insurrectionary mind—gives way in the face of the ambiguities surrounding the authorship of *Confessions*. Supposedly narrated by Turner and transcribed by Gray, we do not know whether this text is, as accompanying affidavits promise, Turner's own uncoerced and unadulterated testimony. Given the political urgency surrounding it, we can imagine that Gray was tempted to recast Turner's story in any number of ways. And if Turner did tell his own story, he may well have embellished or distorted it.

The narrative begins with a disagreement between Turner and Gray that only intensifies the reader's interpretive difficulties. In his preface, Gray recalls visiting Nat in prison when "without being questioned at all, he commenced his narrative" (44). Gray presents this document as Turner's spontaneous self-expression. Indeed, Gray can only claim to offer an accurate picture of the insurrectionary mind if Turner tells his story willingly and Gray transcribes it accurately. But the confession itself immediately calls both Turner's willingness and Gray's neutrality into question. Turner's account begins with this address to Gray: "Sir,—You have asked me to give a history of the motives which induced me to undertake the late insurrection, as you call it" (44). Turner implies that he is not offering this narrative "freely" but responding to Gray's interrogation. Turner again asks us to take stock of Gray's presence when he notes that Gray calls Turner's uprising "the late insurrection," implying that he himself would call it something else, though he does not tell us what. One imagines that Gray would have every interest in suppressing an opening statement that directly contradicts his own account of how this document came into being. Thus we wonder why Gray might have decided to let Turner's disruptive remark stand. Even more confounding, we cannot rule out the possibility that Gray himself may have invented or chosen to foreground this important difference between Turner and himself. Either Turner or Gray or both of them want to emphasize Gray's presence at the scene of narration and thus heighten questions of narrative authority that trouble the work.

Certainly, it is tempting to read this as a hybrid text, in which Gray's and Turner's motives concur and conflict, and to attempt to disentangle the complex weave of style and intention as we go. But can we do this? For example, Turner's tone, described by Tony Horwitz as "icy and unrepentant," may imply Gray's effort to deny sympathy to the condemned prisoner or Turner's unwillingness to offer a public apology.[49] If one reads "Nat Turner" as a function of Gray's own imagination, the text appears to be an effort to reduce the black insurrectionary to a type by elaborating on his dangerousness. If, however, one reads "Nat Turner" as Turner's own creation, his blunt recounting of the violence he committed and witnessed appears to resist the disciplinary imperatives of the confession genre. Once we acknowledge that it is impossible to trace the text's features to the motives of either man, we witness the emergence of a composite voice and intentionality that belongs only to the narrator "Nat Turner." We can begin to appreciate the peculiar nature of this text, which, while it presents a rare case study in the dynamics of racial violence, cannot be read through the racial identity of either of its authors. The uncertainties surrounding the production of this text demand a reader who can embrace the condition of not knowing and resist the urge to read the text as an expression of the author's identity. In return, she will witness the genesis of an insurrectionary voice that floats free of the exigencies of personality and fulfills, as nearly as any text can, an apocalyptic urge to self-forgetting.

If one admits that it is impossible to determine which of these men shapes the voice of "Nat Tuner" at any given point, a peculiar feature of the text comes to the fore. The ethnological premise that provides the occasion for *Confessions* breaks down as Nat Turner secures the role of interpreter and Thomas Gray emerges as the story's author *and* its object: this text refuses to objectify the body or the mind of the black insurgent. Nat Turner (and I speak here of a narrative voice that cannot be traced to an individual author) resists the ethnologist's gaze not, as one might expect, by humanizing the scene of empirical observation with a resonant account of his own experience, but rather by reproducing the ethnologist's interpretive egotism and its power to deflect attention.

If Gray wants to document the "operations" of Turner's mind, only Turner himself, the insurrection's "contriver and head," can detail the thought process that resulted in violent revolt. While Gray's preface and Turner's text disagree over whether or not *Confessions* was spontaneously offered by Turner, they are in perfect agreement when it comes to the subject of the narrative. This is first and foremost a story of Nat Turner's intellect—how his mind works and how the workings of his mind led to insurrection. Turner begins his narrative by remarking that his violent acts can be traced directly to an incident from his childhood. Turner remembers that when he was a young boy his mother overheard him telling his friends stories of things that had happened before he was born. His parents recognize, and celebrate, the gift of prophecy, and from then on Turner is regarded with great expectation by his family and community

(44). The story of how Turner learns to read is in keeping with this emphasis on his early prescience: "I have no recollection whatever of learning the alphabet—but to the astonishment of the family, one day, when a book was shewn me to keep me from crying, I began spelling the names of different objects" (45).

For Turner, learning is a matter of recognizing what he already knows, and this experience of recognition, which exceeds his own volition, offers the best evidence that he has been chosen by God. In this regard, *Confessions* presents a striking contrast to *Narrative of the Life of Frederick Douglass* (1845). Douglass's *Narrative* tells the story of how Douglass learned to read and write. Explaining how he came to write his narrative "by himself," Douglass accounts for his anomalous status as ex-slave and author. Refuting the assumption that slaves are intellectually inferior, he argues for their emancipation and integration into society. The story of how Douglass acquires literacy is also the story of his developing consciousness. In the process of learning to read and then to write, Douglass becomes aware of his powerlessness and determined to find a way to free himself. While white abolitionists dwell on the slave's bodily suffering, Douglass focuses on the growth of intellect and, consequently, of character.

Douglass's intellectual development, a register of his experience, is the subject of his *Narrative*. By contrast, *The Confessions of Nat Turner* offers a narrative voice that is not bound by the imperatives of self-reflection or self-revelation. *Confessions* eschews a sentimental approach to slave experience, which foregrounds the slave's emotional and physical anguish, as well as an individualist approach, exemplified by Douglass's narrative, which documents the slave's development and consequent autonomy firsthand. Instead, Turner, an antinomian figure whose private experience of divinity justifies his lawbreaking, portrays his own mind as a static repository of divine knowledge. A series of visions confirms Turner in his role as a rebel and a prophet, revealing to him that the time has come to strike out against slavery. When "hieroglyphic characters, and numbers, with the forms of men in different attitudes" appear on leaves in the woods, Turner recognizes "the figures I had seen before in the heavens" (47). When he sees "drops of blood on the corn," he recognizes the blood of Christ "returning to earth again in the form of dew" (47). These visions make it clear to Turner that the "time was fast approaching when the first should be the last and the last should be the first," and that he must take up Christ's "yoke" and "fight against the Serpent" (47–48). Once again, Turner takes these signs as evidence of what he already knows with certainty: his intended role in the coming apocalypse.

While ethnologists confidently interpreted physical features as signs of character, from our vantage point it appears that far from deciphering interiority or, more impressively, the record of God's creation, they produced a body of knowledge in accordance with their own beliefs. Like the ethnologist, Turner turns a blind eye to the difficulties of interpretation, refusing to entertain the possibility that rather than reading God's will in the signs of nature he is projecting his own assumptions onto the world of natural forms. (The difference, of course, is that the certainty with which Turner takes external signs to confirm his own prior knowledge goes under the name "fanaticism," while the ethnologist's interpretive confidence was dubbed "science.") If African American writers challenge the ethnologist's claim to objectivity, Turner does these authors one better: rather than calling the observer's neutrality into question, he claims omniscience for himself.

While Gray's "Preface" promises to describe Turner's frame of mind as he contemplated violent revolt, the body of the text, with its emphasis on the gradual revelation of God's will, makes such an analysis impossible. Because *Confessions* does not offer a narrative of cause and effect in which Turner responds, as Douglass does, to the conditions of enslavement, it becomes difficult to account for his behavior. For example, Turner remarks that he had nothing against his master Joseph Travis, the first victim of Turner's band. Indeed, he remembers Travis as a "kind master" who gave him "no cause to complain of his treatment" (48). Turner is not motivated to kill by rage, hatred, or a sense of injustice: he kills because God tells him to. In this way, the structure of prophecy, in which all knowledge points toward a divine presence that cannot be interrogated, makes it impossible to characterize Turner's violence as a function of his circumstances or his emotional state.

While Turner's thoughts, like the structure of prophecy itself, remain perfectly self-enclosed, Gray's mind emerges as an object of analysis. If Turner reads the world around him as an ethnologist would, arrogantly interpreting worldly appearances as expressions of divine will, Gray's perspective on Turner is vacillating and contradictory. Just as the narrative begins with Turner's assertion that Gray demanded this narrative, it concludes with a reminder that it is Gray, not Turner, who relates the story. Turner tells Gray, "During the time I was pursued, I had many hair breadth escapes, which your time will not permit *you to relate*" (53, emphasis added). Turner reminds us that it is not Turner's "I" but Gray's "you" that "relates" this narrative. Far from trying to wrest narrative control from Gray, Turner refuses to present himself as an author; in this way, he calls attention to Gray's authorial agency.

These sentences precede Gray's overt reclamation of the narrative voice. Following this abrupt transition from "I" to "you," the narrative shifts from Turner's voice to Gray's without structural transition: "I here proceeded to make some inquiries of him" (54). Wholly abandoning the premise of Turner's narrative autonomy, Gray goes on to conclude *Confessions* with an account of Turner's character that is so inconsistent that it cannot help calling Gray's authorial competence into question. According to Gray, Turner is brave, intelligent, and virtuous. Gray refutes claims that Turner attacked his victims in order to rob them and that he displayed cowardice by allowing himself to be captured by a single man. In the next breath, however, Gray calls on the inflated language of sensational fiction to describe Turner as a bloodthirsty fiend. He writes, "The calm, deliberate composure with which he spoke of his late deeds and intentions, the expression of his fiend-like face when excited by enthusiasm, still bearing the stains of the blood of helpless innocence about him; clothed with rags and covered with chains; yet daring to raise his manacled hands to heaven, with a spirit soaring above the attributes of man; I looked on him and my blood curdled in my veins" (54–55). Gray's description of Turner, marred by inconsistency, reveals his ambiguous and contradictory thoughts about his subject.

It is tempting to be impressed by the way that Turner effects this role reversal. Refusing to offer himself as the object of scrutiny, he shines light on Gray's intellectual shortcomings. But the desire to discover a canny and resistant black subject who will face Gray down in print must itself be regarded with some suspicion. To make Turner's brilliance the object of this analysis would be to forget that we do not know who shapes Turner's narrative and would reinstate the very interest in black subjectivity that *The Confessions of Nat Turner* strangely resists.[50] Instead, I would simply note that insurrection—which threatens a reversal in the order of things—provides the occasion for rethinking the position of the white investigator. Ostensibly the agent of investigation, Thomas Gray, once he is explicitly identified as the author of this text, becomes its object. As in the other texts I have discussed, when the problem of perspective is introduced to the scene of ethnological contemplation, the act of interpretation is revealed as a form of authorship and the interpreter's own conclusions become an object of critical inquiry.

While the fate of Turner's corpse is impossible to determine, legend has it that his body was dissected and then circulated among white residents of Southampton. William Drewry, who interviewed Southampton residents in 1900, recounts that before it was "misplaced" Turner's corpse was used by doctors who "skinned it and made grease of the flesh." Parts of his body, most significantly his skull, were passed from hand to hand. According to Drewry, there were those who still recalled the particulars of Turner's skull: "It was very peculiarly shaped, resembling the head of a sheep, and at least three-quarters of an inch thick."[51] Critics have used the fate of Turner's corpse as a figure for his inscrutability. Peter Wood writes, "Ever since he was hanged and cut apart in 1831, this unknown black leader has been largely shrouded from view, despite the best efforts of researchers. Perhaps soon they will be able to restore substantial flesh to the living bones of the historical Nat Turner."[52] Instead, I think we should regard the rumored dissection and dissemination of Turner's corpse as a common historical practice with particular objectives: the insurrectionary was dissected so that no one could anticipate his Christlike resurrection; he was dissected in order to legitimate a view of the black body as a useful instrument; and he was dissected so that his body might be scrutinized for abnormalities that would in turn provide an apolitical explanation for his insurgency.

By contrast, *Confessions* creates an absence where the black subject would typically be found scrutinized and objectified. Mystery attaches not to the fate of Turner's bones but to the state of his mind before, during, and after the Southampton insurrection. Freed from the conventions of an authenticating autobiographical discourse, "Nat Turner" expresses a rage that threatens to flatten the known world. *Confessions* divorces the violence of the Southampton insurrection, and the wider violence it intimates, from coherent psychological intent; in consequence, there is no one to punish or to know, and our attention shifts from the scrutiny of the insurrectionary subject to the devastation he left behind. The descriptive, documentary quality of *Confessions* is, in the end, its most salient property. What we see finally is not Turner, but what Turner saw: signs in the sky, bodies on the ground. In this instance, the power to deflect narration, scrutiny, and objectification goes hand in hand with the power to record the world-altering effects of violence.

≈ Although he went to Harpers Ferry with a band of black and white men, facing death Copeland chose to take his place in a genealogy of black martyrs. In a letter written to his brother six days before his execution, Copeland tries to determine how his participation in the raid and his consequent punishment will be remembered:

My Dear Brother:
I now take my pen to write you a few lines to let you know how I am . . . I am, it is true, so situated at present as scarcely to know how to commence writing; not that my mind is filled with fear or that it has become shattered in view of my near approach to death. Not that I am terrified by the gallows which I see staring me in the face, and upon which I am so soon to stand and suffer death for doing what George Washington, the so-called father of this great but slave-cursed country, was made a hero for doing while he lived. . . . And now, brother, for having lent my aid to a General no less brave, and engaged in a cause no less honorable and glorious, I am to suffer death. Washington entered the field to fight for the freedom of the American people — not for the white man alone, but for both black and white. Nor were they white men alone who fought for the freedom of this country. The blood of black men flowed as freely as that of white men. Yes, the very first blood that was spilt was that of a negro. It was the blood of that heroic man, (though black he was) Cyrus Attuck [sic]. And some of the very last blood shed was that of black men. . . . It is true that black men did an equal share of the fighting for American Independence, and they were assured by the whites that they should share equal benefits for so doing. But after having performed their part honorably, they were by the whites most treacherously deceived — they refusing to fulfill their part of the contract. But this you know as well as I do, and I will therefore say no more in reference to the claims which we, as colored men, have on the American people.[53]

Copeland finds a precedent for his own violence in the American Revolution. Invoking Washington as a model, he asserts the injustice of his pending execution. In the face of this double standard, Copeland allies himself with those black men, most notably Crispus Attucks, who fought and died in the Revolutionary struggle.

Copeland's recourse to the language of blood sacrifice recalls John Brown's courtroom speech. In this speech Brown used the figure of common blood to imagine his own children and millions of suffering slaves as members of a single family. But Copeland invokes the rhetoric of blood sacrifice only to refuse it in favor of an alternative account of black heroism. Far from imagining a unified biracial army, Copeland distinguishes between black and white blood in an effort to quantify black participation in the Revolutionary war: in this letter, the language of martyrdom quickly gives way to the language of legal contract. As he sees it, black self-sacrifice sealed a contractual exchange between black and white Americans. Asking to be remembered as the offspring of Crispus Attucks, Copeland asserts that equality is not a utopian prospect envisioned by the founders, but a right, already secured by black participation in the Revolutionary effort.[54] The heroic presence of African Americans at the scene of revolution drives home the injustice of their continued enslavement. In the face of this injustice, Copeland appears willing to forgo inclusion in a family of white Americans.

Facing death on the scaffold, Copeland turns to Attucks in an effort to articulate a model of national culture in which one generation of black martyrs inspires the next. It appears that Attucks, like Copeland, was a victim of postmortem violence. London's Wellcome Institute for the History of Medicine holds in its collection a small notebook purportedly bound in Attucks's skin. While the Wellcome Institute's catalog identifies this object with the title "Notebook Bound in Human Skin," the notebook itself bears a more specific inscription. The first page reads: "cover of tanned skin of Negro whose execution caused War of Independence." When Copeland identified himself as Attucks's descendant, he meant to construct a narrative of revolutionary agency that belonged exclusively to black men. The exertion of such agency was, of course, punished in particular ways. Postmortem dissection, as I have argued, excludes the dead from the commemorative circle of family and friends as well as producing knowledge that abstracts and universalizes that exclusion. Copeland left a record that tries to reinstate his place in both familial and political communities. His companion Shields Green, however, was not literate and had no access to the press. It fell to James Monroe to commemorate and record the circumstances of his death.

Monroe had time to kill before his train departed for Ohio, so he decided to pay a final visit to the dissecting rooms of the Winchester Medical College. There he found the corpse of "another Oberlin neighbor" whom he had "often met upon our streets, a colored man named Shields Green." Neither the zealous medical students nor Monroe himself appear to have had much interest in Green's corpse. While Monroe was commissioned to travel to Winchester to get Copeland's body, the corpse of Shields Green, an uneducated ex-slave with no family or friends to represent him, was carelessly abandoned. Monroe took a moment, however, to devote his attention to this unclaimed body. He describes the corpse as a "fine, athletic figure . . . lying on his back—the unclosed, wistful eyes staring wildly upward, as if seeking, in a better world, for some solution to the dark problems of horror and oppression so hard to be explained in this."[55]

Monroe transforms Green's inert body into an active, speculating mind. He focuses on Green's eyes, which, he imagines, strain to see beyond the "horror" of the present. Monroe offers up Green's unclaimed corpse for a last look, tentatively restoring the conventions of commemorative ritual. This gaze, however, is quickly inverted. As in the conclusion of Melville's "Benito Cereno," the reader who gazes on the body of the dead insurgent suddenly finds herself looking through his eyes. Monroe leaves us with this problem to solve: what exactly does Shields Green see? When we view African American writing of the antebellum period in relation to the practice of dissection, a radical literature that identified the practice of enslavement with the production of knowledge emerges. The writers I have discussed in this chapter not only work to render perceived truths uncertain but also to construct a visionary black subject who, in the privacy of his own mind, works to imagine a different future. The practices intended to define and enforce racial difference helped to generate a body of writing that seeks change not in the liberation of the fettered body but in the far-reaching gaze of the critical mind.

"THIS COMPOST"

DEATH AND REGENERATION
IN CIVIL WAR POETRY

3

Whitman's 1856 "Poem of Wonder at the Resurrection of
the Wheat" begins "Something startles me where I thought
I was safest." Sickening at the sudden realization that the
earth teems with rotting corpses, the poet withdraws from
the natural world. Suspecting that he has been deceived by
the earth's apparent bounty, he decides to turn up the soil
and "expose some of the foul meat" lying underneath. He
finds, however, that the "sour dead" are wonderfully transformed. Far from contaminating the soil, they are the source
of new life: "What chemistry!" The poet celebrates the process of organic renewal that turns death into life with an ex-
ultant description of spring's arrival: new wheat rises, calves
are born, birds resume their song, and the poet is free to return to the natural world to bathe, eat, and loaf. Yet in the
wake of this happy resolution the poem takes another sudden turn. Reassured, the poet is also "terrified" by the earth,
which "grows such sweet things out of such corruptions."
In the final lines of the poem Whitman describes the earth
as a machine that "turns harmless and stainless on its axis"
as it produces "sumptuous crops" from "endless successions
of diseas'd corpses." In the end, the poet succumbs to the
power of a machine able to unite life and death, health and
disease, ugliness and beauty in a process of consumption and
reproduction that proceeds without end.[1]

"Poem of Wonder" appears to prophesy the spectacle of
mass death that would, five years later, leave hundreds of
thousands of corpses rotting beneath the earth's surface.
During the Civil War, the disposal and commemoration of
the dead became a national project. Describing new life as
the result of death, organic metaphor affiliates two of the
chief aims of wartime culture: mourning the dead and mo-

bilizing the living. Uniting the ritual observance of loss—the burial of the dead—with nature's power to produce, representations of the dead body as a source of fertility consoled grieving individuals while helping to reconstitute the fragile bonds of national community. In order to continue to fight, die, and grieve, people needed to believe that something worthwhile, even beautiful, could grow from their suffering. The plant life that springs up from the graves of dead soldiers provides a ready image for the willingness of soldiers and civilians to continue to support the war effort in the face of massive losses. At the same time, by projecting expansion—in the form of growth—as the natural trajectory of political community, organic metaphors characterize violent death as the source of the nation's increasing strength.

After the war, Whitman renamed the poem "This Compost," thus emphasizing not only the corpse's materiality (as opposed to the miraculous appearance of new wheat) but also the process of decomposition through which death would renew the natural world. During the war, organic metaphors were used to construe violence as an instrument of natural progress and, on this basis, to lend mass death an aura of beauty and inevitability. Although it is tempting to imagine that Whitman's graphic and erotically charged portrayals of dead and wounded bodies resist institutional efforts to categorize, and rationalize, war-torn flesh, it seems to me that Whitman was determined to give death a transcendent purpose that is very much in keeping with the interests of the state.[2] The specificity of his descriptions of the wounded and dead, while they suggest the difficulty of finding redemptive meaning in the massive casualties of wartime, do not detract from this effort. Whitman's wartime poetry and prose at once renders wounded and dead bodies in detail and uses the figure of the anonymous or unknown soldier to abstract them. Representing the harm done to individual bodies, Whitman treats the wounded and dead with great tenderness while placing them in an overarching scheme that sentimentalizes the state as the apotheosis of wartime heroism.

If Whitman uses the metaphor of composting to describe the burial of the dead as a means to collective renewal, he prescribes silence as the appropriate attitude of the mourner in the face of these losses. Indeed, an organic model of national community often went hand in hand with a rhetoric of unrepresentability that interpreted silence as evidence of the gravity and grandeur of death in war. Declaring that the Civil War could not be described, writers and politicians implied that the public performance of silence was one way that citizens could participate in a regenerated national community. Abraham Lincoln, who appeared at Gettysburg dressed in mourning for his own young son, told the assembled that words could not possibly compete with the deeds of dead soldiers. At his own funeral, large and silent crowds provided further evidence of the martyr's power to create political community. Canvassing the art of the Civil War, we find that representations of unanimity, so vital to the state's objectives, use silence to signify the devotion of citizens to the cause of war.

In this chapter, I will consider Whitman's contribution to a nationalist aesthetic of silence and abstraction, founded on the bodies of the wounded and the dead, as well as occasional poetry that resists abstraction by focusing on the material conditions of war and the mechanics of cultural production in constrained circumstances. While Whitman's war writing takes the disappearance of the dead into the earth as a central figure for the production of nationhood out of individual suffering, a vast body of poetry authored by anonymous, or virtually unknown, occasional poets attempts, more modestly, to document the circumstantial detail of war. Viewing the conflict through the lens of specific places and events, anthologies of occasional poetry, published in the years following the war, short-circuit the rhetoric of transformation that will make easy use of corpses. Though many individual poems celebrate the war effort, taken together these poems convey a fragmentary account of the conflict that cuts against the grain of nationalist representations of common purpose and institutional expansion. The mourner who pauses, humbled, at the soldier's grave, provides a model for the reader of Whitman's poetry, as well as for the student of Civil War history, awed by a spectacle she cannot fully comprehend. The imprisoned Southern colonel who scribbles a poem on the wall of his cell before committing suicide suggests a very different kind of poetic practice: executed in a state of emergency, occasional poetry uses simple and highly accessible conventions to describe the extraordinary circumstances of war. Documenting not only the conditions of war, but also the mechanics of transmitting them, these poems trade a rhetoric of commonality for a record of experiential diversity.

⬩ Recalling Henry James's comment that the war was an "immense and prolonged outwardness" that made it difficult to "live inwardly," Neil Schmitz observes that "the text the Civil War principally produced is a vast photography, an archive of views we are still assembling and sorting. What significant writing there is—several speeches, brief takes, small pieces, short poems—scans like photography, is other-directed, memorial, documentary."[3] Scholars have described the Civil War as a catalyst for the development of postwar realism. According to this view, the war produced seismic changes in technology and social organization that, in turn, demanded new modes of representation. Confronting Americans with bloodshed on an unprecedented scale, the conflict shook artists out of a transcendentalist reverie, in which they contemplated the affinity of self, nature, and God, and urged them to document a rapidly changing world.

If we pause to consider representations of the dead before and during the war, however, arguments concerning the advent of realism in the postbellum period appear partial. Antebellum Americans surrounded themselves with images of dead people that are so graphic that they often offend contemporary viewers. An antebellum "culture of death" beautified and objectified the dead body in the process of memorializing it. Grieving relatives displayed the dead body, carefully tended, before burial; they gathered keepsakes from the corpse, making jewelry, for example, out of the hair of the deceased; they took postmortem photographs that portrayed the dead—eyes open, sitting erect—as if they were still alive. Mourning portraits, sometimes drawn from daguerreotypes of the subject, were also characterized by a meticulous attention to physical detail: in some instances, the corpse was carefully measured so that the portrait would be life-size.[4]

Antebellum mourners employed a realist aesthetic to repress death's material effects. Lingering over the dead body, they cultivated its lifelike appearance, thus expressing their ongoing emotional attachment to the dead. The circumstances of death in war did not, however, conform to realist modes of representation. Once the war began, the military found it difficult to identify the bodies of dead soldiers, let alone transport them home for burial.[5] As a result, Northern civilians often mourned soldiers in the absence of their corpses. As I have argued, to be unclaimed in death was an anathema that differentiated disenfranchised people from those more secure in the comforts of middle-class domesticity. The uncertain fate of soldiers' corpses intensified the anguish of grieving families, and it may at times have raised uncomfortable questions about the status of soldiering itself.

At the same time that the war made it difficult for Northern civilians to individuate the dead, it challenged them to imagine mass death and to feel sorrow, if they could, for countless unidentified bodies. The unprecedented scale of war violence called for forms of representation that could help people grieve for a large, undifferentiated group. If antebellum death rituals helped mourners remember the dead in vivid detail, during the war descriptions of the dead tended toward a universalizing abstraction.[6] Organic images that described the regenerative effect of the decaying body located the significance of wartime death not in the body-as-object but in the gradual deterioration of body's form. In this way, they offered a commemorative figure that might encompass all the absent dead.

Addressing the impact of war on Whitman's career, Betsy Erkkila remarks that it "had the effect of jolting literary America out of romance and into realism," and transforming Whitman, the "poet-prophet," into a "poet-historian." In discussing Whitman's war poems, Erkkila, like Schmitz, emphasizes the ascendance of the image. She writes, "The immediacy and brutality of the war shocked Whitman into a new realism in which painting and the snapshot rather than oratory and opera became the primary artistic analogues of his poems."[7] Indeed, *Specimen Days*, which recounts Whitman's experience tending the sick, wounded, and dying in Washington's military hospitals, contains some of the most graphic representations of wounded and dead bodies to be found in the literature of the Civil War. Unlike mourning portraiture, however, which uses the dead body to produce an enduring image of a living person, Whitman's descriptions of the dead fuel a nationalist romance in which the remains of the body are absorbed by a greater whole. Although Whitman describes the scenes of war in great detail, an emphasis on the documentary aims of his wartime prose and poetry overlooks the ease with which he used a model of organic transformation to incorporate the seemingly intractable particulars of war into a narrative of national regeneration.

In "The Million Dead, Too, Summ'd Up," the penultimate entry in the war-related section of *Specimen Days*, Whitman surveys the "varieties of strayed dead" left behind by the war. The entry experiments with different ways of imagining what becomes of dead bodies. Whitman writes, "The dead in this war—there they lie, strewing the fields and woods and valleys and battle-fields of the south—Virginia, the Peninsula—Malvern hill and Fair Oaks—the banks of the Chickahominy—the terraces of Fredericksburgh—Antietam bridge—the grisly ravines of Manassas—the bloody promenade of the Wilderness."[8] Whitman begins by emphasizing the massive extent of death, giving the impression that bodies fill the Southern landscape. Dashes pile locations, like bodies themselves, one on top of another, conveying a sense of disorder and neglect. Whitman interrupts this list with a parenthetical aside in which he rehearses the War Department's own count of the unburied, or inadequately buried, dead: "(the estimate of the War department is 25,000 national soldiers kill'd in battle and never buried at all, 5,000 drown'd — 15,000 inhumed by strangers, or on the march in haste, in hitherto unfound localities — 2,000 graves cover'd by sand and mud by Mississippi freshets, 3,000 carried away by caving-in of banks, &c.,)" (800). The horror entailed by the particulars of the body's disappearance is played off against the "&c.," which implies the callousness of institutional efforts to count the dead, as well as their futility: this list, it seems, could go on indefinitely. As well as signifying the government's inability to account for the dead, "&c." calls for a different kind of institutional approach to commemoration, one that acknowledges, even elevates, the impossibility of representing dead soldiers. Whitman concludes "The Million Dead, Too, Summ'd Up" by describing the "soldiers Cemeteries of the Nation" that pervade "all the peaceful quarters of the land" in the years following the conflict. In these cemeteries, "we see, and ages yet may see, on monuments and gravestones, singly or in masses, to thousands or tens of thousands, the significant word UNKNOWN" (801).

"Counting," James Dawes writes, "is the epistemology of war." While numbers contain an otherwise "borderless trauma," they also convey the massive extent of death in war.[9] Dawes praises Whitman for avoiding sentimental strategies that reinterpret mass violence by way of individual suffering. Instead, Whitman attempts "to create a new genre of war writing, a genre appropriate to the unprecedented multiplicative array of national action." He continues, "For Whitman, a national memory properly constituted must body forth from a skeletal structure built out of numbers rather than narration, out of counting rather than history" (54–55). Dawes offers "The Million Dead, Too, Summ'd Up" as an example of Whitman's effort to communicate the extent of war violence through enumeration rather than individuation. And yet the number Whitman arrives at — one million dead — is grossly exaggerated.[10] Numbers mount toward an apocalyptic figure that impresses by virtue of its inaccuracy. Throughout, Whitman conveys the breadth of death in war by converting its hard particulars — words or numbers — into capacious abstractions. In the end, "UNKNOWN" provides another way of "summing up" when numbers fail and intimates one powerful aim of Whitman's wartime writing: not to know the dead but to unknow them, to enumerate the particulars of dying and death in order to arrive at a sum that is truly greater than its parts — the awesome whole that in its entirety resists description.

Whitman's final war entry announces that "future years will never know the seething hell and the black infernal background of countless minor scenes and interiors." He continues, "*And it is best they should not*—the real war will never get into the books" (802, emphasis mine). *Specimen Days* begs the question: how to reconcile the assertion that the war should not be represented with the graphic nature of Whitman's descriptive prose? Shuttling, as so much of Whitman's writing does, between the particular and the abstract, "The Million Dead, Too, Summ'd Up" suggests an answer to this question. On the one hand, Whitman presents us with material remnants of the dead: one might yet discover the "bleach'd bones, tufts of hair, buttons, fragments of clothing" left behind in secluded spots where soldiers "crawl'd to die, alone" (801). On the other hand, he describes the complete disappearance of the dead into a landscape "saturated, perfumed, with their impalpable ashes' exhalation in Nature's chemistry distill'd" (801). While commemorative objects embody the dead, organic metaphor allows Whitman to represent the influence of the dead—manifest "in every future grain of wheat and ear of corn, and every flower that grows, and every breath we draw"—as it grows and changes over time.

Whitman describes (at the very least) two different ways of conceptualizing the dead and our relation to them: we can hold tightly to the relic, the material trace (however inscrutable) of a particular life; or, we can take the absence of the corpse—most powerfully signified by the land's fertility and beauty—as an occasion to affirm the ongoing presence of the dead. Here and elsewhere Whitman uses the figure of decay to imagine these two modes of commemoration as part of a single process. While the body decomposes and disappears into the soil, fragments are left behind. These fragments, in turn, force us to recognize what cannot be fully known or remembered. The claim that the real war will never get into the books, generally taken to indicate the inadequacy of language, signals instead its power; the elaboration of detail produces an intense, nearly visceral experience of all that falls outside the realm of observation and memory. Whitman uses fragments of the dead body—amputated limbs or scraps of clothing—to indicate his own inability to represent the dead. In doing so, he demonstrates the power of documentary representation to produce a keen awareness of its own limits. In the end, "&c." intimates the particulars that have been lost to time and circumstance. When dignified with the "significant word UNKNOWN," this absence attaches the mourner more firmly to an idealized nation that translates the lives of individuals into a motivating aura—impossible to describe—of life without end.

Whitman's "The Million Dead, Too, Summ'd Up" could be describing the War Department's own efforts to figure out how to best commemorate the dead under new and trying conditions. During wartime, responsibility for tending and burying the dead fell to the state. The task of honoring hundreds of thousands of corpses was inextricably related to the state's ability to produce enthusiasm for the war effort: how to dispose of the dead in a way that would dignify the war itself, ensuring the continued contribution of soldiers and civilians? In 1863, the Gettysburg and Antietam battlefields became the first national cemeteries for the Union dead. They provide examples of state-sponsored culture struggling to invest dead bodies with common meaning. Whereas antebellum commemorative practices celebrated the particulars of character, identity, and appearance, the national cemetery at Gettysburg eschewed precise identification, honoring the individual soldier by assigning him a place in a well-ordered assembly. William Saunders, the architect appointed to design the cemetery, held that in order to "produce an expression of grandeur" it would be necessary to "avoid intricacy and great variety of parts."[11] Accordingly, the dead were buried in graves of uniform size that were grouped by state and marked by identical headstones that recorded name, company, and regiment. Saunders abandoned an aesthetic of specificity out of necessity—many of the dead could not be identified. Yet by representing the subordination of dead individuals to a greater cause these generic headstones served a political purpose.

While nineteenth-century headstones typically recorded a history of particulars—date of birth, relation to loved ones, a line from a favorite poem—the war dead were commemorated en masse. During the Civil War, an emphasis on the corpse's particular features was supplanted by a tendency to view the dead as featureless, or unknown: the elaboration of anonymity as a function of national identity is perhaps the national cemetery's most important contribution to the art of war. A democratic gesture that refuses to reinstate military (and implicitly class) hierarchy, the anonymity of state burial also implies the leveling effect of death itself. It seems possible, however, that the generic cast of the cemetery at Gettysburg could be taken as a sign of indifference on the part of the state that failed to recognize dead individuals. Perhaps to avoid any appearance of callousness in the design, David Wills, Pennsylvania governor Andrew Curtin's representative in Gettysburg, asked Lincoln to attend the cemetery's commemoration in order to assure soldiers that they would be well treated in death. Lincoln's presence, he wrote, would "kindle anew in the breasts of the comrades of these brave dead, who are now in the tented field or nobly meeting the foe in the front, a confidence that they who sleep in death on the battle-field are not forgotten by those highest in authority; and they will feel that, should their fate be the same, their remains will not be uncared for."[12]

Forgoing any elaboration of the particulars of the battle, Lincoln's "Gettysburg Address" mirrored the design of the cemetery itself.[13] Lincoln attempted to justify this approach by explaining, "The world will little note, nor long remember what we say here, but it can never forget what they did here."[14] While the speech uses language to spectacular effect, it elevates the actions of the dead by denigrating the power of the living to "consecrate" the war in words. We might imagine that the much-noted brevity of Lincoln's speech was the closest he could come to calling for a moment of silence. Indeed, when the speech was over (almost as soon as it was begun) the audience was left dumbstruck. The scene at Gettysburg—simple headstones arranged in orderly ranks, the president paying homage to a generic heroism—suggests the contours of a nationalist aesthetic that favors abstraction over detail and vies with commemorative traditions that dwell on the material properties of the corpse.

❧ The claim that the Civil War stimulated the development of postwar realism stands, somewhat uneasily, alongside the contention that it failed to produce "great" art. Even as they attempt to account for the interesting, if occasional, texts that the war left behind, literary critics note that many of the nineteenth century's most celebrated American writers remained silent on the subject of war. Most notably, Daniel Aaron's *The Unwritten War* offers an exhaustive survey of literary responses to the conflict while maintaining that writers failed to say anything "revealing" about the causes, or the meaning, of the Civil War.[15] In Aaron's view, the inability of writers to illuminate the war testifies to its monumental violence and the paralyzing impact this violence had on the imagination. He writes, "The thrill of fear after the first exultation and the abrupt change from haphazard engagements to massive and machine-made slaughter stunned the imagination. . . . It took time . . . to adjust to the enormous scale of the War and to tally its material and human cost" (336).

While Aaron does not dwell on the effect that technological change had on cultural production at any length, scholars who study the wars and genocides of the twentieth century have theorized this relationship more fully. Discussions of modern war describe the ways that the advent of new killing technologies, designed to destroy ever-larger groups of people more efficiently, alternately paralyzed the imagination and provoked it to invent new forms. Attempting to convey disorientation, disbelief, and mental and emotional paralysis, twentieth-century writers often rejected representational conventions designed to make the world appear ordered and coherent.[16] Indiscriminate and far-reaching destructiveness found formal expression as artists tried to communicate the power of war to cripple and destroy language. Represented silence offered one way to convey the failure of language in the face of pain and suffering.

Analyses of twentieth-century representations of war, which emphasize both the power of war to deconstruct language and artistic attempts to reconstruct it in new and politicized ways, are instructive in their failure to describe the literature of the Civil War. Indeed, what remains disquieting about the culture of this war is how rarely, and incompletely, it protests war violence. Civil War writing does not regard silence as evidence of the debilitating effect of violence on the individual's power of self-expression, but rather as testimony to the war's monumentality— its power not to shock and disturb but to awe and inspire. If twentieth-century authors often broke with literary conventions in an attempt to describe the impact of trauma on individual consciousness, Civil War writers used highly conventionalized declarations of the war's unrepresentability to express grief and pay homage to the war effort.

Forsaking the abundant detail of *Specimen Days*, Whitman's wartime poetry aestheticizes the carnage of war. In *Drum-Taps*, Whitman uses the informal, often improvised burials that occurred on the battlefield and in the hospital to structure a narrative of triumphant nationalism. While the volume as a whole narrates the emergence of a robust, unified nation from the chaos of war, poems that describe the burial of the dead demonstrate the role of ritualized silence in establishing the citizen's attachment to the state. Unlike *Specimen Days*, which devotes a great deal of attention to the dying soldier, *Drum-Taps* focuses on the spectator who "beholds" the war and, particularly, the mourner who contemplates the bodies of the wounded and the dead. Poems of death and mourning offer up simple, unelaborated images of the dead. Formulating a poetic practice commensurate with the claim that the real war should not get into the books, these poems conjure brief moments of silence amid the cacophony of the conflict as a means of ordering war's diversity and directing its affective power.

As scholars have argued, *Drum-Taps* expresses Whitman's deep ambivalence about the Civil War.[17] Clearly, it was difficult for him to reconcile the grandeur of the war effort with the dead and wounded bodies it produced: while some poems celebrate the advent of war others recoil from its horrors. Over time, however, Whitman reworked the volume in significant ways, using poems of death and mourning to enlarge, rather than detract from, a sense of the war's overarching purpose. Ruminating on war in retrospect, the final edition of *Drum-Taps* uses the reverential encounter between mourner and corpse to structure and dignify a narrative of war as the mechanism of national progress.

Michael Moon takes the tension between "war-rhetoric" and "elegiac rhetoric," which characterizes the first edition of *Drum-Taps*, to indicate how Whitman's view of war changed when he began working in Washington military hospitals.[18] During the first two years of the war, Whitman anticipated a brief and successful conflict at a safe distance from the battlefield. During these years he produced his patriotic poems, which urge participation in the war effort. "First O Songs for a Prelude" (called "Drum-Taps" in the original edition), which opens both early and late versions of *Drum-Taps*, provides one example. This poem re-creates the cacophony of the early days of the conflict as whole cities shift their attention from the routines of daily life to the project of war. Against the backdrop of the Manhattan cityscape, people emerge from interior spaces— houses, workshops, stores, and churches—to congregate in the street. As the title implies, sound provides the main motif for the poem: this noisy scene reminds us of a chorus warming up, testing its lungs with the round, empty "O" of the poem's title. What we hear in the rumble of artillery, the cheers of the crowd, the drum struck lightly is not the orchestrated tune but the "mutter of preparation."[19]

After his arrival in Washington, where he spent three years nursing soldiers, Whitman's outlook changed: the poetry of these years focuses on the sick, wounded, and dead. If the recruitment poems take marching as their central image for the engagement of individuals in the war effort and the consequent progress of the nation as it moves forward in history, these later poems pause the action of war in order to describe the soldier-spectator who gazes on the dead. The earlier poems emphasize sound as they strive to re-create the invigorating accompaniment of martial tunes; the later poems emphasize visual detail as they portray the poet's silent encounter with damaged bodies.[20]

In its two earliest versions—published in a separate volume as *Drum-Taps and Sequel to Drum-Taps* in 1865 and annexed to *Leaves of Grass* in 1867—the collection is marked by an unsteadiness of tone and purpose. Poems that celebrate the war effort clash with somber meditations on dead bodies. These are awkwardly juxtaposed to very brief descriptive poems that seem to bear little or no relevance to the subject of war

("Mother and Babe," "A Farm Picture," "The Torch"). While the volume as a whole captures the sense of excitation and restless energy that, in Whitman's view, characterizes the early days of the war, it defies the order and steady rhythm of the military march—the volume's ostensible framing device. Indeed, because the poems seem to follow one another in nearly arbitrary ways the volume has a staccato quality—like tap-tapping on a drum—but these bursts of sound, and attendant pauses, never cohere in a fluid and sustainable rhythm.

By contrast, the final edition of *Drum-Taps* (1891–92) represents the mourner's encounter with the dead as a necessary, if painful, step in the development of national community.[21] This volume takes on a narrative shape that moves from the "militant exultation" of the recruitment poems, to the imagistic, highly controlled poems of death and mourning, to the final poems, which offer a "justification of the war as part of the 'throes of democracy' in its march toward the future."[22] Whitman helps to achieve this effect by bringing together—and placing them near the center of the volume—four poems that describe the poet-soldier's confrontation with the dead and wounded: "Vigil Strange I Kept on the Field One Night," "A Sight in Camp in the Daybreak Gray and Dim," "As Toilsome I Wander'd Virginia's Woods," and "A March in the Ranks Hard Prest." In each of these poems, the narrator is brought up short by an unexpected encounter with a dead body. He pauses to pay tribute and then continues on his way. In "Vigil Strange," for example, a soldier sees his comrade drop on the battlefield. He continues fighting and then, during the night, returns to find that his friend has died. He sits all night with the body and buries it at dawn. He does not cry or speak ("not even a long-drawn sigh") but gazes on the corpse in silence. The word "vigil," repeated throughout, suggests both devotional watching and wakefulness, implying that even in mourning the soldier remains alert to danger. At daybreak the soldier "rose from the chill ground," wrapped his friend in a blanket, "And buried him where he fell."[23]

In describing a mourner paying homage to a corpse before moving on, these poems enact a ritual devotion that bridges the need to honor the dead with the need to keep fighting. The structure of these poems—movement that pauses and then resumes—is mirrored by the structure of the whole: this cluster of poems works to slow the progress of the volume by building a devotional pause into the triumphant forward motion of the whole. They help Whitman to structure this narrative of war as a well-ordered procession that moves, in a simple, elegant rhythm, from past (innocence) to present (death) to future (unity). In the final version of *Drum-Taps*, the double meaning of the title is realized and put to use: the slow, sad cadence of the funeral march structures and dignifies the progress of war.[24]

As Whitman's wartime writing demonstrates, close scrutiny of the dead does not necessarily temper the project of nation building through war. In "Turn O Libertad," the penultimate poem in *Drum-Taps*, the nation emerges from war "expanding, doubting no more, resolute, sweeping the world."[25] In a wartime setting, mourning often involves a ritualized forgetting that paves the way for future conflict. As the poet-soldier who gazes on the body of his enemy in the poem "Reconciliation" remarks, "Beautiful that war and all its deeds of carnage must in time be utterly lost" (453). Once the dead are buried and forgotten, Whitman can turn to celebrating a robust nation poised for "wars to come" (457). The imperial imagination is the beneficiary of wartime commemoration: a country unified by abstract losses—the untold suffering of unknown soldiers—can more easily project itself into a limitless future.

After burying his friend, the narrator of "Vigil Strange" rises up to return to the work of war. As I have argued, organic metaphor provided a way to describe the living invigorated by wartime death: some went so far as to imagine that violence would produce new populations—masses of people as well as the common identity that united them. Written by James Sloan Gibbons in 1862, "We Are Coming, Father Abraham, Three Hundred Thousand More" describes recruits rising up, like new wheat, from the ground where the dead lie buried:

> We are coming, Father Abraham, three hundred thousand more,
> From Mississippi's winding stream and from New England's shore;
> We leave our plows and workshops, our wives and children dear,
> With hearts too full for utterance, with but a silent tear;
> We dare not look behind us, but steadfastly before,
> We are coming, Father Abraham, three hundred thousand more.
> CHORUS:
> We are coming, coming our union to restore,
> We are coming, Father Abraham, with three hundred thousand
>   more.

> If you look across the hilltops that meet the northern sky.
> Long moving lines of rising dust your vision may descry;
> And now the wind an instant, tears the cloudy veil aside,
> And floats aloft our spangled flag in glory and in pride;

And bayonets in the sunlight gleam, and bands brave music pour,
We are coming, Father Abraham, three hundred thousand more.

If you look all up our valleys, where the growing harvests shine,
You may see our sturdy farmer boys fast forming into line;
And children from their mothers knees are pulling at the weeds,
And learning how to reap and sow, against their country's needs;
And a farewell group stands weeping at every cottage door,
We are coming, Father Abraham, three hundred thousand more.

You have called us and we're coming, by Richmond's bloody tide,
To lay us down for Freedom's sake, our brother's bones beside;
Or from foul treason's savage group to wrench the murd'rous blade,
And in the face of foreign foes its fragments to parade;
Six hundred thousand loyal men and true have gone before—
We are coming, Father Abraham, three hundred thousand more![26]

Gibbons wrote this song in response to Lincoln's request for 300,000 new volunteers. He uses Lincoln's own viewpoint to portray recruitment as a breathtaking natural spectacle: the president, who scans the horizon in anticipation, is barely able to distinguish new recruits from the landscape that appears to produce them. The song also describes the soldier's sad departure from home. We catch a glimpse of the mother left behind teaching her children to pull up weeds, "learning how to reap and sow against their country's needs." Images of fertility link landscape, home, and army in a vision of natural abundance; Gibbons imagines the emergence of 300,000 volunteers as a function of a fertile and well-tended national landscape.

Although "We Are Coming" begins with 300,000 living men growing up from the earth, it ends with them laying themselves down "for freedom's sake, our brothers' bones beside." The "more" of the title acknowledges that these men follow others who have already died in the conflict; the final stanza names the "six hundred thousand loyal men" who have "gone before." As this song demonstrates, wartime culture not only compensates loss with images of prosperity, productivity, and well-being but also imagines death itself as the source of such bounty. Representations of the dead body, gradually decaying, as the source of national identity, find their complement in representations of the miraculous appearance of new populations that give nationhood its public expression.

Benedict Anderson observes that nationalism and religion both provide ways of imagining life without end.[27] While religion offers the promise of immortality to the individual soul, nationalism projects the ongoing life of an abstract "people" and the institutions that govern them. In Gibbons's song the nation's immortality is expressed by its ability to produce fighting men. Lincoln himself imagined that the country could produce an infinite supply of soldiers. In his Annual Messages to Congress, Lincoln celebrated national expansion—territorial, economic, and industrial. On December 6, 1864, he linked these forms of expansion to the growth of "the most important branch of national resources—that of living men." Presenting a detailed comparison between the election returns of 1860 and 1864, Lincoln asserts that despite the mounting death toll the country's population is on the rise: the "important fact remains demonstrated, that we have *more* men *now* than we had when the war *began*; that we are not exhausted, nor in process of exhaustion; that we are *gaining* strength, and may, if need be, maintain the contest indefinitely." Referring to both men and material, he concludes that "national resources, then, are unexhausted, and, as we believe, inexhaustible."[28] Lincoln imagines the war as a generative force that, like a powerful machine or like the earth itself, can produce fighting men "in endless succession."

Lincoln's Annual Message, which describes the production of bodies during wartime as evidence of national strength, implies his broader effort to rethink the nature of state authority. Rejecting British governance, founding authors asserted the primacy of contractual association; the Declaration of Independence insisted that the textual elaboration of collective grievances and common interests legitimated the new nation. In order to neutralize obvious analogies between colonists and secessionists, Unionists needed to demonstrate the failure of the founding texts— especially the Constitution—as a basis for political community and to offer an alternative. They often turned to an organicism that viewed bodies, like plants, as part of a regenerative cycle in order to imagine a nation that preceded, and would outlast, the consent of its citizens. Although Lincoln at times insisted that protecting the Constitution was his chief object, his First Inaugural Address describes the Constitution as an outgrowth of the Union. He argues, in a maddeningly circular fashion, that it is "safe to assert that no government proper, ever had a provision in its organic law for its own termination" (217). Lincoln's "new" nationalism, born of necessity, trades an Enlightenment emphasis on rational consent for an ill-defined "organic law" that takes expansion, rather than stability, as the natural trajectory of political community.

During times of war, and especially civil war, a nation's legitimacy and

its future are called into question. Insisting that the nation was producing men at an increased clip, Lincoln refused to acknowledge that, at
points, the machine of state nearly ground to a halt. His Annual Message,
like Gibbons's song, masks the crisis of authority faced by a government
unable to count on the enthusiastic participation of its citizens. After all,
Lincoln had to ask for volunteers because the example of many thousands dead was not inspiring enough: the enlargement of federal power
during the war was occasioned by a shortage, rather than an abundance,
of manpower.

The Civil War witnessed the marked and permanent expansion of federal authority. James McPherson describes this remarkable structural
transformation: "The old federal republic in which the national government had rarely touched the average citizen except through the post-
office gave way to a more centralized polity that taxed the people directly
and created an internal revenue bureau to collect these taxes, drafted
men into the army, expanded the jurisdiction of federal courts, created a national currency and a national banking system, and established
the first national agency for social welfare—the Freedmen's Bureau."[29]
Lincoln was the principal agent, as well as the chief theorist, of these
changes. Three important instances of the controversial exercise of state
power occurred during the second year of the war (1862-63): the first
military draft in U.S. history, the nationwide suspension of the writ of
habeas corpus, and the Emancipation Proclamation. At Gettysburg Lincoln asserted that the dead had the power to "dedicate" the living to the
"unfinished work" of war.[30] In fact, quite the opposite was true. All three
measures were, according to Lincoln, responses to a crisis in manpower.
In 1862, the Union army was depleted, and potential recruits were far
from eager to join up. Losses from combat, disease, and desertion were
compounded by the expiration of enlistments. In response to this shortage of fighting men, Lincoln undertook the expansion of federal power
that he regarded as necessary to obtain and retain new soldiers.

Lincoln's wartime writing is characterized by a certain contradiction:
does the soldier's self-sacrifice renew and expand the influence of the
state, as Lincoln suggests at Gettysburg, or does the state, which needs
more fighting men, enlarge itself by finding ways to obtain them? In his
Opinion on the Draft, written in September 1863, Lincoln justified the
draft as a military necessity. He wrote, "We already have, and have had
in the service, as appears, substantially all that can be obtained upon this
voluntary weighing of motives. And yet we must somehow obtain more.
. . . To meet this necessity the law of the draft has been enacted. You

who do not wish to be soldiers, do not like this law."[31] Lincoln described emancipation as, like the draft, a response to a labor shortage. In numerous letters, he explains that he issued the Emancipation Proclamation in order to provide the army with a new source of recruits. On April 4, 1864, he writes that faced with the prospect of "surrendering the Union, and with it, the Constitution," he decided instead to place a "strong hand upon the colored element." Over a year later, the military "shows a gain of quite a hundred and thirty thousand soldiers, seamen, and laborers." He concludes, "We have the men; and we could not have had them without the measure" (586). In light of his remarks on conscription and emancipation, the production of fighting men appears not to be the expression of a prolific national landscape fertilized by dead soldiers, but rather the result of decisive and unorthodox assertions of state power.

The assassination of Abraham Lincoln, and the subsequent spectacle of national mourning, contributed enormously to the belief that death in war produced national unity. In "Death of Abraham Lincoln" (1887), a lecture that Whitman delivered annually on the anniversary of Lincoln's assassination, the poet claims that Lincoln's death gave birth to a "homogenous Union, compact, born again, consistent with itself."[32] Toward the end of the lecture he turns to Lincoln's "prairie-grave," where "Crumbled and wordless now lie his remains long buried," to describe the awesome influence of Lincoln's death. Whitman writes, "The final use of a heroic-eminent life—especially of a heroic-eminent death—is its indirect filtering into the nation. . . . Then there is a cement to the whole People, subtler, more underlying, than any thing in written Constitution, or courts or armies—namely, the cement of a first-class tragic incident thoroughly identified with that People, at its head, and for its sake. Strange, (is it not?) that battles, martyrs, blood, even assassination, should so condense—perhaps only really, lastingly condense—a Nationality" (12). Once again, the Constitution comes up short when compared to that "subtler, more underlying" form of social cohesion produced by blood sacrifice. The president's death stands in for the myriad individual losses of wartime, and his power to orchestrate war pales in comparison to his representative vulnerability.

Whitman, like Lincoln, imagined that violence would produce an infinite supply of living soldiers. Echoing Lincoln's claim that "national resources, then, are unexhausted, and, as we believe, inexhaustible," Whitman wrote, "I strengthen and comfort myself much with the certainty that the capacity for just such regiments, (hundreds, thousands of them) is inexhaustible in the United States, and that there isn't a county nor a township in the republic—nor a street in any city—but could turn out, and, on occasion, would turn out, lots of just such typical soldiers, whenever wanted."[33] Descriptions of the living who rise up in the wake of the dead metaphorize death as growth, inverting the material effects of war. During war, soldiers kill people. They rape women, demolish buildings, burn crops, and destroy culture. But while war obliterates bodies, objects, and memories, it also produces meaning—the sense of a worthy cause—that compensates for material losses. Whitman's claim that the "United States" can generate an infinite supply of "typical soldiers" not only represses war's destruction but also provides a powerful figure for the genesis of meaning; these masses embody the mobilizing influence of nationalist abstractions disseminated by wartime culture.

I would suggest that people were able to use the dead body as an occasion for collective rededication because they believed that dead people would be reborn, that the body retained some essential significance that was not extinguished in death but was freed to circulate. Lincoln's death provides a case in point. While James Gibbons describes "father Abraham" straining to see 300,000 soldiers mustering in the distance, at least that number went out of their way to catch a glimpse of the dead president as his body made its way across the countryside. Concluding a period of civil conflict, Lincoln's death occasioned an outpouring of nationalist feeling as enormous, peaceful crowds gathered in Northern cities to pay their respects. Over the course of two weeks, Lincoln's funeral procession, which began in Washington, D.C., stopped in Baltimore, Harrisburg, Philadelphia, New York, Albany, Buffalo, Cleveland, Columbus, Indianapolis, and Chicago, before arriving in Springfield. In each city, people turned out in unprecedented numbers for street processions and stood in line for many hours in order to have a chance to file past Lincoln's open casket.[34] All along the route, they gathered in groups, small and large, to sing and pray. These crowds provided evidence of Lincoln's authority, now disseminated through the body politic in the form of common feeling.[35]

Visual depictions of the event stress the impressive spectacle of these huge, peaceful crowds. While photographs show Lincoln's catafalque surrounded by an unwieldy mass of people (fig. 3.1), prints and wood engravings give form and structure to the crowds (fig. 3.2). Like visual representations, first-person accounts dwell on the size of the crowds that gathered to mourn the president. They emphasize the length of the lines, attempt to estimate the number of people in attendance, and often

FIGURE 3.1. *Lincoln's funeral procession. Brown University Library.*

marvel at the silence that characterized these huge and potentially unruly groups. Describing Washington on the day of Lincoln's funeral, one spectator remarked that "the scene in the White House, the street, and the Capitol today, was the strongest evidence the war afforded of the stability of our institutions and the worthiness and magnanimous power of our people."[36] Representations of Lincoln's funeral procession, in which enormous and immobile crowds gather to pay their respects, exemplify, in microcosm, the power of the dead to produce civic unity out of civil war.

While representations of Lincoln's death affirmed a popular narrative of the regenerative effect of self-sacrifice, a great deal of war-

THE 25TH OF APRIL 1865 IN NEW YORK.

FIGURE 3.2. *"The 25th of April 1865 in New York." Brown University Library.*

time art did not readily contribute to this vision of a unified and inexhaustible public. In the years following the war, anthologists gathered a diverse body of poetry that cannot be read through the lens of homogenizing nationalist abstractions. Rather than describing a mass of people animated by a single will, these anthologies investigate a wide range of responses to the war. Sallie Brock prefaced her anthology of Southern wartime poetry, *The Southern Amaranth*, with the following remarks: "The design of this work was conceived in an individual desire to offer a testimonial of gratitude to the memories of the brave men who perished in the late ineffectual effort for SOUTHERN INDEPENDENCE; as well as in a wish to render to my Southern sisters some assistance in gathering up the remains of the CONFEDERATE DEAD, from the numberless battle-fields over which they were scattered, and placing them where the rude ploughshares may not upturn their bleaching bones, and where sorrowing friends may at least drop a tear and lay a flower upon the grass-covered hillocks that mark their resting places."[37] Analogizing these collected poems to bone fragments, Brock describes the process of recovering obscure, occasional poems, written in a time of crisis, as a form of mourning that was not possible during the war. Published in New York in 1869, *The Southern Amaranth* is one of many anthologies that appeared in the years following the Civil War. These collections use the occasional expressions of wartime culture in an effort to rebuild national community. Unlike Whitman, who assimilates the particulars of war into a narrative of triumphant national unity, these anthologies narrate the war through the accumulation and juxtaposition of discrete instances of poetic expression. Attempting to recover the homely particulars of wartime poetry, they reverse the process of abstraction vital to the development of Civil War nationalism.

Mary Louise Kete has examined the role that poetry played in shaping community during the nineteenth century. She describes the production and exchange of sentimental poetry as a form of mourning that helped middle-class Americans shore up their sense of self and community in the face of death and dislocation. Her analysis centers on "Harriet Gould's Book": originally blank, Gould's book was filled with occasional verse, inscribed by family and friends, over the course of a lifetime. Containing poems to mark a variety of occasions, such books chronicled an individual's life through the words of her intimate circle. Some of the poems in Gould's book are original, some are copied from other sources, and some are lifted and rewritten without attribution. It seems that these poems were not valued for their originality, or viewed as the property of individual authors. Instead, they were gifts that strengthened communal bonds as they passed from hand to hand.[38] In important respects, anthologies of war poetry resemble the albums that Kete discusses. In order to include poems by famous authors and anonymous ones, devotional poems and irreverent satires, poems that applaud the war and those that call it into question, anthologists cast a wide net. They subordinate coherence to comprehensiveness and representative genius to idiosyncratic self-expression.

Introducing a retrospective account of the war that proceeds by way of accumulation rather than synthesis, these anthologies necessarily meditate on the relationship between war and art, implicitly asking what kind of poetry best represents, and most respectfully commemorates, the events of war. Instead of imagining a community constituted by representative acts of suffering, they stress the material nature of poetry itself, asserting, as "Harriet Gould's Book" does, that culture is produced by individuals, as well as groups, on particular occasions. Far from applauding art for transcending circumstance, they describe circumstance as the ground of culture. Indeed, anthologists defended wartime poetry against the attacks of critics, real or imagined, who valued formal refinement too dearly. While Daniel Aaron notes that "almost immediately after Appomattox Northern commentators began to complain about the failure of American writers to do justice to the recent strife," some complained about those who mounted such criticism.[39] Oliver Wendell Holmes, for example, began his lecture on the poetry of war, delivered on November 21, 1865, by addressing "those who would save me all trouble by the assertion that there has been no real poetry produced during the war."[40] Holmes does not leap to defend the literary merit of war poetry, or to call standards of judgment into question. Instead, he maintains that the unique circumstances of wartime, particularly advances in the technologies that produce and circulate print material, call for a certain kind of poetry. Unlike the days when "everything had to be written out by hand, and . . . parchment was very dear," now "printing is cheap; paper is cheap. The gods are dethroned, men are less exclusive, and the columns of the daily, weekly and monthly press require a standing army of moderately good poets" (3). Punning on "columns," Holmes links advances in the publishing industry to efforts to wage war on the cultural front, and argues that the poetry of a democratic war, implicitly a war waged against the "exclusive" institution of slavery, will be authored by amateur poets.

As Holmes suggests, the vast body of wartime poetry was published in daily newspapers and illustrated magazines. These poems were written with a sense of urgency—often in response to a particular battle or event—and rushed off for publication. Those who witnessed the war firsthand wanted to convey their experience to civilians, while civilians translated secondhand accounts of the war that they found in newspapers, magazines, and bulletins into poetry.[41] The hasty production and mass publication of a lot of poetry was part of a much larger effort to maintain communication between the battlefield and the home front—a process inevitably plagued by rumor and hypothesis. In keeping with these conditions, anthologists asserted that the value of occasional poetry lay not in its beauty, its complexity, or its ability to transmute the circumstances of war, but rather in the power of the poems, when collected, to reproduce war's cacophony.

Drawing attention to the unevenness and inconsistency of their volumes, anthologists suggested that in order to adequately convey the reality of war a collection of poems *must* be mediocre. Introducing a volume of his own poems that had already been published in newspapers, Henry Howard Brownell remarks that because his poems were "penned, for the most part, on occasion, from day to day," and often in the midst of crisis, his collection will be marred by "instances of diffuseness, contradiction, or repetition."[42] Introducing his 1866 anthology, Richard White acknowledges that in selecting a representative collection of Civil War verse "poetical merit has not been the only consideration." Indeed, "fastidiousness in these respects would be much out of place." Rather than choosing his poems on the basis of literary merit, he has "looked through the street ballads as well as the monthly magazines, and . . . taken as readily what was printed upon a broadside, or written for negro minstrels, as what came from Bryant, Longfellow, Lowell, or Boker."[43] Anthologists do not, however, forgo claims to representativeness. They insist that when gathered together these poems convey the will and the mood of the American people during wartime. Thus aesthetic mediocrity goes hand in hand with a volume's power to embody the evanescent spirit of a people at a particular moment in time. Brownell describes his verse as "spray . . . flung up by the strong Tide-Rip of Public Trouble" which will "present the Time more nearly, perhaps, than they do the writer" (iii). And White portrays his volume as a "poetical reflex of the mind of a whole people under the excitement of a war lasting four years."[44]

Anthologies do not embody a people at war by synthesizing, abstracting, or homogenizing the conflict's particulars but rather by collecting individual poems, each indebted to its own urgent occasion, and letting them stand side by side. In the aftermath of the Civil War, these anthologies suggest how difficult it was to arrive at a common understanding of the recent conflict. Their response to the nationalist imperative of shared remembrance is hesitant at best: proposing the accumulation of occasional verse, in all its diversity and artistic unevenness, as the best way to describe the war, these collections trade a vision of seamless union for an account of political community that remains divided by circumstance.

When reading through collections of Civil War poetry, however, I hardly feel that I am brought face to face with the conditions of war. Ideologically motivated and highly conventional, these poems often blend into one another. Those that stand out, able to convey a sense of immediacy over time, are distinguished not by content but by context. For example, "What tho' These Limbs," written by a Confederate prisoner of war, appeared in the anthology *War Lyrics and Songs of the South* (1866):

What tho' these limbs be bound with iron cords,
Still I am free!
For liberty can dwell amidst the clank of chains,
And in the gloom of dungeons,
As well as 'neath the leafy arches
Of the boundless forest.

Who can fetter the undying spirit,
Or circumscribe the limits of the mind?
Far out beyond these prison walls
I roam adown the vistas
Of imagination—and still am free![45]

This poem pivots on the conventional trope of slavery and freedom often found in Confederate and Union poetry. What will catch a reader's attention, however, is the brief description that precedes the poem: "Written by Col. Ben Anderson of Louisville, Kentucky, on the prison wall in Cincinnati, shortly before committing suicide." The fact that this poem was written by a prisoner of war, or that it was intended as a suicide note, can only heighten its affective power. The emotional intensity produced by these particulars is inseparable from the poem's dramatic appearance on the wall of a prison cell. Similarly, an editorial note that introduces "Too Good to Be Lost"—a poem that meditates on the worthlessness of Confederate currency—explains that "the following lines were found written on the back of a five hundred dollar Confederate note."

These contextualizing remarks draw attention to the importance of spatial settings—actual and imagined—to the production and reproduction of war poetry. Whether or not Colonel Anderson actually wrote his verse on the wall of a prison cell, this text imagines that wartime poets write in desperate circumstances, making use of all available surfaces. Poetry is not an instrument of refined expression but a form that responds impulsively to an unprecedented crisis and proceeds by way of improvisation. The reality of war, in this context, does not attach to the graphic representation of bodily pain but to the production of poetry itself. In contrast to Whitman's efforts to convey the failure of representation, this poetry takes an optimistic view of the power of language to record the circumstances of war. While the dead body, subject to certain decay, is the appropriate object for an aesthetics of forgetfulness, the materiality of unlikely spaces of production furthers the anthologist's effort to secure the war in memory.

I would like to turn now to a particular compilation of occasional poetry that documents the war's symbolic conclusion—the assassination of Abraham Lincoln. In the days after Lincoln was killed, an observer walked, pen in hand, through the streets of Manhattan and recorded in a notebook all the occasional poetry and sketch art that appeared in the windows of storefronts, churches, schools, and homes.[46] Although this is a private document, most likely not intended for publication, it underscores the role that carefully recorded detail plays in helping to orient the observer in a world suddenly transformed by violence. Reading this notebook, one begins to imagine the streets of New York papered with expressions of sorrow, shock, and revenge.[47] Most frequently, the poems express sadness. In the window of Frederick's Gallery: "In sorrowing tears the nation's grief is spent / Mankind has lost a friend, and we a President." At 843 Broadway: "The tear that we shed, / Though in secret it rolls, / Shall long keep his memory / Green in our souls." Many verses are, like these, lilting and predictable in their rhymes; others, like this one, are more awkward: "A martyr to the cause of man / His blood is freedom's eucharist / And in the world's great hero list, / His name shall lead the van." Threats of revenge also appear with frequency, though not in poetic form. At 663 Broadway a sign reads: "Woe to the hand that shed this costly blood." More pointedly, 18 Bowery declares, "Death to Assassins." Throughout, poetry is accompanied by discursive prose that tends to be somewhat more idiosyncratic. At 544 Broadway: "There was in this man something that could create, subvert, or reform: an understanding, a spirit, and an eloquence, to summon mankind to society, or to break the bonds of slavery asunder, and to rule a wilderness of free minds with unbounded authority, something that could establish and overwhelm an empire, and strike a blow in the world that resound [sic] through the universe." In addition, we find drawings of weeping willows and tombstones, quotes from Shakespeare, and a passage from a speech by Andrew Johnson announcing that if he were president all traitors would be arrested and hanged.[48]

This anthologist also recorded the context in which these poems, drawings, and aphorisms appeared, not only noting the street address and often the type of establishment where they were posted, but also the relationship of a given text to its material context. One verse is followed by a note remarking that it appeared in "white letters on black ground"; a passage from Lincoln's Second Inaugural Address is surrounded by a sketch of a wreath and then, in handwriting, "green wreath"; a written description of an image accompanies a poem — "Goddess of Liberty holding the olive branch, the frame was draped with black crape and white rosettes with this inscription." The anthologist tries to reproduce as nearly as possible the public space of the city filled with the particulars of occasional art. The blurring of forms — poetry, prayer, drawing, aphorism — is accompanied by the blurring of the boundaries between the text and the physical context in which it appears.

In the wake of Lincoln's assassination, the streets and storefronts of

New York resembled the pages of "Harriet Gould's Book," covered with an eclectic array of poetry and prose that favored quotation and juxtaposition over originality. In *City Reading*, Kevin Henkin describes the proliferation of ephemeral public texts in antebellum New York: "Disparate urban texts marked the streets as a site of public reading, a palimpsest of shared information upon which claims to personal authority blurred into one another and receded into a larger verbal collage."[49] According to Henkin, the expressions of grief and rage that filled New York after Lincoln's death were reproduced in the city's major newspapers. Like the private notebook I have described, the *New York Times* not only reprinted messages posted in windows and on storefronts but also tried to convey a sense of the varied settings in which these texts appeared: "From every window in every street . . . from the spires of our churches, from the domes of our halls, from every flag-staff, from every pane of glass, on the lappel [sic] of the millionaire, about the arm of the laborer . . . are the insignia of grief."[50]

As Henkin demonstrates, during the nineteenth century public culture was increasingly permeated by anonymous and ephemeral printed texts. Insisting that occasional poetry must exceed the bounds of great art if it were to capture the reality of war, anthologists also scrambled distinctions between high and low art, between poems by famous authors and those by anonymous authors, between poetry and song. In recording poems with an eye to context—where and how did these poems originally appear?—anthologists drew attention not only to the material properties of occasional poems but also to the difficulty of producing art during wartime. In the view of anthologists, the real war did not, as Whitman claimed, fail to get into the books. Instead, it was captured by poetry of a certain sort—poetry that responded to the exigencies of the moment by recording the events of war on the page, in the margins of the page, on the walls of prison cells, and on city streets.

Published in 1866, Herman Melville's *Battle-Pieces and Aspects of the War* is dedicated "To the Memory of the Three Hundred Thousand who in the War for the Maintenance of the Union Fell Devotedly under the Flag of Their Fathers."[51] This dedication might prepare us for a narrative of suffering and redemption, but while Melville does pay tribute to the heroism of soldiers and the grand purpose of the war in some poems, in others he laments war's pointlessness. Like the volumes of occasional poetry that I have discussed, and like the first edition of *Drum-Taps*, this book is willfully eclectic: drawing on various poetic styles and popular forms, Melville refuses to unify the scenes of war. In composing *Battle-Pieces*, Melville relied on *The Rebellion Record*, a thirteen-volume collection of newspaper articles, speeches, maps, and other sources.[52] His poems not only feature well-known battles, military leaders, and events, they also draw on the forms of communication—photographs, ballads, newspaper reports—that gave descriptions of the war their particular texture. The fragmented quality of the work—emphasized by the "pieces" and "aspects" of its title—is one effect of its documentary method.

Foregrounding his dependence on an array of external sources, Melville acknowledges the mediated and indeterminate nature of his relation to the Civil War. Throughout, he calls attention to the inconclusive particulars of war, repudiating an organicist vision of war as part of a natural cycle of death and regeneration.[53] Whitman's war writing is characterized by a momentum that breeds interconnection: soldiers march, the death toll mounts, memory recurs, as the war builds toward its inevitable conclusion. Combining an easy antiformalism with a romantic investment in the feeling subject, many of the poems in *Drum-Taps* produce a sense of linguistic and emotional abundance. The poems in *Battle-Pieces*, by contrast, are "grim, carefully crafted, aesthetic objects."[54] Despite Melville's claim that he simply drew on themes that "chanced to imprint themselves upon the mind," the volume's formal diversity, adherence to prescribed poetic form, and obvious debt to other sources communicate the effort that goes into writing these poems.[55]

If Melville's wartime poetry stands in stark contrast to Whitman's, it is formally, if not ideologically, affiliated with popular poetry of the period. The anthologies I have discussed are embedded in circumstances that cannot be reduced to, or redeemed by, political unities; *Battle-Pieces* intensifies the eclectic and improvisational nature of the genre. But unlike popular anthologies in which such diversity, taken to characterize the mood of the people, is an end in itself, *Battle-Pieces* uses formal multiplicity to reflect on redemptive narratives like Whitman's own.

If *Drum-Taps* takes the intimacy between the living and the dead as a source of political unity, *Battle-Pieces* takes the standoff between North and South to characterize relations of many sorts—between civilian and soldier, observer and object, reader and text, past and future—as conflicted and incomplete. The poem "Donelson," drawn from *The Rebellion Record* accounts of the battle at Fort Donelson, takes the difficulty of conveying information from the battlefield to the home front as its subject. Describing a group of people who gather around a bulletin board during a winter storm to find out what is happening in the battle over Fort Donelson, the poem dramatizes the imprecise nature of wartime communication.[56] It is divided between sections that describe civilians responding to a series of news bulletins and sections that comprise the reports, narrating the battle itself. Throughout, an attention to context runs counter to the representation of unanimity or coherence. We are reminded of the reporter who does his best to compile his dispatch "from varied sources" and of the vagaries of technology when transmission is disrupted by a storm in the west (41, 49). Melville emphasizes the unreliability of communication and, by extension, the unbridgeable distance between battle and home fronts.

The divide that separates soldiers and civilians also characterizes the relationship between the living and the dead. Far from sentimentalizing battlefield death as a source of civic commitment, Melville stresses the difference between the living and the dead by objectifying corpses and mocking the conventions meant to elevate them. Unlike the narrator of Whitman's "Reconciliation," who leans over to kiss the lips of his dead enemy, Melville's "Magnanimity Baffled" describes the Northern "victor" who reaches out to his Southern foe only to find himself grasping the hand of a corpse (156).

In much of the popular culture of war, the absence of the corpse, and of language commensurate to its demise, allows the mourner's feelings of affection and longing for the dead to be transferred to the state. This displacement of feeling obscures the workings of power as well as the historicity of the circumstances that produce suffering. But the reconstruction of historical context, which situates suffering in place and time, may fail to do justice to wartime experiences that do not conform to the observations of documentary description any more than they conform to nationalist narratives of heroism and transcendence. As Margot Norris has observed, survivors witness "the deconstruction not only of their material world but also of their conceptual universe." As a result, when one is documenting war, the "effects of irreality" may become tools of "historical explanation."[57]

At times, Melville uses images of the body's resistant materiality to produce this very effect. In "Donelson," a dozen wounded soldiers freeze to death on the battlefield. Melville describes their "ice-glazed corpses, each a stone" (43). This image of bodies frozen solid neatly links the two worlds of the poem: they remind the reader of the "shards" of freezing rain that pummel civilians gathered for news, as well as the fragments of information they receive. Melville's corpses fail to yield knowledge or consolation. At one point, Melville describes the civilian's emotional response to death in war as a brittle object not unlike the corpses of dead soldiers, or Melville's own poems. Having read the latest posting from the front, the reader looks "To find in himself some bitter thing, / Some hardness in his lot as harrowing / As Donelson" (46). Rather than using a rhetoric of transformation to harmonize the living and the dead, Melville uses the dead body's material and epistemological recalcitrance to describe the fragmenting effect of violence on the survivor's consciousness.

While collections of occasional poetry focus on detail in an attempt to reproduce context, they do not use these details to describe the war's impact on perception. Using brittle fragments—stone, shards, ice—to depict both external conditions and internal states, Melville contemplates the impact of physical violence on subjectivity, reminding us of modernist efforts to use the shards of language—curtailed and incomplete— to describe war's effect on the mind. In my view, the representations that most powerfully convey the damage done by the war are those that in their emphatic materiality resist narration or contextualization, thus communicating the alien and incomprehensible nature of wartime suffering. Defying assimilation of any kind, these texts imply that death is final and loss cannot be redeemed. I find one example in the collection of photographs taken by Reed Bontecue, Civil War physician and photographer, at Harewood Hospital in Washington. Portraying sick and wounded soldiers, who look at the camera or refuse to meet its stare, these portraits meditate on the power and limits of the diagnostic gaze; graphically portraying wounded body parts while also studying the powerfully expressive faces of these soldiers, they consider the impact of amputation and disfigurement on the psychologized subject (see fig. 3.3).[58]

One unusual photograph, however, portrays the result of wounding in the absence of appropriate context: it presents a fragment of bone mounted on a small pedestal (fig. 3.4). If this image were not accompanied by a written description, and juxtaposed to photographs of amputees, John Miller's leg bone would appear a stray piece of stone, a geologist's find. We might wonder where it came from and why someone saw fit to photograph it. Then again, its interest might be self-evident: a brittle substance, riddled with pockmarks, with an oval hole in the middle, and tapered to a point. Reading the caption that originally accompanied the photograph, we learn that this is a bone fragment, six inches in length, "drawn from the end of the stump" of one John Miller, a private in the 118th Pennsylvania Volunteers who was shot in the knee in October 1864 somewhere near Petersburg, Virginia. These details do not qualify the

FIGURE 3.3. *John Miller, hospital number 18,450.*
Yale University, Harvey Cushing/John Hay Whitney Medical Library.

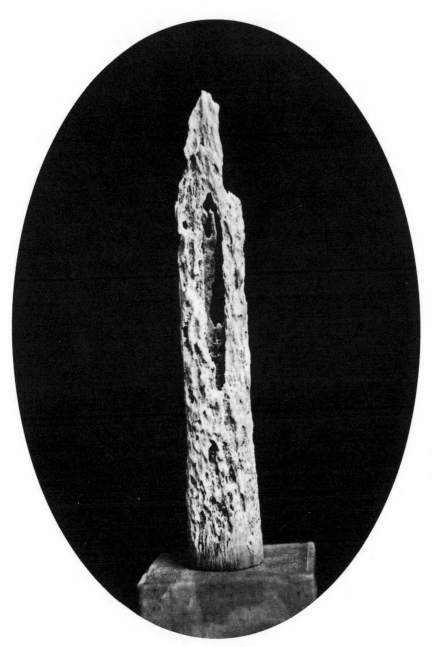

FIGURE 3.4. *John Miller's leg.*
Yale University, Harvey Cushing/John Hay Whitney Medical Library.

impenetrable materiality of this photograph. If anything, they exaggerate it. Looking at this piece of bone one comes no closer to imagining what it was like to fight in Petersburg on an October day, or to be wounded there. In their resistant ahistoricity, such fragments reproduce a fundamental disorientation on the part of the viewer that, if it does not resemble the disorientation of wartime experience, certainly testifies to the impact of time on historical inquiry: this bone fragment reminds us that the thing that we are looking for—John Miller, his experience of war, the war itself—no longer exists. In this instance, the referential content of the wounded body floats free, suggesting that war is best expressed by pieces of the broken body that cannot be reassembled, let alone resurrected.[59]

While Whitman's "This Compost" points toward the war's stupendous death toll and rehearses the narrative of organic transformation that will help to rationalize it, the poem also suggests a certain tension in wartime culture. Time and again in poems and songs, essays and speeches, battlefield death is viewed as one stage in an inevitable, and virtually unaccountable, natural process. Yet in the midst of these affirmations we sometimes hear the hum of a sturdy machine—the machine of state—at work. When we do, it is difficult not to pause and observe that state-sanctioned death may not lead forward—to redemption, renewal, or even social progress—but may, to the contrary, be an end in itself. Melville concludes "Donelson" not by envisioning the body's fruitful decomposition but rather by evoking the decaying machinery of war:

> The battle flag-staff fall athwart
> The curs'd ravine, and wither; naught
>   Be left of trench or gun;
> The bastion, let it ebb away,
> Washed with the river bed; and Day
>   In vain seek Donelson. (52)

Melville imagines the power of nature turned against the instruments of war. Unlike Whitman, who uses organic imagery to ennoble state power, Melville is glad that the machines that produce wounded and dead bodies will, in time, erode and disappear. His poetry of brittle particulars reveals that there is no object, belief, or figure commensurate with the war; instead, such poetry intimates the debris war leaves behind, fragments that, at the very least, dissociate the act of interpretation from the affirmation of triumphant rebirth.

PHOTOGRAPHING
THE WAR DEAD

4

During the Civil War, Americans viewed photographs of dead soldiers for the first time. Images of contorted corpses, severed limbs, bodies heaped in mass graves documented the effect of violence on the soldier's body and testified to the particular conditions of battlefield death. These photographs posed a challenge to popular conventions for representing death in war: when we look at them we see corpses that will never decompose and thus never regenerate. In the last chapter, I examined the tendency to describe violent death as an expression of nature—cyclical, productive, and benevolent. Here I will argue that photographs, unlike poetry, allow us to see wartime death as decidedly unnatural. Organic imagery, which views death as part of a process of deterioration and growth that unfolds over time, describes war as a means to spiritual and social progress. While organic metaphors portray change, no matter how dramatic, as inevitable and assimilable, photographs show us that cherished beliefs, habits, and routines can be shattered by events.

With little evidence as to how photographs of dead soldiers were received, scholars have tried to understand their impact on perceptions of death, violence, and representation both during the war and after. Often they assume that antebellum viewers were shocked, and their view of war transformed, by these photographs: such gruesome images, they argue, could not help calling romantic notions of heroic self-sacrifice and collective rededication into question. William Stapp, for example, asserts that these "unflinching, unsentimentalized" photographs "forever destroyed the cherished myth of the soldier's glorious death in battle and made palpable to those who actually saw them the reality of the human cost of the Rebellion."[1]

Such analyses construe nineteenth-century responses through the lens of our own tendency to be shocked by images of dead bodies. Too often they assume that viewers were unaccustomed to looking at photographs of dead people and were likely to see them (as we do) as evidence of the war's reality. In an era in which we rarely see, let alone handle, dead bodies, photographed corpses provide contemporary photojournalism with a powerful sign of presence. The precision achieved by documentary photography during the twentieth century contributes to the experience of verisimilitude. I will contend that nineteenth-century viewers, by contrast, were not likely to be shocked by the sight of corpses or to expect unadulterated realism from photographs. To the contrary, during the Civil War the imprecision of photographic technology embodied the distance that separated soldiers from their families as well as the difficulties civilians faced when trying to follow the events of war.

By the time the war began, photographs of corpses were commonplace, as middle-class Americans routinely employed professionals to take portraits of dead family members. Postmortem photographs, typically daguerreotypes that could not be reproduced, provided one popular way to memorialize the dead. Representing the dead as if they were still alive, postmortem photographs served as relics endowed with the aura of the once-living person. They also testified to the ongoing devotion of the living who washed, groomed, and posed the corpse in preparation for the photograph. Carefully staged, these images remind us that nineteenth-century Americans viewed both photographs and corpses as vehicles of self-expression, capable of giving form to imagined as well as actual states. If postmortem photographs reaffirmed familial love in the face of death, photographs of soldiers who died alone and decayed in the open air confronted Northern viewers with their inability to care for their dead. Drawing on the familiar genre of postmortem photography, these photographs dramatized the impossibility of honoring dead soldiers in accustomed ways.

Photographs of the dead soldiers were extraordinary, not only because they showed corpses stripped of all signs of ritual devotion, but also because they circulated to an audience of strangers. Postmortem daguerreotypes, while they might be shared with acquaintances or exhibited in portrait galleries, were essentially private objects that embodied individual grief. The mid-1850s saw the introduction of techniques for reproducing photographs as well as the advent of illustrated magazines.

Once the war began, people bought *cartes de visites* and stereoviews of dead soldiers, and encountered wood engravings that reproduced these images in the illustrated press. These new conditions allowed for the emergence of the corpse as a journalistic subject: death scenes were distributed far and wide as one means of informing people about the war. A nascent photojournalism potentially clashed, however, with the memorial function of the daguerreotype. Because photographs of the battlefield dead represented corpses in the absence of grieving family members, they lacked a way to ensure the appropriate emotional response in a viewing audience. As a result, these images threatened to build national community bound not by common sorrow but by a newfound detachment in the face of mass death.

Photographs of the battlefield dead failed to facilitate individual grief or its dissemination to a larger community. They also dramatized the limitations of the photograph as a tool of war reporting. If the impulse behind photojournalism is to document events as they occur, Civil War photographers were necessarily thwarted. Because the camera could not yet record moving objects, it was impossible to photograph men fighting. In the context of wartime journalism, photographs of the battlefield dead stood in for the "newsworthy" event—killing and wounding in battle—that could not be documented.

For many reasons, then, a rhetoric of presence, which informs both nineteenth- and twentieth-century accounts of the advent of photography, cannot fully account for the impact of photographs of dead soldiers. Among others, Roland Barthes has theorized the ways that the photograph embodies forms of distance, or absence, that at their most extreme intimate death itself. Barthes describes the photograph's deconstruction of linear time as an expression of its fundamental relation to death. In Barthes view, the "catastrophe" witnessed by every photograph is the death of the photographed subject.[2] When we look at an old photograph, in particular, we see a person who is on the verge of the future and, at the same time, already dead. The photograph brings us in contact with the past as it looks out on an unrealized future and at the same time produces a keen awareness that this future is already finished. It disrupts narrative time in which one event leads to another and in which through retrospection we can reconstruct the genesis of our own present. In doing so, the photographic image produces a form of subjectivity characterized not by insight but by incomprehension.[3]

War itself disrupts the expectation that the future will unfold in the image of a familiar past. By virtue of its formal properties, the photograph captures the power of war to disrupt continuity, dividing past from future by destroying familiar objects and routines. In this chapter, I will argue that during the Civil War the relatively new and inexact technology of photography was uniquely able to portray the way that war uproots things as they are, rendering traditions and routines inoperable while failing to offer new forms of political and representational certainty. Far from assuring people that war was a form of progress and that death strengthened national community, photographs of the battlefield dead implied that violence breeds isolation. They did so, however, not by awakening civilians to the truth of death in war but by depriving them of the means of expressing, and elaborating, the reality of death as they knew it.

Portrayed photographically, battlefield death undermined the very habits of thought and representation that transformed individual loss into spiritual and political community. At the same time, the isolated corpse, stripped of signs of affection and grief, directs us toward the twentieth century's reliance on the dead body as a sign of truth and, more broadly, on documentary observation as a source of collective knowledge. These photographs, and the texts that accompany them, take up the failure of familiar forms of artifice to invest the dead with meaning while pointing tentatively toward the emergence of the body as an object that speaks for itself.

≈ Primed by their knowledge of Roger Fenton's photographs of the Crimean War, exhibited in Britain in 1855 and 1856, American photographers went to great lengths to document the Civil War. Between September 18 and September 22, 1862, Alexander Gardner, assisted by James Gibson, photographed the aftermath of the battle of Antietam.[4] Among the first known photographs of dead soldiers, these images reached a Northern public quickly: within a month they were exhibited in Mathew Brady's New York gallery and reproduced in *Harper's Weekly*.[5] Based on a handful of available sources, scholars ascribe terrific impact to these images, arguing that the unprecedented realism of the Antietam photographs upset viewers accustomed to a romantic view of war. Often they cite a review of the exhibit published in the *New York Times* to substantiate the powerful effect of these photographs on the viewing public.[6] A close examination of this piece, however, suggests that these images were unsettling not because they conveyed the reality of war but because they failed to elicit an appropriate emotional response from viewers.

While the review cannot tell us how exhibition goers actually reacted to the Antietam photographs, it in effect cautions us against assuming that they were shocked by them. The essay opens with the problem of civilian apathy: "As it is, the dead of the battlefield come up to us very rarely, even in dreams. We see the list in the morning paper at breakfast, but dismiss its recollection with coffee. There is a confused mass of names, but they are all strangers; we forget the horrible significance that swells amid the jumble of type."[7] The reviewer laments the civilian's inability to feel enduring sorrow over battlefield losses. He imagines, however, that such feeling could be aroused by the presence of the dead body itself. "Our sensations might be different," he speculates "if the newspaper carrier left the names on the battle-field and the bodies at our door instead." Contrasting the negligible impact of print with the immediacy of the photograph, the reviewer claims that Brady may not have "brought bodies and laid them in our door-yards" but "has done something very like it."

The review goes on to describe crowds dwelling, fascinated, over images of the dead. They bend down to get a better look, "chained by the strange spell that dwells in dead men's eyes." As if to underscore the "terrible distinctness" of these images, the reviewer notes that with "the aid of the magnifying-glass, the very features of the slain may be distinguished." Yet Gardner's Antietam photographs would seem to repudiate this intimate gaze (see fig. 4.1). They depict small groups of contorted bodies, corpses strewn indiscriminately across the battlefield, and bodies piled in mass graves awaiting burial. Most of the images were taken from a distance and subordinate the particular features of individual corpses, emphasizing instead the extent and anonymity of battlefield death. When we take the nature of these images into consideration, the reviewer's use of the magnifying glass appears to compensate for the failure of these photographs to capture the dead man's face, his eyes, and, by implication, his identity.

Stressing the alien nature of the dead, the Antietam photographs also examine the attitude that the living take toward these barely recognizable forms. Seven photographs from this series show the dead in the company of the living. (By contrast, while a number of Gettysburg images show the dead gathered for burial, none of them shows the dead with living soldiers.) One photograph depicts soldiers gathered to bury the dead (fig. 4.2). They seem to take a casual attitude toward the work at hand. One soldier works while the rest appear relaxed, leaning on their tools or lounging on the ground. While some look at the dead, others look at the camera or the ground. Far from demonstrating the intimacy between the living and the dead, these photographs dwell on the problem

FIGURE 4.1. *Confederate dead by a fence on the Hagerstown Road,*
Antietam, Maryland, 1862. Library of Congress.

of disposal: burying their former comrades is a chore, nothing more, that
these soldiers approach with marked disinterest.

A similar disregard characterizes an image titled "A Contrast: Federal buried, Confederate unburied, where they fell on the Battle-field of
Antietam" (fig. 4.3). In this photograph a man looks down at a freshly
dug grave. His posture and expression suggest casual curiosity at best.
He does not attend to what one might expect would be shocking about
the scene—no one has bothered to bury the Confederate soldier's body.
When this image was reproduced in *Harper's Weekly* (October 18, 1862)
the dead Confederate soldier was described as a "little-drummer boy"
and the fact that his body had not been buried seemed inexplicable: "How
it happens that it should have been left uninterred, while the last honors
were paid to one of his comrades, we are unable to explain." Likewise, the
man standing by the grave (probably a soldier) was portrayed as a civilian,
gazing on the body with a "pitying interest." The article speculates that it

FIGURE 4.2. *"Burying the Dead after the Battle of Antietam." Alexander Gardner,*
1862. PR-065-788-12, Collection of The New-York Historical Society.

had probably been some time since this "seedy, shiftless-looking" fellow
had his "blunted nature . . . moved by such deep emotion as it betrays
at this mournful sight." This interpretation suggests the impropriety of
the photograph, which reveals that some corpses are hastily buried and
casually regarded while others, ignored altogether, are left exposed. By
remaking the spectator's response along sentimental lines—a hardened
man is moved to feel—the article avoids acknowledging that witnesses
to wartime slaughter, including visitors to Brady's gallery, might look on
the dead and feel nothing at all.

It is not unlikely that people who visited the Antietam exhibit had
photographs of corpses perched on the mantelpiece at home. These photographs, however, looked nothing like Gardner's images. If we consider

FIGURE 4.3. *"A Contrast: Federal Buried, Confederate Unburied, Where They Fell on the Battle Field of Antietam." Alexander Gardner, 1863. PR-065-788-1, Collection of The New-York Historical Society.*

photographs of the battlefield dead in relation to the popular tradition of postmortem photography, we see the strain war placed on conventional methods of representing the dead. Postmortem photographs, most often featuring children, portrayed the dead as if they were still alive and the grieving family as if it were still intact. By tending and carefully posing the body, photographers tried to reproduce the appearance of life. As Jay Ruby notes, postmortem photographs made before 1880 concentrate on the facial features of the dead, most often employing the "last sleep" pose in which the dead subject appears to rest peacefully (see fig. 4.4).[8] Postmortem photographs underscore the continuity between life and death not only by making the dead look as though they are alive but also by dwelling on familiar domestic objects. A dead child might be

FIGURE 4.4. *Postmortem, unidentified young girl. Southworth and Hawes, ca. 1850.*
Courtesy George Eastman House, Gift of Alden Scott Boyer.

photographed in her cradle, flanked by a favorite doll, or holding flowers
from the garden. Likewise, family ties appear unbroken in these images:
dead children are posed alongside their loved ones—sitting on a mother's
lap, or cradled in the arms of a sibling. Taken at home and adorned by
the props of daily life, postmortem photographs, like other forms of commemoration, portrayed death as a familiar aspect of domestic routine.

Reproducing the regularity of domestic life and an atmosphere of familial love, postmortem photographs commemorated the dead by expressing the survivor's desire for eventual reunion. In her discussion
of postmortem photographs of children, Karen Sánchez-Eppler writes,
"From the first, photography has been understood as a miracle of memorialization: the capacity to let us see again, as it was, a moment that
is in all other ways irretrievably past."[9] Unlike journalistic photographs
that portray subjects outside the viewer's experience, postmortem photographs give form to private memory. Invested with the desire of living
relatives to see their dead again, postmortem photographs function as
sentimental objects. In its preoccupation with broken families and lost
homes, sentimentality takes up home and family as a memory of what

FIGURE 4.5. *Postmortem portrait, woman holding baby. Unidentified photographer, ca. 1855. Courtesy George Eastman House, Gift of Mr. Donald Weber.*

has been and what might be restored. Antebellum attitudes toward death are, in this sense, wholly sentimental in that they view death as a transitional state in which the living and the dead endure a painful separation before celebrating a joyous reunion.

Photographs of dead children use the sentimental dyad of mother and child to figure this ongoing relatedness. Often mothers posed with their dead children (see fig. 4.5). If the mother did not appear in the image, her influence was signified by the objects—toys, flowers, rosary beads—that accompanied the dead child or by the carefully groomed corpse itself. The mother's presence—actual or implied—interpolates the viewer as a familiar who regards the corpse, as the mother does, with love and sorrow. Thus the grieving mother mends the potential discontinuity between life and death, past and present, private grief and its public articulation.

My students, who are used to seeing photographs of dead people that they have never met, are horrified by nineteenth-century postmortem photographs. They find photographs of dead children posed with their mothers especially offensive. The physical proximity of living and dead bodies disturbs them. To put it more bluntly, they are repulsed by the sight of living people touching dead flesh. Once the processes of sickness, death, and dying were removed from the home, death and life came to seem fundamentally opposed; in this context, the thought of handling a corpse seems strange and frightening. But while modern viewers are shocked by physical intimacy between the living and the dead, a nineteenth-century audience, accustomed to accompanying their loved ones through illness and death, may have been disturbed to see corpses out of reach of loving hands. While war photographers could soften the appearance of wounding, dismemberment, and death, they could not make these bodies appear as if they were alive, nor could they include the accoutrements of domestic comfort and affection that helped antebellum mourners figure death as a temporary, if difficult, separation.

During the Civil War, the focus of photography itself shifted from the familiar setting of the parlor or portrait studio to the unfamiliar world of camp and battlefield. The increasing foreignness of the subject matter coincided with new technologies that allowed for the reproduction of images. Most antebellum postmortem photographs were daguerreotypes that could not be replicated. With the introduction of the wet-plate negative in 1855, photographs could be reproduced and widely disseminated. This transformation in photographic technology nearly coincided with the crisis of mass death in war. Whereas postmortem photographs were used to identify the mourner's grief to a larger community of friends and acquaintances, photographs of the battlefield dead circulated among an audience of strangers.

Civilians who were able, for the first time, to see photographs of dead strangers were unable to buy postmortem portraits of their own dead sons. Because the government could not send soldiers' corpses home for burial, most familiar avenues for memorializing the dead were barred to mourning families. Accordingly, the *New York Times* review describes the failure of photographs to fully capture the experience of wartime loss. "Broken hearts," the reviewer laments, "cannot be photographed." The Antietam archive provides a sort of composite portrait of the corpse that might belong to any dead soldier—or to all of them. In this regard they are of little use in reproducing the feelings of those who have experienced the death of their loved ones firsthand. The review dramatizes this failure when it concludes by imagining a woman who recognizes one of the photographed corpses as her own beloved son. "We would scarce choose to be in the gallery, when one of the women bending over them should recognize a husband, a son, or a brother in the still, lifeless lines of bodies that lie ready for the gaping trenches." The audience that lingers over images of the mangled dead recoils from the public display of maternal grief:

> How can a mother bear to know that the boy whose slumbers she has cradled, and whose head her bosom pillowed until the rolling drum called him forth—whose poor, pale face, could she reach it, should find the same pillow again—whose corpse should be strewn with the rarest flowers that Spring brings or Summer leaves—when, but for the privilege of touching that corpse, of kissing once more the lips though white and cold, of smoothing back the hair from the brow and cleansing it of blood stains, she would give all the remaining years of life that Heaven has allotted her—how can this mother bear to know that in a shallow trench, hastily dug, rude hands have thrown him. She would have handled the poor corpse so tenderly, have prized the boon of caring for it so dearly—yes, even the Imperative office of hiding the dead from sight has been done by those who thought it trouble, and were only glad when their work ended.

Looking at a photograph of her dead son, this mother grieves not only his death but also the fact that she did not have a chance to touch, kiss, and wash his corpse. Far from consoling her, as a postmortem photograph might, this image reenacts her intolerable distance from the corpse and heightens her emotional pain.

It was not uncommon for wartime texts to ask people to experience the sorrow conjured by representations of the dead as, in essence, a mother's grief over the loss of her son, given up in the interest of the state. The painful separation of mother and child that, as Philip Fisher argues, establishes slavery as one of the natural subjects of sentimentality, also provided a figure for the common experience of wartime loss.[10] Photographs of the war dead, lacking any sign of maternal devotion, demonstrate the power of war to undermine these sentimental conventions. The carelessness of this soldier's burial—thrown into a hastily dug trench by the "rude hands" of strangers—intensifies the problem that the review deals with throughout: the public's unfeeling response to wartime death. The mother's arrival disrupts a nascent intimacy between the unidentified corpse and the curious spectator, keeping alive the question of how, and whether, strangers can use photographs to mourn the war dead.

Like postmortem images, Gardner and Gibson's Antietam photographs focus on the relationship between the living and the dead. They make it impossible, however, to view dead bodies with tenderness. Indeed, these photographs raise the terrifying possibility that during wartime the living come to view the dead with antagonism. The wet-plate collodion process, which allowed for the reproduction and circulation of war scenes, expanded a viewing audience without ensuring that they would identify with the grief felt by the living relatives of dead soldiers. While postmortem daguerreotypes preserved the dead in family memory, they also brought viewers into the mourning process. The battlefield postmortem, by contrast, depicted the death of an anonymous individual to a community of strangers without any representational mechanism for showing them how to feel about it. The introduction of the mediating figure of the mother in the *New York Times* review indicates only what the photograph leaves out: the mother's singular feeling for her dead son and the possibility that those feelings could be widely shared.

≫ In preparing his two-volume *Gardner's Photographic Sketch Book of the Civil War* for publication in 1866, Gardner had the chance to select 100 photographs from his archive and order them chronologically.[11] The *Sketch Book* dwells on the war's impact on the South. Specifically, Gardner documents the destruction of the Southern landscape by Northern weaponry. Like *Drum-Taps*, the *Sketch Book* narrates the war as a means to national power. Here, however, progress is viewed not as part of a natural process but rather as the result of human ingenuity. The collection exults over the technological innovations of the Army of the Potomac—pontoon bridges, telegraph lines, wagon trains—that help the Union reduce Southern gas works, bridges, and arsenals to rubble.

Gardner favors a documentary portrait of the institutions and technologies that secure Northern victory to an organicized rendering of destruction and rebirth that might universalize the South's fate and provide a basis for postwar reconciliation. A narrative of organic change in which nature, disrupted by war, regenerates in time is frequently the subject of captions in the first volume. In some instances, individuals rebuild the ravaged landscape; in others, nature grows over the wreckage soldiers leave behind. In the second volume, however, these concerns are super-seded by a narrative of technological progress in which the implements of war provide a foothold for Northern hegemony. The second volume focuses on institutions and the technologies that enable them. Opening with a photograph of a Sanitary Commission office, it proceeds to docu-ment the Headquarters of the Christian Commission, the Army of the Potomac's Commissary Department and Headquarters, a field hospital, a medical supply boat, and an army repair shop. Not surprisingly, the sec-ond volume devotes some attention to communication systems. As well as a photograph of the headquarters of the *New York Herald*, Gardner in-cludes two of the military telegraph. The first shows men perched on tall poles, stringing up telegraph wire, while the second shows the battery wagon where telegraphic messages were received. In the caption to this photograph Gardner observes, "No feature of the Army of the Potomac contributed more to its success than the field telegraph" (*Sketch Book*, plates 56, 62, 73).

The Union army's ability to move men, supplies, and information across vast spaces with unprecedented efficiency contributed to its even-tual success. Although the flow of goods was an unqualified boon to the Union army, the transmission of information was more problem-atic. Even as the telegraph and the photograph provided information to civilians eager for news, the free flow of information posed a strate-gic liability. At times, information gathered at the battlefront was kept secret. While Gardner's photographs, reproduced as wood engravings, circulated widely in the illustrated press, he also worked for the military, copying maps and charts and taking photographs to help the Secret Ser-vice catch spies.[12] Without naming the issue of censorship, the *Sketch Book* describes secrecy, even duplicity, as an inescapable feature of the photographic record.

Timothy Sweet observes that while "newspaper reports were often censored by the War Department, no research to date has suggested any government interference with the commercial operations of photo-graphic galleries."[13] In Sweet's view, however, these photographs would hardly have required government censorship, as their depictions of battlefield death tend to support the aims of the state. Sweet argues that war photographers used pastoral conventions, drawn from landscape painting, to legitimize the state project of controlling land through war. When considering photographs of dead bodies, Sweet emphasizes their subordination to the natural world and, implicitly, a narrative of American exceptionalism rooted in spectacular landscape. In this account, visual (like poetic) organicism forecloses any exploration of cause and effect that might have helped people to understand the political ideas and policies that led to war (117). This obfuscation is compounded by the tendency of the photograph to conceal its own representational status. "Of all representational media," Sweet writes, "photography was the most prone to efface its own status *as* representation . . . hence the rhetoric of 'truth to nature' in which early accounts of the medium were shrouded" (102).

While Sweet maintains that the photograph, disguising its own nature, conceals and rationalizes the government's power to wage war, throughout the *Sketch Book* Gardner uses both images and captions to expose the photograph's artificiality as well as the role of the photographer in controlling the dissemination of vital information to the viewing public. Although the sequential structure of the *Sketch Book* gives Gardner a chance to tell a story of the war that advances by degrees, in the end it is the dyadic structure of the two volumes that is most relevant: the division between the two parts of the work, punctuated by the title of plate 50, "The Halt," can be read in relation to the divide between battle and home fronts, past and future, North and South. The *Sketch Book* depicts war not as a source of continuity but as a conflict that divides, destroys, and empowers. Gardner demonstrates the ways that photographs trouble the flow of information, intensifying the Northern civilian's distance from the battlefield by withholding valued knowledge.

During the antebellum period, a preoccupation with radical forms of communication characterized sentimentality, transcendentalism, spiritualism, and the pseudosciences. While sentimentalists and reformers put great stock in the transformative power of experience—passed from one person to another in the form of feeling—pseudoscientists literalized the concept of circulation on which sympathy, in all its guises, depends. Mesmerists, for example, theorized that all objects, animate and inanimate, were interconnected by an electrical medium that they dubbed "universal fluid." They magnetized the bodies of their patients in order to restore the flow of universal fluid that joined disparate bodies and objects. Similarly, electrotherapists applied batteries to patients with both physical and psychological ailments in an attempt to correct obstructions to the flow of electricity through their bodies.

Such experiments in physical and psychic relatedness were, in part, responses to territorial and economic expansion. As the country grew, new methods for bridging distance kept pace: the early nineteenth century witnessed developments in communication, particularly the possibility of transmitting information across large distances rapidly, that appeared nothing short of magical. In the early decades of the century the time it took to convey information decreased dramatically. As a result, newspaper readers were able to follow events as they unfolded. News spanned ever greater distances in ever shorter periods of time, cultivating a sense of participation in national events. These trends culminated with the introduction of the telegraph in 1846, which employed electricity to convey messages to distant points instantly.[14]

Initially, Morse's invention was regarded with some skepticism; the telegraph's communicative powers (like the reproductive powers of the camera itself) may have appeared as yet another instance of the fantastic interrelatedness expounded by spiritualists, mesmerists, and the like. Soon enough, however, people began to realize its practical and ideological uses. The power of the telegraph to communicate rapidly between distant places led to increased homogeneity in news coverage. The Associated Press, founded in the mid-1840s, circulated single stories telegraphically to papers with divergent editorial viewpoints. The founding of the Government Printing Office in 1860 spelled the death of party papers and the emergence of a national press that drew coverage from common sources.[15] Rapid communication and increased centralization fostered the experience of simultaneity and commonality. Extolling the impact of the telegraph, James Gordon Bennett, founder of the *New York Herald*, wrote that "the whole nation is impressed with the same idea at the same moment. One feeling and one impulse are thus created and maintained from the center of land to its uttermost extremities."[16]

During the war, Northern noncombatants turned to newspapers for information about their loved ones and the progress of military action. Because the war scattered families across space, the project of collecting and conveying news from the front in a timely fashion was especially urgent. At the same time, government control over the dissemination of information during the war worked to reverse recent trends in newspaper publishing. Confederate officers, like Northern civilians, wanted to know the whereabouts of Union troops. Trying to cater to their readers, Northern newspapers ran the risk of offering up useful information to the enemy army. After taking office early in 1862, Secretary of War Edwin Stanton took control of telegraph lines nationwide. All news stories filed by telegraph came under the scrutiny of government censors. This increased censorship, while never total or wholly effective, made a difference in what the public learned about the war and when they learned it. Stories from the front might arrive days late, disappointing people who had come to expect timeliness from their newspapers.[17] While photographs were not systematically censored, photographers also worked within the limits placed on the news media by the government. Mathew Brady and Alexander Gardner were able to photograph the war, and achieve fame doing so, because the government allowed them to. While Brady's access to the troops was approved by Lincoln himself, Gardner was recommended to the post of chief photographer under the jurisdiction of the United States Topographical Engineers by Secret Service director Allan Pinkerton.

Although it was not until the invention of the half-tone screen in the mid-1880s that it became possible to reproduce photographs in newspapers, Civil War photographs provided a source of visual information to civilians eager for news. In the *Sketch Book*, Gardner uses images of dead soldiers, and accompanying narratives, to demonstrate the ideological indeterminacy of the photograph and its consequent unreliability as a source of information. As in *Drum-Taps*, about a third of the way through the volume we find a sequence of images devoted to the bodies of dead soldiers. There are only seven images of the dead in the *Sketch Book*; five of them are part of a ten-image sequence that documents the aftermath of the battle at Gettysburg (plates 35–44). While Whitman's burial poems are repetitive, creating a pause, full of tender feeling, at the heart of his volume, Gardner's corpse sequence strips the dead body of meaning and relevance.

At the center of this sequence, there are two pairs of two similar images of corpses. "A Harvest of Death" and "Field Where General Reynolds Fell" offer panoramic views of the battlefield strewn with dead bodies, while "A Sharpshooter's Last Sleep" and "The Home of a Rebel Sharpshooter" both depict a lone sharpshooter lying dead with his rifle (plates 36, 37, 40, 41). In both instances the viewer may note that the photographs feature the same bodies. If not, she will at least observe some similarity in the appearance of these corpses, a resemblance that is underscored by their similar postures. The accompanying text, however, creates distinctions between the images that are barely credible. Describing "A Harvest of Death" as an image of Confederate dead, Gardner is punitive: "Killed in the frantic efforts to break the steady lines of an army of patriots, whose heroism only excelled theirs in motive, they paid with life the price of their treason, and when the wicked strife was finished, found nameless graves, far from home and kindred." When he

FIGURE 4.6. *"Field Where General Reynolds Fell, Gettysburg, July 1863."*
Timothy O'Sullivan. Library of Congress.

describes the corpses in the next image, "Field Where General Reynolds
Fell" (fig. 4.6) as Union soldiers, Gardner's tone is reverential and his
view of death optimistic. He writes, "Some of the dead presented an aspect which showed that they had suffered severely just previous to dis-
solution, but these were few in number compared with those who wore a
calm and resigned expression, as though they had passed away in the act
of prayer. Others had a smile on their faces, and looked as if they were
in the act of speaking. . . . The faces of all were pale, as though cut in
marble, and as the wind swept across the battle-field it waved the hair,
and gave the bodies such an appearance of life that a spectator could
hardly help thinking they were about to rise to continue the fight." Gardner stubbornly disavows the content of "Field Where General Reynolds
Fell." While he imagines that the dead might rise up again and carry on

the work of war, the evidence of the photograph tends in the opposite direction: these men have suffered a terrible death that cannot be elevated or redeemed. The text stands in stark contradiction not only to the accompanying image but also to the caption of the previous image. Against the background of generic, indeed identical, bodies Gardner sketches the antinomies of war—the Southern traitor and the Northern hero—from a Unionist perspective. Thus he suggests that these familiar narratives may be useful fictions and, like the bodies they are tenuously attached to, interchangeable.

By showing us that the same corpses can be put to vastly different uses, Gardner emphasizes the referential indeterminacy of both the corpse and the photograph. Elaine Scarry has pointed out that in the aftermath of war this indeterminacy is most extreme: once a war is over, all soldiers appear to have died for the same cause and all serve to substantiate the authority of the victor. Scarry could be describing Gardner's images when she explains that "if the wounded bodies of a Union and a Confederate soldier were placed side by side during the American Civil War, nothing in those wounds themselves would indicate the different political beliefs of the two sides."[18] In the *Sketch Book* we see the evidentiary power of the wounded body put into practice as Gardner uses identical images to punish Confederate soldiers and exalt the Union dead. At the same time, because visual representations of the wounded body convey so little information, they stand ready to expose the arbitrary nature of these political fictions.

When we consider Gardner's archive, and Civil War photography more generally, in relation to the phenomenon of state censorship, the photograph's failure to determine context takes on broader significance. Unlike the newspaper, expressly committed to conveying the events of war as quickly and accurately as possible, photographs offered a record that was by definition fragmented and incomplete. Photographs of the battlefield dead confronted civilians not only with their inability to adequately mourn the war dead, but also with the partial and inadequate nature of the information they received from the battlefront. Nowhere is Gardner's own interest in the power of the photograph—and the photographer—to withhold vital information more evident than in the much-discussed photograph "The Home of a Rebel Sharpshooter" (fig. 4.7). In this image, and the accompanying caption, Gardner takes up the problem of the photographer's relation to the journalistic project of conveying news from the battlefield to the home front.

In order to make "The Home of a Rebel Sharpshooter," cameramen

FIGURE 4.7. *"The Home of a Rebel Sharpshooter."*
Alexander Gardner, 1863. Library of Congress.

carried the body of a young soldier, probably not a sharpshooter, to a new
location in order to produce a dramatic image.[19] The photograph appears
in Gardner's *Sketch Book* after another photograph of the same body—
this one titled "A Sharpshooter's Last Sleep." With its youthful subject in
a sleeping pose, and the accompanying text that describes the mother's
undying hope for their reunion, "The Home of a Rebel Sharpshooter"
closely resembles a postmortem photograph. A stone wall between two
large rocks encloses the sharpshooter's corpse, providing the "home" of
the photograph's title. The dead soldier looks as if he is sleeping—he lies
on his back, stretched between rock walls, his head resting on a blanket
or backpack, his face turned slightly toward the camera. While his di-
sheveled clothing signifies the intense pain he suffered while dying, his
facial expression is peaceful and his body composed.

Since William Frassanito revealed that many Civil War photographs
of the battlefield dead were carefully staged, historians have returned to

these images in an attempt to tally contrivance with a rhetoric of photographic realism. Assuming that no one doubted the veracity of these images, scholars cast nineteenth-century viewers as credulous, subject to the manipulations of crafty photographers.[20] In light of the tradition of postmortem photography, viewers may not have been shocked to learn that photographers posed battlefield corpses. Indeed, this practice was not at odds with a rhetoric of realism that often accompanied the publication of these startling images. Miles Orvell observes that simply drawn distinctions between "reality" and "artifice" would have had little appeal to antebellum consumers. He argues that nineteenth-century photographers and viewers took a more catholic view of the medium and its prospects, "one moment celebrating its capacity for a seemingly literal imitation of reality and the next its use as a vehicle for fantasy and illusion."[21] While antebellum viewers surely recognized the postmortem photograph for what it was—a picture of a corpse—the very habit of posing the dead as if they were sleeping indicates that they did not associate the dead body, as we do, with the difficult fact of death. Embodying the power of the spirit to outlast death, the corpse provided an expressive medium that people shaped in the attempt to signify a state that was neither wholly accessible nor entirely alien. Postmortem photographs employed artifice unabashedly in order to portray a reality that lay just beyond the bounds of human perception.

Although Gardner at times uses a rhetoric of realism, touting the power of the photograph to "speak for itself," the *Sketch Book* as a whole foregrounds its artificiality, allying the image with other forms of technology that definitively alter the Southern landscape. The theatrical imagery that introduces the work, the staged intermission between the two volumes, the tension between images and captions—all ask us to consider photographs with strategy in mind. While he does not admit to staging "The Home of a Rebel Sharpshooter," Gardner does little to mask his involvement in the process of photographic production. Indeed, the narrative that accompanies this image dramatizes the presence of a less-than-reliable photographer who interprets battlefield carnage for a civilian audience.

Gardner describes "the artist" who "passing over the scene of the previous days' engagements, found in a lonely place the covert of a rebel sharpshooter, and photographed the scene presented here." He goes on to narrate the artist's return to Gettysburg four months later to attend the consecration of the national cemetery: he goes back to the sharpshooter's home and finds the scene unchanged. The "musket, rusted by many storms, still leaned against the rock, and the skeleton of the soldier lay undisturbed within the mouldering uniform." Gardner remarks, "None of those who went up and down the fields to bury the fallen, had found him."

None, of course, except Gardner himself who, by his own account, found the body twice. Unlike the poet-narrator of *Drum-Taps*, intent on giving an adequate burial to friends and strangers alike, Gardner refuses to look after the sharpshooter's remains. Gardner's Antietam photographs capture the lack of interest on the part of soldiers charged with caring for the dead. Here it is the photographer himself who neglects the soldier's corpse. In the context of a culture that valued burial and dreaded the body's exposure, Gardner's neglect seems callous, and his decision to publicize it is puzzling. When we take into consideration the likelihood that the story of his return to the site is, like the image itself, fabricated, it appears that Gardner goes out of his way to portray himself as a heartless professional.[22] In "The Home of a Rebel Sharpshooter," Gardner's exaggerated rendering of professional indifference stands in stark contrast to the boy's thoughts of home and to the experience of his mother with which Gardner concludes. He writes, "'Missing,' was all that could have been known of him at home, and some mother may yet be patiently watching for the return of her boy, whose bones lie bleaching, unrecognized and alone, between the rocks at Gettysburg."

Like Whitman's "Come Up from the Fields Father," Gardner's "The Home of a Rebel Sharpshooter" triangulates the relationship between the artist, the mother, and her dead son. In Whitman's poem, however, an omniscient narrator shares the mother's intuitive knowledge that her son is dead.[23] Unlike Whitman, who takes the amanuensis as one figure for his poetic project—to create union during wartime—the photographer divides the sharpshooter from his mother. If the mother in "Come Up from the Fields Father" instantly understands that her son is dead, the mother in Gardner's narrative remains ignorant. Gardner possesses information that she does not share, knowledge that gives him a certain voyeuristic power as he imagines both the boy's dying thoughts and the mother's own.

Gardner's image and the narrative that accompanies it are indebted to sentimental iconography that takes the mother's grief as a paradigm for collective sorrow.[24] In "The Home of a Rebel Sharpshooter," Gardner employs the sentimental frame of a lost home. More narrowly, he invokes the separation between mother and child that drives sentimental narration. He does so, however, in order to dramatize the photographer's role in intensifying the mother's difficulties. While the image, like other battlefield postmortems, interpolates the viewer as the dead soldier's own mother, Gardner juxtaposes this sentimental figure to the forward-looking photographer who harbors secrets at the mother's expense. The artfully composed scene, in combination with the text that calls attention to Gardner's meddlesome role in the process of photographic memorialization, suggests his effort to heighten, rather than conceal, the representational status of the photograph.

The posed corpse produces authentic feeling as well as demonstrating the way that those feelings can be manipulated. Unlike poetry or song, widely practiced forms that provided avenues for collective expression, photography was the province of a handful of experts. When brought to the viewer's attention, this expertise compromised the supposed transparency of the image. Far from cloaking state agency in the guise of nature, Gardner's *Sketch Book* demonstrates the power of new technologies, sponsored by the state, to win the war. In doing so, it allows us to speculate on the role of the photograph—and of the photographer— in the war effort. Dramatizing the photographer's efforts to manipulate photographic meaning, Gardner emphasizes the artificial nature of the image and asks us to consider censorship as a feature of photographic representation.

In the context of the emergence of photography, "nature" did not connote the process of growth and decay but rather the world of forms that the photograph was, quite remarkably, able to reproduce. But, as Oliver Wendell Holmes observed, once nature was reproduced photographically it ceased to exert its hold on us. Ruminating on how the future will be shaped by photography, Holmes announced, "Form is henceforth divorced from matter." Replicating reality, the photograph invites the abandonment, perhaps the destruction, of the world as we know it: "Give us a few negatives of a thing worth seeing, taken from different points of view, and that is all we want of it. Pull it down or burn it up, if you please."[25] This observation has special relevance to thinking about war photography: what does it mean to reproduce the material world at the very moment that world is being destroyed?

During the Civil War the nearly magical reproductive capacities of the camera opened onto new ways of seeing; at times the photograph embodied a reality that seemed as strange and incomprehensible as death itself.[26] Unlike narrative, which is implicitly governed by the logic of development, the photograph manifests history as a series of traumatic interruptions. Expanding on the relationship between photography and catastrophe, Eduardo Cadava describes the photograph as "seizing and tearing an image from its context" and, in doing so, "immobilizing the flow of history." The photograph refuses to naturalize death but presents it, instead, as a "shock," impossible to fully assimilate or believe, analogous to the catastrophic events that punctuate, or puncture, our sense of the fluidity of time unfolding.[27] The shock that confronts us when we look at a photograph reproduces the "opacity" of our own lived experience; the unbridgeable distance between subject and object, staged so dramatically by nineteenth-century photographs, is true to life only insofar as it captures our inability to understand the world around us. In this way, photographs intimate the difficulty of living helplessly in time rather than triumphantly through it.

Sentimental narration, occupied with distance, prods the reader to find ways to project herself into the text and, in doing so, to make connections between representation and reality that provide a model for formulating other kinds of interrelatedness. Early documentary photographs, by contrast, dramatize the difficulty of establishing correspondences between representation and reality. Far from asking the viewer to bring representation into existence (either through the process of interpretation or through action in the world), the photograph allows her to meditate on the way that reality, depicted photographically, trumps her sense of agency.

Alan Trachtenberg describes the "near-impossibility of seeing and knowing simultaneously," experienced during wartime by soldiers and civilians. The confusion faced by Civil War soldiers as they attempted to maneuver on "battlefields thick with smoke" resembled the incomprehension of civilians confronted with the "inevitable fragmentation of the photographic report." In Trachtenberg's view, the schism between perception and cognition indicates a new understanding of time and event as they were refashioned by war and photography at midcentury: photographs of the battlefield dead convey the subject's paralysis in the face of historical events that appear to unfold without design.[28]

The battlefield corpse stands in for what Civil War photographs cannot represent—soldiers fighting, the grief of mourning relatives, and, more broadly, the subject's inability to comprehend the causes and events of war. Embodying these pressing omissions and failures, the corpse takes on a vital presence. Signaling the inadequacy of antebellum death rituals, photographs of the battlefield dead also provide an inaugural moment in the history of photojournalism. While postmortem photographs give evidence of the efforts of the living to soften the effects of death on the body, photographs of the war dead show the impact of violence in the absence of any mitigating human agency. In this way, they point us toward a documentary tradition that takes the violated body as a measure of the impersonal and implicitly social forces that the camera cannot represent.

Victims of violent crime, natural disasters, accident, and war have provided photojournalism, which banks on the unmediated equation of image and actuality, with its peculiar claim to transparency. Because photographs of the wounded and the dead impart experiential intensity in the face of epistemological uncertainty, they have become privileged signifiers of war's reality. The intensity of the viewer's experience, which results in part from her inability to refer the represented crisis to any outside source, ratifies the photograph's claim to objective truth.[29]

Although a comprehensive account of the rise of documentary journalism is beyond the scope of this book, I would contend that the conditions governing the circulation of information during the Civil War played a part in the emergence of the dead body as a sign of unmediated reality. The quality of uncertainty, even suspense, that characterizes war was redoubled by government censorship. David Mindich argues that while Stanton's censorship policies created a vacuum for news, this vacuum was in turn filled by authoritative accounts emanating from the government (some of them written by Stanton himself) and circulated by the Associated Press.[30] The widespread use of the telegraph, the emergence of the wire services, and government censorship all resulted in increased centralization. The value placed on objectivity, Mindich argues, was one result of these changes. As the government had more power to control and streamline news, the myriad details and narrative exuberance that characterized earlier journalism were gradually supplanted by fewer and ostensibly more reliable facts that were given more weight and consumed more readily as truth.

The power of the state to determine not only the progress of war but also individual perceptions of it is nowhere evident in photographs of the battlefield dead. I would suggest, however, that the emergence of the body as an object that signifies truth rather than artifice is one expression of broader transformations in how news circulated and how people were asked to consume it. Journalistic objectivity subordinates the process of interpretation to facts that appear self-evident or complete. As increasingly homogeneous and widely disseminated news stories received the stamp of objectivity, the victimized body emerged as a material analog for fact.

FIGURE 4.8. *Dead Confederate soldier in the trenches at Fort Mahone.*
Thomas Roche, 1865. Library of Congress.

Unlike photographs of the war dead that emphasize the corpse's alien
appearance, Thomas Roche's photographs—to my mind the most affect-
ing of the war—create a sense of intimacy between the viewer and the
dead soldier. Roche, a civilian war photographer, took pictures of the
Confederate dead at Fort Mahone, outside Petersburg, in April 1865.[31]
His images draw heavily on the conventions of postmortem photography.
Trenches provide enclosures that, like the sharpshooter's home, shelter
the dead. Many appear in the "last sleep" pose of postmortem photographs (see fig. 4.8); in some instances they are curled up in the fetal position and appear nearly childlike. Most importantly, these photographs

FIGURE 4.9. *Confederate soldier killed in the trenches, at the storming of Petersburg. Thomas Roche, 1865. PR-065-811-4, Collection of The New-York Historical Society.*

dwell on the features of the corpse's face, making it easier for viewers to feel grief. By enabling the viewer to observe the corpse closely, and in nearly total isolation, these photographs individuate the battlefield dead.

Because they document soldiers' wounds in unusual detail, these are also among the most graphic photographs produced during the Civil War; Roche's images, at once poignant and repulsive, elicit strong feeling by way of close observation. In order to produce this effect, Roche had to photograph the dead at close range (see fig. 4.9). Frassanito observes that the "series is undeniably a powerful one, specifically because of its deliberate focus on individual corpses."[32] Dwelling on the isolated corpse, Roche sidelines questions of context in order to produce an experience of certainty, of an end (albeit grim) already achieved. Thus he suggests the power of the documentary photograph to impart a very little difficult knowledge by keeping the viewer's gaze focused narrowly on the victim's body.

These photographs further decontextualize the dead by excluding living subjects; Roche is not interested in how the living handle or represent the dead. Many battlefield postmortems emphasize the horizontal plane, aligning both viewer and corpse with the diverse and cluttered landscape of war. In Roche's Fort Mahone photographs, the viewer looks down on the corpse. This position of spiritualized omniscience allows the viewer a fullness of feeling reminiscent of Whitman's burial poems in which the surviving soldier gazes down on his dead comrade. Intensifying the absence of context, verticality creates a powerful intimacy between the viewer and the corpse. As the dead body comes to fill the photograph, however, the complexities of this relationship—questions concerning the viewer's obligations to the dead—are pushed out of the frame. These images reintroduce emotion to the scene of death without revitalizing the viewer's agency in relation to the dead. Indeed, the modest scope of these photographs conveys a radically circumscribed view of how the living and the dead are interrelated. Like the newspaper reader, the viewer receives knowledge that is ostensibly more complete—both the soldier's wounds and his face are represented in unprecedented detail—while her potential responses to this information are curtailed.

By short-circuiting emotional and cognitive habit, photographs of the battlefield dead conveyed the toll that war took on a utopian vision of interrelatedness, particularly between the living and the dead. At the same time, they embodied a future in which the victimized body would stand in for all the burnt and destroyed objects—books, buildings, people—that over the years would become increasingly difficult to visualize and remember. While antebellum sources ruminate over what the photograph cannot reveal, in time these images, and others like them, have come to represent the reality of war. As the enduring popularity of Civil War photographs indicates, our tendency to accept the corpse as a sign of truth that might, in its felt intensity, encompass the whole of war is one important outcome of a conflict in which death took an unprecedented form.

In this chapter, I have examined visual and written texts that worry over the failure of wartime photography to adhere to the conventions of antebellum commemorative practice and, by extension, to adequately represent the dead. In the war's aftermath, however, these photographs have often been taken to describe the nature of death in war. In their original context, photographs of the battlefield dead meditated on the impact of war violence on civilians who experienced it from afar. These images, and the commentary surrounding them, used the corpse to demonstrate how war destroys ways of managing, honoring, and understanding the dead, practices that, to a significant extent, shape the very contours of reality. Out of the reach of intimates, the corpse could not provide a medium for expressing the sadness and desire of grieving individuals. Instead, it fell into the hands of professional journalists who, documenting its woeful isolation, intimated a future in which portraits of dead strangers, wrenching and complete, would tell us all we need to know about the circumstances of distant suffering.[33]

AFTER
EMANCIPATION

5

Edward Zwick's 1989 film *Glory*, gives a fictionalized account of the Massachusetts 54th, the first regiment of free black men to enlist in the Union army. Mustered in February 1863, a month after Lincoln signed the Emancipation Proclamation, the 54th attained enduring renown when it lost nearly half its number in an ill-conceived assault on Fort Wagner in South Carolina. In an important early scene set in training camp, the regiment's commander, Colonel Robert Gould Shaw, receives news that the Confederate Congress has issued a proclamation threatening to execute black soldiers, as well as their white officers, upon capture. He assembles his troops on a stormy night, reads them the proclamation, and offers a discharge to any soldier who wants one. The next morning he finds his men waiting in formation, ready for another day of drill; not a single soldier has chosen to leave his command. The Confederate threat, another instance of the injustice these men enlisted to fight against, only strengthens their resolve. Awed by the willingness of his troops to face death at the hands of their captors, Shaw murmurs, "Glory hallelujah." The title of the movie itself, drawn from this scene, pays homage to the willingness of black soldiers to sacrifice themselves in the name of freedom.[1]

Thanks, in part, to Zwick's efforts, the Massachusetts 54th has become a symbol of black heroism during the Civil War; commentators praise *Glory* for asserting the importance of black participation in a war too often remembered as a noble fight between white countrymen. The film dramatizes the evolution of commitment, to the cause and to each other, in a disparate group of soldiers. The conflicted relationships between Shaw, his longtime friend and second in command, and four black enlisted men provide the backdrop for this story of personal and social transformation. In the tradition of combat films, each character is identified by certain idiosyncrasies that are, in the end, abandoned in favor of loyalty to the regiment and, by extension, the cause. Throughout, the process of maturation—through which "boys" become "men"—provides a figure for the development of individual courage and collective bonds: under pressure, these boys—impulsive, rebellious, naive—become skilled and loyal fighting men.[2]

Well aware of the double meaning of "boy," which simultaneously connotes Shaw's immaturity, a function of privilege, and the degradation long suffered by his soldiers, the film ties the transformation of both the individual and the regiment to the problem of oppression. Zwick contends that in the case of black soldiers the threat of violence at the hands of the enemy was compounded by the oppressive conditions they faced in the Union army. As portrayed by the film, the men of the 54th were refused adequate clothing, equal pay, and the privilege to serve as officers; they were whipped without cause; they were denied the opportunity to fight, only to be sent out on a suicide mission at the whim of their commanding officer. Although Zwick may underestimate the wrongs endured by black Union soldiers, he nonetheless describes their military service as a series of humiliations and inequities.

How then can we believe the film's central premise—that black soldiers were ennobled and liberated through their military experience? Attempting to elaborate, rather than resolve, this dilemma, the film dwells on the role of discipline. In a series of scenes of physical and psychological abuse that leads up to the final scene of death in battle, *Glory* simultaneously advocates discipline as the means by which soldiers learn to fight and condemns it as the means by which the Union army perpetuates the practices of enslavement.[3] These two accounts of discipline are difficult to reconcile. They speak to an inherent tension between the ideal of soldierly devotion and the lived experience of Civil War soldiers, black and white.

As Kirk Savage observes, military life did not, for the most part, call for singular acts of heroism but rather the soldier's unquestioning obedience to authority. He writes, "On the one hand, to be a soldier was to test one's manhood. . . . On the other hand, to be a soldier was to become a virtual slave, to forfeit the very sense of personal responsibility and agency supposed to define manhood."[4] The possibility that military service most resembled enslavement, and that the soldier who fought, and perhaps died, for his country did not exemplify heroic agency so much as effective subordination, was exacerbated by the introduction of the first draft in

U.S. history and by the enlistment of nearly 200,000 African American soldiers, many of them ex-slaves, into the Union army. As the problem of desertion, which increased over the course of the war, implied, many soldiers were willing to face violent death only if forced to do so.

And yet it is difficult to find representations of the soldier's subordination to a powerful, potentially coercive, military regime. Indeed, the songs, poems, essays, and speeches produced during the Civil War typically represent violent death as an expression of individual agency and a source of national unity. In wartime art, white soldiers die so that the nation might be reborn, while black soldiers die in a heroic effort to liberate themselves. Viewed in this context, visual representations of Union army executions cut against the grain. If white soldiers died willingly, in order to save the union, what were viewers to make of the spectacle of the army killing its own? Likewise, how could one believe that black men earned their freedom by becoming soldiers when confronted with the harsh punishment inflicted on black enlistees? In this chapter, I will argue that military executions constitute a crisis in which the soldier's relationship to the state appears structured not by participation but by the exercise of violence. Establishing the intentional violence of the state, inflicted on its own emissaries, as an object of contemplation, visual images of state-sanctioned executions challenge popular understandings of wartime death as an act of heroism and a means to progress.

Glory directs us to reconsider Civil War culture with the practice of military discipline in mind. In this light, the experience of black soldiers functions as both the exception and the rule. Black soldiers were punished more often, more severely, and for fundamentally different reasons than white soldiers. For this reason, the wartime discipline of black soldiers speaks to a history of racial violence, at once recalling the abuses of enslavement while directing us toward the rise of Southern lynching in the decades after emancipation. Yet as Savage suggests, the threat of punishment—at the hands of both armies—tempered the experience, and behavior, of soldiers generally. From this perspective, the experience of black soldiers is representative. Indeed, I will argue that, by the time the war began, corporal punishment was associated not only with the violence of slaveholders but also with the ways that violence had infiltrated the society at large. At times, visual representations of military execution go so far as to analogize the unrestrained exercise of state power to the brutal practices of slaveholders, thus defining soldiering itself as a form of enslavement. More modestly, they suggest that the soldier's devotion may be the effect of his subordination to a powerful military authority and, like Zwick's portrait of black soldiering, make it difficult to accept the nobility of battlefield death as an article of faith.

In 1848, William Wells Brown included a woodcut by African American artist Patrick Reason (fig. 5.1) at the beginning of his anthology of antislavery songs, *The Anti-Slavery Harp*. Reason depicts a black man tied by his hands and feet to a flagpole; the American flag waves above his head as he is readied for punishment. Transforming the flagpole into a whipping tree, Reason calls on the metonymic relation between whipping and enslavement to boldly denounce slavery as a national crime from which the insignia of collective identity—the stars and stripes— derives. Thomas Campbell's verse elaborates:

United States, your banner wears
Two emblems,—one of fame;
Alas, the other that it bears,
Reminds us of your shame.
The white man's liberty entype
Stands blazoned by your stars;
But what's the meaning of your stripes?
They mean your Negro-scars.[5]

Racial violence, woven into the very fabric of collective identity, is the distinguishing trait of American nationhood. Reason uses the scene of corporal punishment not to signify the brutality of Southern slavery but rather the national character of racial oppression.

While Reason offers an especially damning account of the relationship between racial violence and national identity, he was hardly alone in viewing slavery as a defining feature of life in the United States. From the country's inception, people feared that slavery would have a corrosive influence on the young republic. How would the legally sanctioned cruelty inflicted on slaves affect the way that white Americans treated one another? And might the differences between slaveholding and nonslaveholding states grow, eventually proving intractable? Often writers and artists used depictions of the corporal punishment of slaves, which dramatized both the victim's suffering and its impact on spectators, to address these concerns.

From the late eighteenth century on, the use of public, corporal punishment was a source of controversy and debate. Those who argued against public punishment held sway, and incarceration came to replace physical violence as the state's primary response to criminal transgres-

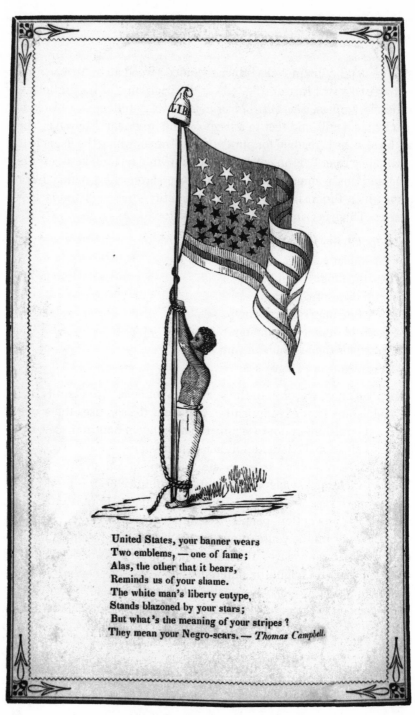

United States, your banner wears
Two emblems, — one of fame;
Alas, the other that it bears,
Reminds us of your shame.
The white man's liberty entype,
Stands blazoned by your stars;
But what's the meaning of your stripes?
They mean your Negro-scars. — *Thomas Campbell*

FIGURE 5.1. *Patrick Reason's American flag.*
Special Collections, University of Virginia.

sion. Post-Revolutionary opponents of public punishment focused on the impact of state-sanctioned violence on the viewing public. They argued that far from ensuring obedience these spectacles would produce hatred for the government and increase the spirit of lawlessness. In *Enquiry into the Effects of Public Punishments*, Benjamin Rush describes the universal response to suffering: "By an immutable law of our nature, distress of all kinds, when *seen*, produces sympathy, and a disposition to relieve it."[6] The spectator, necessarily moved by the criminal's suffering, will "secretly condemn the law which inflicts the punishment—hence arises a want of respect for laws in general, and a more feeble union of the great ties of government" (7).

The stigma surrounding public punishment provided a resource for abolitionist critiques of slavery, and depictions of the corporal punishment of slaves became a staple of antislavery discourse. Abolitionists often used whipping, in particular, to symbolize the array of injustices intrinsic to slavery.[7] Putting Rush's account to the test, abolitionists circulated representations of corporal punishment in order to produce sympathy for slaves and hatred for the laws that protected the peculiar institution. They did not, however, intend to alienate citizens from the government so much as dedicate them to its improvement. Generally, abolitionists dramatized the pain inflicted on slaves in an effort to bolster arguments for institutional reform.

Reason's critique of slavery alerts us to a different strain in antislavery thought. Portraying the flag as an instrument of torture, Reason nationalizes the violence of enslavement, turning the flag itself into a source of revulsion. In some instances, the violence inflicted by slaveholders, and sanctioned by law, could be used, as Rush feared, to dismantle the individual's affection for the nation. Written before the Revolution, J. Hector St. Jean de Crevecoeur's *Letters from an American Farmer* offers an early example of how sympathy for the suffering slave, particularly the victim of corporal punishment, might destroy the individual's allegiance to the larger community. After celebrating the transformation of the destitute immigrant into a prosperous American farmer, James, the narrator of Crevecoeur's *Letters*, recounts the erosion of his own commitment to civic life in the New World, a decline that is initiated by his encounter with a brutalized slave. In the widely canonized Letter 3, "What Is an American?," Crevecoeur sings the virtues of life in America. The "distressed European" who leaves behind grotesque extremes of wealth and poverty, finds himself transformed upon arrival in North America.[8] While in their native countries the poor of Europe are nothing but "useless plants . . . mowed down by want, hunger, and war," in the New World "they are become men" (43). Throughout, James celebrates wage labor as the means by which the immigrant achieves autonomy, the mark of manhood. If the American farmer is "honest, sober and industrious," he will reap the substantial rewards of "ease and independence" (66).

When James visits Charles-Town (Charleston, South Carolina), however, he finds that Southern life is characterized by the old extremes of idle luxury and fruitless labor: slaveholders enjoy a life of festivity and pleasure, while slaves are "driven to toil, to starve, and to languish" on their behalf (154). The myriad abuses of enslavement are dramatized by one terrible encounter. Walking through the woods on his way to dine with a local planter, James comes upon a slave who has been mutilated and left in a cage suspended from a tree. He recounts, "I shudder when I recollect that the birds had already picked out his eyes; his cheek bones were bare; his arms had been attacked in several places, and his body seemed covered with a multitude of wounds. From the edges of the hollow sockets, and from the lacerations with which he was disfigured, the blood slowly dropped, and tinged the ground beneath" (164). It would be difficult to find an equally graphic description of slave suffering in all of antislavery writing. The farmer responds sympathetically: "I found myself suddenly arrested by the power of affright and terror; my nerves were convulsed; I trembled, I stood motionless, involuntarily contemplating the fate of this negro in all its dismal latitude" (164). James's response imitates the victim's bodily pain and, in doing so, registers its powerful impact.

Later abolitionist writers will employ highly conventionalized portraits of slave suffering to inspire their readers to action; in these texts, the sympathetic spectator is motivated by her intense response to the pain of others. In this instance, however, the farmer is incapacitated by what he sees: lacking a bullet to kill the suffering man, the farmer offers him a drink of water and then walks away. At the planter's dinner table he learns that the slave was punished for killing the overseer of the plantation. Although he seems unimpressed by this explanation, James does not express outrage. Instead, the letter concludes on a note of resignation as he chooses not to "trouble" his reader with his host's self-justifying arguments (165).

Rush worried that the spectacle of punishment would turn the citizen against the government not only by eroding his respect for the law but also by destroying his very capacity to feel sympathy for others. He remarks that the "principle of sympathy, after being often opposed by the law of the state, which forbids it to relieve the distress it commiserates, will cease to act altogether; and, from this defect of action, and the habit arising from it, will soon lose its place in the human breast."[9] Corporal punishment threatens the law, which articulates the obligations of citizens to one another, by producing a sympathy that has no constructive outlet and thus serves only to alienate people from one another and from the government that ideally unites them.

James's encounter with the dying slave leads him to reflect not only on the evils of slavery but also on the destructive nature of human society. He writes, "Every where one part of the human species is taught the art of shedding the blood of the other: of setting fire to their dwellings; of levelling the works of their industry: half of the existence of nations regularly employed in destroying other nations. . . . Republics, kingdoms, monarchies, founded either on fraud or successful violence, increase by pursuing the steps of the same policy, until they are destroyed, in their turn, either by the influence of their own crimes, or by more successful but equally criminal enemies" (162). The spectacle of racial violence prompts James to imagine mass bloodshed as nation-states make war on one another. Unlike abolitionists, who used similar scenes to make utopian arguments for social change, Crevecoeur takes the scene of racial violence to emblematize life in America, and ultimately social relatedness itself. His encounter with slave suffering initiates a process of alienation, the converse of the transformation that the immigrant farmer undergoes in becoming an American, and James withdraws into psychic and physical isolation.

Crevecoeur observes that if universalized the practices of enslavement would result in total war. Increasingly, antebellum Americans shared this perspective as the conflict over slavery appeared to be the source of widespread and potentially catastrophic public unrest. The controversy was marked by any number of violent, widely publicized episodes that captured the public imagination and fueled a sense that the struggle could only escalate. Although opponents of public punishment argued that the spectacle of state-sponsored revenge would fuel a spirit of lawlessness, the problem of public violence only grew as incarceration supplanted corporal punishment during the first half of the nineteenth century. Historians have documented the increased incidence and virulence of mob violence during this period.[10] This violence was directed against a variety of victims—Mormons, Catholics, immigrants, free blacks, and slaves. It erupted most frequently, however, in response to the political struggle over slavery.[11] Attacks on abolitionists, skirmishes over fugitive slaves, race riots—all attested to the polarization of pro- and antislavery forces, as well as the increasing viciousness of white on black violence in the Northern states.

In his 1838 Address to the Young Men's Lyceum of Springfield, Abraham Lincoln responded to a rash of mob violence in the mid-1830s. He warned against "the increasing disregard for law" expressed by "the growing disposition to substitute the wild and furious passions, in lieu of the sober judgment of Courts; and the worse than savage mobs, for the executive ministers of justice."[12] Even as he deplores vigilantism, however, the seemingly indiscriminate nature of mob violence provides a resource for Lincoln as he searches for an enduring basis for national identity. Lincoln describes a series of lynchings in Vicksburg, Mississippi. First, gamblers hang, then blacks suspected of plotting insurrection, then white men in league with blacks, and finally strangers unlucky enough to be in the wrong place at the wrong time. He concludes, "Thus went on this process of hanging, from gamblers to negroes, from negroes to white citizens, and from these to strangers; till, dead men were seen literally dangling from the boughs of trees upon every road side; and in numbers almost sufficient, to rival the native Spanish moss of the country, as a drapery of the forest" (30). Lincoln's mob is characterized by the excessive, proliferating tendencies of nature itself as the tree, which provides the apparatus for the mob's rushed and makeshift operations, becomes an emblem for uncontrollable violence. In Lincoln's description of the Vicksburg hangings, the instrumentality of lynch law disappears and disobedience itself is literalized as a feature of the moody and exotic native landscape.

Lincoln's description of mob violence spreading, irresistibly, effectively transmutes racial conflict into a national condition and reflects a sense that the controversy over slavery was transforming the very nature of public life in the Northern states. When Lincoln includes black insurrectionists and their white sympathizers in his list of victims, he alludes to the racist character of mob law. Lincoln refuses, however, to analyze the relationship between antislavery agitation, mob violence, and sectional antagonism. Searching for a secure basis for the perpetuation of civic order, Lincoln is briefly tempted to describe mob violence itself as the ground for national belonging: the mobs that "spring up" across the land are not peculiar to the "eternal snows" of New England or to the "burning suns" of Louisiana but are "common to the whole country" (29). In a speech that asks citizens to embrace the law as "the political religion of the nation," vigilante justice emerges, strangely enough, as an alternative source of collective identity.[13]

Lincoln, Reason, and Crevecoeur describe racial violence as the defining trait of an immoderate or lawless nation. They do so, however, to very different effect. Reason and Crevecoeur nationalize racial violence in order to indict slavery more forcefully. Lincoln's denunciation of lawlessness, by contrast, draws on the volatility of the public conflict over slavery while working to obscure the centrality of slavery to national life. During the antebellum period, corporal punishment was often associated with the unchecked violence of slaveholders and lawless mobs. The question remains: when spectacular state punishments are taken up once again, will the prerogatives of a government at war outweigh the stigma that attaches to corporal discipline in the years preceding the conflict?

On December 13, 1861, Private William Johnson was shot for desertion. *Harper's Weekly* described his execution—the Union army's first—in some detail. Johnson was escorted to his execution by a funeral procession: "The Provost Marshal, mounted and wearing a crimson scarf across his breast, led the mournful cortege. He was immediately followed by the buglers of the regiment, four abreast, dismounted. Then came the twelve men—one from each company in the regiment, selected by ballot—who constituted the firing party . . . the coffin, which was of pine wood stained, and without any inscription, came next, in a one-horse wagon. Immediately behind followed the unfortunate man, in an open wagon."[14] Once the entourage arrived at the execution site, the casket was taken off the wagon, and Johnson stood next to it as he faced the firing squad. (Often, an open grave waited alongside the condemned prisoner.) When the execution was over, soldiers were marched by the corpse. The account of Johnson's execution concludes: "The troops then all marched round, and each man looked on the bloody corpse of his late comrade, who had proved a traitor to his country." After the dead soldier had been viewed by his fellows, he was placed face down in the coffin and buried in an unmarked grave.[15]

During the Civil War, the Union army executed 267 soldiers.[16] The number of executions increased each year: whereas nine soldiers were condemned to death in 1861, ninety-six were executed in 1864.[17] The unprecedented number of executions might have been a source of embarrassment for the army and, by extension, the federal government. As soldiers were most commonly shot for desertion, the dramatic increase in military executions implied, among other things, dissatisfaction with military life. Yet there was nothing sheepish about the way the army conducted executions. To the contrary, these public affairs gave the military a chance to flex its muscle. At a time when executions were increasingly conducted privately in front of a handful of witnesses, the Union army put soldiers to death in full view of large gatherings of troops and civilians. On one occasion an estimated 25,000 spectators attended the execution of five deserters.[18]

The studied theatrics of military execution, designed to intensify the mental suffering of the condemned, were an anomaly in the United States at midcentury.[19] By the time of the Civil War, executions were generally conducted in private, behind penitentiary walls, and imprisonment was increasingly favored over corporal punishment as a means of transforming criminal character. Widely publicized episodes of mob violence contributed to a sense that corporal punishment was not a means of preserving social order but rather an expression of disorder. As public punishment became associated with the lawless mob, the state itself ran the risk of appearing unrestrained when it took aim at the criminal's body.

How then do we account for the spectacular military executions that survive this transition? Rehabilitative efforts to inculcate self-discipline appear inadequate to conditions of wartime in which extraordinary demands are placed on soldiers. The mass mobilization necessary for fighting the Civil War brought with it the prospect of mass disobedience, a threat intensified by the precedent of Confederate secession. The draft, necessary to compel reluctant citizens to become soldiers, was itself a source of violent unrest. Military executions, anachronistic in their public and highly theatrical character, provided a far-reaching source of discipline during a time of crisis.

In his *Treatise on Military Law*, Captain Stephen Vincent Benét asserted that the death sentence should be made "as extensively useful as possible, by the publicity which attends its execution."[20] The Union army used executions to produce obedience and to display it to the public at large. Typically, soldiers were positioned at the site of the execution in the shape of a "hollow square" as stipulated by military regulation.[21] This three-sided formation ensured that each soldier would have a clear view of the condemned man, who was placed in the open side of the square. Standing at attention these soldiers provided evidence of the disciplinary effect of public punishment. In turn, they presented a threatening spectacle of military power that might be easily unleashed against the enemy.

The display of military discipline was disseminated to crowds gathered at the site of execution and circulated to a mass public by the illustrated

FIGURE 5.2. *"Execution of Private Lanahan."* Harper's Weekly, *January 25, 1862.*
Special Collections, University of Virginia.

press. During the war, *Harper's Weekly* and *Frank Leslie's Illustrated
Newspaper* published numerous sketches of military executions accompanied by articles providing detailed narratives.[22] These illustrations generally take a wide view, showing the impact of capital punishment on
crowds of soldiers and civilians.[23] As in renderings of John Brown's execution, these images portray the condemned man (or men) from a distance: between the viewer and the scaffold stands a vast military display.

To be sure, representations in illustrated weeklies do not neatly conform to the army's disciplinary intentions. Mass-produced illustrations
of executions often include civilian spectators who appear to take only a
casual interest in the spectacle at hand. Even as they display the impressive spectacle of well-organized troops, ready for action, these illustrations do not ask their viewers to identify with obedient soldiers. "Execution of Private Lanahan" (fig. 5.2), which appeared in *Harper's Weekly* on
January 25, 1862, employs the gap in troop formation, mandated by military regulation, to offer a handful of onlookers access to the scene. These
are the most carefully drawn figures in the image and, in their various
attitudes, delimit the viewer's responses to the spectacle at hand. Generally, the range of civilian response in such illustrations is quite narrow:

FIGURE 5.3. *Private William Johnson, executed by a firing squad, December 1861.*
Frank Leslie's Illustrated Newspaper, *January 4, 1862.*
West Virginia State Archives, Boyd B. Stutler Collection.

they are mildly interested or they are distracted; revulsion, rage, and rapt attention do not figure as potential reactions. Indeed, these spectators appear to view the execution as a source of amusement. Their attitude intimates the aim of illustrated magazines in publishing these images: to entertain a mass audience with pictures of military executions that, while reassuring in their representation of military order, dissociate the spectator from the disciplinary process.

As I have observed, the popular figure of the devoted soldier who willingly, even happily, gives up his life out of love for his country obscured the conditions of military service in which some soldiers were drafted into the army and kept there under threat of punishment. Gary Laderman argues that military executions provided a corrective to the mayhem of war. He writes, "In the midst of chaotic battles, uncontrolled violence, and thoughtless killing, the formal spectacle of the military execution signified the primacy of law, order, and the Union cause."[24] And yet William Johnson's fate—shot and then buried in an unmarked grave—was identical to that of most soldiers who died in battle. An unusual image published by *Frank Leslie's Illustrated Newspaper* on January 4, 1862, shows Johnson's corpse in the posture common to photographs of the battlefield dead (fig. 5.3). Limbs splayed, shirt open, face upturned—this corpse can only be distinguished from those of other soldiers by the coffin at its feet. Magazine illustrations avoid focusing on the body of the condemned, dwelling instead on the crowd that is constituted, ordered, and entertained by military punishment. When the exe-

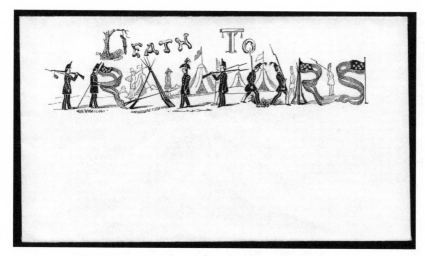

FIGURE 5.4. *"Death to Traitors." E. Cogan. PR-022-3-91-14,*
Collection of The New-York Historical Society.

cuted corpse comes into view, however, the fate of the deserter appears emblematic. At times, images of military executions reveal that death on the battlefield, while it may appear chaotic or disorganized, is an effect of state power.

Portraying military punishment as the source of a robust federal authority, pictorial envelopes offer a far more inflammatory rendering of military discipline. Early in the war, a craze for patriotic envelopes took hold in both the North and South. Alice Fahs remarks that these envelopes were "initially popular because they provided individuals with a means of displaying—and sending—their patriotism."[25] Pictorial envelopes offered a wide range of war-related images—patriotic emblems, portraits of war heroes, battle and camp scenes among them—that were often drawn from broadsides, cards, and illustrated magazines. It is in their tendency toward caricature, however, that these images are most suggestive.[26]

"Death to Traitors" is a popular theme of the more cartoonlike and satirical envelopes. One envelope, for example, uses this slogan to ponder the disciplinary function of military executions. In this image (fig. 5.4), the bodies of drilling soldiers contort to shape the letters of the words "Death to Traitors." Resembling the flags and the guns that they hold, soldiers' bodies are transformed into instruments of violence and emblems of national power. As in Reason's image, the flag's relation to the disciplined body calls the nature of state power into question: this

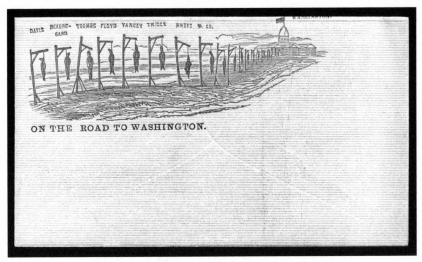

ON THE ROAD TO WASHINGTON.

FIGURE 5.5. *"On the Road to Washington." PR-022-3-91-19,*
Collection of The New-York Historical Society.

envelope implies that executions give the army a chance to inculcate obedience, making the soldier over in the very image of state authority. The sinister implications of this analogy are only heightened by the juxtaposition of the hanging tree (the letter "D") to the scaffold (the letter "T"), which threatens to undermine this playful rendering of military justice altogether. The hanging tree recalls the atrocities committed by Southern slaveholders, as well as the vigilantism that was increasingly associated with the conflict over slavery during the antebellum period. Thus the envelope poses this question: does the scaffold represent the army's power to manage disobedience or does it suggest that military justice is vigilantism by another name?

"On the Road to Washington" (fig. 5.5) threatens Southern leaders with state executions that bear a striking resemblance to vigilante murders. In this image, the comparison between scaffold and tree recurs, if in a subtler form: these makeshift scaffolds resemble nothing so much as stately trees lining the boulevard that leads to the Capitol. The proliferation of dead bodies, in the absence of any perpetrator or witness, intensifies the threatening quality of the scene; metaphorized as a function of the natural world, violent death appears ungovernable. At the same time, the presence of the Capitol, flag flying, at the end of the line makes it clear that this mass execution is not an expression of nature but of

FIGURE 5.6. *"Agriculture, Manufactures, Fine Arts."* PR-022-3-87-9,
Collection of The New-York Historical Society.

federal authority. Introducing a sign of state power—the Capitol—to the
scene of execution, this image implies that during wartime the disreputable methods of the mob attach to the government itself. Drawing on
natural imagery to suggest a process that is out of control while including
an emblem of institutional authority, these scaffolds signify state power
run amok.

"Agriculture, Manufactures, Fine Arts" (fig. 5.6) forgoes any sign of
state power—Capitol, flag, gun, obedient soldier, or the dead body itself.
Instead we find a demystified, indeed comical, Uncle Sam making the
rope that will be used to put traitors to death.[27] Here the indiscriminate
nature of state-sponsored execution is indicated by the caption on the
spinning wheel: "hemp for traitors north or south." The process of producing rope to hang enemies of the state is the same regardless of their
sectional affiliation. The commentary offered by this image is especially
direct: in its eagerness to execute, the federal government wars on secessionists and citizens alike. As the designation "Fine Arts" implies, far
from naturalizing state power this image demonstrates that both noose
and scaffold are cultural artifacts, the product of human hands.

Unlike magazine illustrations, which view military executions from a
distance, these pictorial envelopes consider the instrumental character
of punishments that produce discipline, vitalize emblems of state power,
and express the vengeful attitude of a people at war. Denaturalizing the

relationship between violence and state power, they suggest that wartime executions institutionalized the extralegal violence of the prewar years.

〜 In a speech delivered in Louisville in 1883, Frederick Douglass remarked, "There are occasional cases in which white men are lynched, but one sparrow does not make a summer. Everyone knows that what is called Lynch law is peculiarly the law for colored people and for nobody else."[28] While vigilantes had long targeted ethnic and religious minorities, it was not until the postbellum period that "lynching" became synonymous with the murder of African Americans at the hands of white mobs.[29] Although representations of black soldiers celebrated the reciprocity that allied black men and the federal government after emancipation, military discipline reproduced many of the inequities long suffered by black people, enslaved and free. The punishment of black soldiers in the Union army provides one chapter, largely untold, in the evolving history of punishment as an instrument of racial oppression.

Punishment has proved a versatile mechanism for barring black advancement. While the illegal violence of lynch mobs in the postbellum South appropriated and mocked the prerogatives of the law, the legalized criminalization of African American men and women, accelerated by the "Black Laws" of the Reconstruction years, continues unabated today. The loophole in the Thirteenth Amendment to the Constitution, which abolishes slavery "except as a punishment for crime whereof the party shall have been duly convicted," established punishment, particularly incarceration, as a primary means of oppressing black people. The mistreatment of black soldiers in the Union army that, at its most extreme, entailed the execution of black soldiers on thin pretext, set a precedent for a postbellum order in which African Americans were marginalized by new forms of discipline.

On June 20, 1864, another private named William Johnson was put to death by the Union army. This African American soldier had been convicted eleven days earlier for the attempted rape of a white woman. A team of photographers working for Mathew Brady and one working for Alexander Gardner photographed Johnson's execution.[30] The result is a series of photographs that have been widely reproduced in the years since the Civil War: one represents Johnson's corpse hanging from the scaffold in the absence of any other human figures; one shows a soldier tying Johnson's hands, while another stands at attention; another, taken from a greater distance, shows a large group gathered to watch the execution; one, taken by Timothy O'Sullivan, shows a few men watching John-

FIGURE 5.7. *Private William Johnson, executed by hanging, June 1864.*
Library of Congress.

son's execution from under a tree (fig. 5.7). All of these images indicate
the entire absence of formal military display that typically characterized
military executions. There are no orderly troops standing at attention, no
display of the army disciplined by the spectacle of capital punishment.
In this instance, military execution was not an opportunity to reassert
the army's might in the face of the enemy. To the contrary, the Union
army offered up the spectacle of William Johnson's death to Confederate troops in a gesture of prospective reconciliation. Remarkably, a white
flag was flown at Johnson's execution, and he was hanged in plain view
of both Union and nearby Confederate troops.[31]

Although Civil War photographers produced an enormous archive, including many images of dead soldiers, there are very few photographs
of wartime executions.[32] The presence of sketch artists and journalists
at these executions, and of photographers at so many other war-related
sites, suggests that photographers were not forbidden to cover execu-

tions. Instead, it appears that the scene did not invite photographic documentation and was perhaps, in the photographer's view, unmarketable. When large crowds of soldiers gathered in front of the scaffold, it must have been difficult, if not impossible, for photographers to get close enough to capture the distinguishing detail, and attendant drama, available in magazine illustrations.

It seems likely that Johnson's execution was interesting to photographers precisely because troops did not block access to the scaffold: in the absence of a vast audience, the camera dwells on Johnson's body. The corpse, subordinated or entirely absent from most representations of military executions, dominates these photographs. The focus on Johnson's body gives these images their dizzying historical scope: recollecting the abuses of slavery while pointing toward the lynchings of the post-bellum period, they collapse historical time, halting the march of progress and revealing racial violence as the single, repetitive keynote of American expansion. In these photographs, the exercise of state power cannot be easily distinguished from the relatively spontaneous violence of the mob: stripped of the trappings of state ceremony, Johnson's execution suggests the aim of wartime punishment when directed against African Americans. Rather than dwelling on the majesty of the Union army, O'Sullivan's photograph—closely focused on the errant soldier's corpse—directs our attention to systematic efforts, both during the war and after, to use the threat of violence to check the newly gained autonomy of emancipated slaves.[33]

The emancipation of slaves, and subsequent enlistment of black soldiers, has often been described as a benevolent, indeed revolutionary, expression of federal authority. Without denying the gains brought by emancipation, we need to recognize that, from the first, new freedoms for black men entailed "new forms of compulsion."[34] As Lincoln recalled in 1864, the Emancipation Proclamation allowed him to place a "strong hand upon the colored element."[35] Emancipation was part of a mass mobilization in which the federal government compelled men, both black and white, to fight and die in war.

Early in the war it was clear that the manpower of slaves was a vital resource. In May 1861, Benjamin Butler declared that the slaves entering his command at Fort Monroe, Virginia, were "contraband of war." The term maintained the status of slaves as property while underscoring their value to the Union war effort. In August, Congress followed Butler's lead when it passed the First Confiscation Act, which affirmed the military's right to confiscate slaves if they had been working for the Confederate army. This act did not address the status of fugitive slaves, and it stopped short of officially freeing contrabands or enlisting them as soldiers. In July 1862, Congress passed the Second Confiscation Act, which proclaimed captured and fugitive slaves "forever free" and allowed them to enlist. In August, Secretary of War Edwin Stanton authorized the formation of black troops on the South Carolina Sea Islands, and for the first time ex-slaves were employed as Union soldiers.[36]

Although emancipation was, in large part, a military necessity, once black soldiers were allowed to fight in the Union army they represented the national project of war in a way that white soldiers could not. After emancipation, the Civil War was increasingly defined as a war against slavery. If the war gave the nation an opportunity to disenthrall itself from the interests of Southern slaveholders and from an ignoble past, black soldiers, particularly ex-slaves who gained their liberty through military service, could best represent these changes. While an organic imagery of decay and renewal exemplifies the celebration of white self-sacrifice, images of liberation characterize wartime celebrations of black soldiering. The slave-turned-soldier—freed by the act of enlisting—gains independence that is neatly equated with "manhood" and, in turn, with the nation's own rededication to the cause of equality.[37]

As Fahs observes, depictions of blacks soldiers in popular culture "explored the idea that the war brought a fundamental transformation to black male identity."[38] In visual culture, this transformation was often expressed by the juxtaposition of "before-and-after" images that show the black man as a slave and then a soldier. The triptych of the slave Gordon (fig. 5.8) offers one example; the three images, drawn from photographs, illustrate an essay, "A Typical Negro," published in *Harper's Weekly* on July 4, 1863. The essay begins by describing Gordon's trials as he flees his master and crosses over into the Union camp at Baton Rouge. The trio of images shows Gordon after arriving in camp, his "clothes torn and covered with mud and dirt"; undergoing surgical examination, the scars from a recent whipping on display; and in uniform, prepared for military service. According to Fahs, the "trope of transformation" that governs the rhetoric of black soldiering, "allowed the past always to be implicit in the present" (169). In the case of this triptych, the foregrounded image of the slave's lacerated back ensures that Gordon's identity as a victimized slave takes precedence over "his new identity as a soldier" (171).

Yet even as they testify to past abuse, scars also represent a provocation to future transformation: the violence exercised by black soldiers represented a decisive break with the slave past. In January 1863, shortly after

|A TYPICAL NEGRO.|

We publish herewith three portraits, from photographs by M'Pherson and Oliver, of the negro GORDON, who escaped from his master in Mississippi, and came into our lines at Baton Rouge in March last. One of these portraits represents the man as he entered our lines, with clothes torn and covered with mud and dirt from his long race through the swamps and bayous, chased as he had been for days and nights by his master with several neighbors and a pack of blood-hounds; another shows him as he underwent the surgical examination previous to being mustered into the service—his back furrowed and scarred with the traces of a whipping administered on Christmas-day last; and the third represents him in United States uniform, bearing the musket and prepared for duty.

This negro displayed unusual intelligence and energy. In order to foil the scent of the blood-hounds who were chasing him he took from his plantation onions, which he carried in his pockets. After crossing each creek or swamp he rubbed his body freely with these onions, and thus, no doubt, frequently threw the dogs off his scent.

At one time in Louisiana he served our troops as guide, and on one expedition was unfortunately taken prisoner by the rebels, who, infuriated beyond measure, tied him up and beat him, leaving him for dead. He came to life, however, and once more made his escape to our lines.

By way of illustrating the degree of brutality which slavery has developed among the whites in the section of country from which this negro came, we append the following extract from a letter in the New York *Times*, recounting what was told by the refugees from Mrs. GILLESPIE's estate on Black River:

The treatment of the slaves, they say, has been grower and worse for the last six or seven years.

Flogging with a leather strap on the naked body is mon; also, paddling the body with a hand-saw until skin is a mass of blisters, and then breaking the bli with the teeth of the saw. They have "very often" slaves stretched out upon the ground with hands and held down by fellow-slaves, or lashed to stakes drive the ground for "burning." Handfuls of dry corn-h are then lighted, and the burning embers are whipp with a stick so as to fall in showers of live sparks up naked back. This is continued until the victim is co with blisters. If in his writhings of torture the slave his hands free to brush off the fire, the burning bra applied to them.

Another method of punishment, which is inflicte the higher order of crimes, such as running away, or er refractory conduct, is to dig a hole in the ground enough for the slave to squat or lie down in. The v is then stripped naked and placed in the hole, and a ering or grating of green sticks is laid over the ope Upon this a quick fire is built, and the live embers through upon the naked flesh of the slave, until his is blistered and swollen almost to bursting. With enough of life to enable him to crawl, the slave is allowed to recover from his wounds if he can, or to his sufferings by death.

"Charley Sloo" and "Overton," two hands, were murdered by these cruel tortures. "Sloo" was wh to death, dying under the infliction, or soon after p ment. "Overton" was laid naked upon his face and ed as above described, so that the cords of his legs an

GORDON AS HE ENTERED OUR LINES.

GORDON UNDER MEDICAL INSPECTION.

GORDON IN HIS UNIFORM AS A U.S. SOLD

FIGURE 5.8. *Gordon, before and after.*
Harper's Weekly, *July 4, 1863.*
Special Collections, University of Virginia.

the Emancipation Proclamation went into effect, Massachusetts governor John Andrew received authorization to raise the first regiments of free Northern blacks. Frederick Douglass, appointed as a recruitment agent by Boston abolitionist George Stearns, threw himself into recruiting soldiers for the Massachusetts regiments. After enlisting his own sons, Charles and Lewis, Douglass spent the spring and summer traveling the lecture circuit trying to convince young black men to sign up.

On July 6, 1863, Douglass spoke at a recruitment meeting in Philadelphia. The Honorable W. D. Kelley introduced Douglass to an audience of black and white men and women in this way: "The speaker about to address you illustrated in his person . . . [h]ow personal estate may convert itself into a man. He was a thing, a chattel, part of the personal estate of Thomas Auld, a Maryland planter, but under the inspiration of freedom has been converted into an accomplished gentleman, a pungent and finished writer, and glowing and potent orator. I present to you Mr. Frederick

Douglass, of Rochester, N.Y."[39] Indeed, the transformation of the slave, defined as property, into a "man," defined by self-ownership, is the subject of Douglass's *Narrative of the Life of Frederick Douglass* (1845). In his account of his residence on the Covey plantation, Douglass describes, in microcosm, the process that turns a man into a "brute" and its reversal. Covey uses the whip to push his slaves to labor at the limit of physical endurance. This exhausting regime breaks Douglass "in body, soul, and spirit."[40] When Douglass confronts Covey with violence, and beats him, the process is reversed. Douglass describes his "battle" with Covey as the "turning-point" in his "career as a slave." He writes, "I now resolved that, however long I might remain a slave in form, the day had passed forever when I could be a slave in fact. I did not hesitate to let it be known of me, that the white man who expected to succeed in whipping, must also succeed in killing me" (113). Through the exercise of violence, Douglass convinces both Covey and himself that he is determined to gain his freedom. A utopian act, his violence produces the experience of freedom before that freedom exists "in fact."

Years later, when Douglass urged black men to fight for the Union, he drew on the same certainty that there is "something ennobling in the possession of arms."[41] Douglass's personal history provided a prototype for the slave who frees himself by fighting. Whether appealing to Northern abolitionists or prospective foot soldiers, Douglass described violence as evidence of an essential, inborn freedom as well as a means of demanding that freedom be recognized. This narrative of independence achieved through violence may have been less compelling, however, to men in Douglass's audience who were already free. For slaves, enlistment provided a means to emancipation. They were eager to enlist and in the end made up an estimated 141,000 of the 179,000 black soldiers who joined the Union military.[42] As these numbers imply, soldiering was less attractive to Northern blacks, who were already free and may have been more skeptical about the promise of military service as a means to equality.

While popular representations of black soldiers portrayed the typical soldier as an ex-slave, and twinned his liberation with the country's own, arguments for recruitment that circulated in the Northern states were often pragmatic, aiming to convince blacks and whites that black enlistment served their interests. Douglass's recruitment speeches offer a dizzying array of arguments—practical, ethical, psychological—for enlistment. At the heart of his approach, however, is the appeal to the prospective black soldier's self-interest *and* his patriotism.[43] From the first,

Douglass insisted that the North could not win the war without the aid of black soldiers and that, in order to gain their allegiance, the Union must dedicate itself to abolishing slavery. As a result of military service, black people would benefit: "Nothing can be more plain, nothing more certain than that the speediest and best possible way open to us to manhood, equal rights and elevation, is that we enter this service."[44]

While white soldiers ostensibly died out of love for their country in an act of pure self-sacrifice, black soldiers died in order to get something—freedom, equality, the vote—in return. Conceptualizing the military service of black soldiers in this way, however, admitted a host of obstacles. Early in the process of building black regiments, it became clear that the government intended to deny black soldiers equal pay. In March 1863, Douglass was able to assure prospective recruits that they would receive "the same wages, the same rations, the same equipments, the same protection the same treatment and the same bounty secured to white soldiers."[45] In June, when the War Department reneged on its promise of equal pay, Douglass was reduced to arguing that black men must put their lives on the line in the name of future equality. In his speech in Philadelphia, he discouraged prospective recruits from being "overnice" about the matter of equal pay. After all, he asked, "Don't you work for less every day than white men get?"[46]

Refusing equal pay to black soldiers, the War Department withheld one practical means to the very autonomy typically associated with "manhood." Many black enlistees were unwilling to accept anything less than equal pay from the federal government. Indeed, the pay crisis generated a discontent in the United States Colored Troops that on occasion brought soldiers to the brink of mutiny.[47] On November 19, 1863, William Walker, a sergeant in the Third South Carolina Volunteers, led his men to the tent of his regimental commander where they laid down their arms in protest. In an assertion of as-yet-unrealized power, not unlike Douglass's own strike against slave driver Covey, Walker and his men refused to accept the terms of their service. Unlike Douglass, however, Walker did not triumph over circumstances; convicted of mutiny, he was executed by a firing squad in February 1864.[48]

Douglass's Philadelphia speech, in which he urged black men to fight despite the inequalities they faced in the Union military, was, according to David Blight, "his last attempt for some time to reconcile enlistment with discrimination."[49] Douglass drew the line when it came to the government's unwillingness to protect black soldiers captured by the enemy army: infuriated by Lincoln's silence in response to Confederate massacres of black soldiers at Port Hudson, Milliken's Bend, and Fort Wagner, Douglass tendered his letter of resignation to George Stearns on August 1, 1863. While the Confederacy had mandated death or enslavement for black prisoners as early as November 1862, it was not until July 30, 1863 — two weeks after the assault on Fort Wagner — that Lincoln ordered that "for every soldier of the United States killed in violation of the laws of war, a rebel soldier shall be executed; and for every one enslaved by the enemy or sold into slavery, a rebel soldier shall be placed at hard labor."[50] Apparently unaware of Lincoln's "Order of Retaliation," Douglass, in his letter to Stearns, condemned the government's complicity in the lawless punishment of black soldiers in the strongest terms. "When I plead for recruits I want to do it with all my heart, without qualification," he wrote. "I cannot do that now. The impression settles upon me that colored men have much overrated the enlightenment, justice and generosity of our rulers at Washington."[51]

While Douglass's letter to Stearns focuses on the administration's un-willingness to protect black soldiers from Confederate mistreatment, the Draft Riots played an important role in his growing disenchantment with the recruiting project. The week of July 13 saw riots break out in New York City. Unrest that began as protest against the government's conscription policy escalated, as white rioters mobbed and murdered black civilians.[52] In a scathing editorial, Douglass wrote, "Beat, shoot, hang, stab, kill, burn and destroy the Negro, was the cry of the crowd. Religion has cursed him and the law has enslaved him, and why not the mob kill him? — Such has been our national education on this subject, and that it still has power over Mr. Lincoln seems evident from the fact, that no measures have been openly taken by him to cause the laws of civilized warfare to be ob-served towards his colored soldiers."[53] On Saturday, July 18, the day after the riots were quelled, the Massachusetts 54th was decimated as it led the attack on Fort Wagner. In light of the pay crisis, Lincoln's inaction, and the Draft Riots, the fate of the 54th could only contribute to the in-creasing difficulty that Douglass faced in arguing that military service would lead to equality. Douglass's enthusiasm for the alliance of state interests and the welfare of black people faltered as the events of July 1863 forced him to acknowledge that African Americans were murdered with impunity in the North as well as in the South.

The experiences of black soldiers made it difficult for Douglass, and others, to describe the black man's participation in the Union army as a step in the direction of equality. Like "A Typical Negro," Thomas Water-man Wood's "A Bit of War History," painted in Louisville in 1866, employs the juxtaposition of three images to portray the transformation of the slave turned soldier. A reviewer, writing in 1867, describes the three panels—titled "The Contraband" (fig. 5.9), "The Recruit" (fig. 5.10), and "The Veteran" (fig. 5.11)—in this way:

> In the first the newly-emancipated slave approaches a provost-marshal's office with timid step, seeking to be enrolled among the defenders of his country. This is the genuine "contraband." He has evidently come a long journey on foot. His only baggage is contained in an old silk pocket-handkerchief. He is not past middle age, yet privation and suffering have made him look prematurely old. In the next we see him accepted, accoutred, uniformed, and drilled, standing on guard at the very door where he entered to enlist. This is the "volunteer." His cares have now vanished, and he looks younger, and, it is needless to say, happy and proud. In the third picture he is a one-legged veteran, though two years since we first saw him can scarcely be said to have passed. He approaches the same office to draw his "additional bounty" and pension, or perhaps his back pay.[54]

In this triptych, the emphasis falls on the portrait of the veteran amputee. These images do not tell a straightforward narrative of progress but show the career of the slave-turned-soldier as he moves forward, and back again. The posture of the recruit, who faces to the viewer's right, one foot placed in advance of the other, contributes to the forward motion of the series of images and the implied narrative of historical progress. The veteran faces back to the left, aborting the promised trajectory of the painting and, by analogy, standing as a reminder of the unrealized hopes of black soldiers themselves. His gesture of allegiance, saluting as he applies to the government for money, mirrors the servile gesture of the "contraband" who doffs his hat to the recruiting officer. Far from entitling the black soldier to autonomy, physical suffering leaves him dependent on the federal government.

Representations of black soldiering during the Civil War and beyond contend that the violence inflicted on and by black soldiers reversed the degradations of enslavement, restoring the slave's manhood and the nation's integrity. But the government that took the remarkable step of freeing slaves also drafted and impressed newly freed men into the army, refused to pay them equal wages, and sentenced an inordinate number of them to death. Although African Americans made up less than 8 percent of the Union army, 21 percent of those executed during the war

FIGURE 5.9. *"A Bit of War History: The Contraband."*
The Metropolitan Museum of Art, Gift of Charles Stewart Smith, 1884 (84.12a).
Photograph copyright: The Metropolitan Museum of Art, all rights reserved.

FIGURE 5.10. *"A Bit of War History: The Recruit."*
The Metropolitan Museum of Art, Gift of Charles Stewart Smith, 1884 (84.12b).

FIGURE 5.11. *"A Bit of War History: The Veteran."*
The Metropolitan Museum of Art, Gift of Charles Stewart Smith, 1884 (84.12c).
Photograph copyright: The Metropolitan Museum of Art, all rights reserved.

were black. Whereas white soldiers were most often executed for desertion, the majority of black soldiers were sentenced to death for rape and mutiny. Indeed, African American soldiers made up almost 80 percent of all those executed for mutiny during the Civil War.[55]

Punishment itself was a source of conflict between African American soldiers and their white officers, one that on a number of occasions led to the execution of black soldiers. Implicitly acknowledging the racial history of corporal punishment, Congress outlawed whipping as a military punishment in August 1861. Individual officers, however, continued to whip soldiers, and to use other forms of punishment—hanging soldiers by their thumbs and bucking and gagging—reminiscent of enslavement. Black soldiers often resisted these punishments by restraining their superiors, liberating soldiers undergoing punishment, and going on strike. On a number of occasions, these acts of resistance—both violent and nonviolent—were determined mutinous and punished by death.[56]

While the enlistment of black soldiers was promoted, and continues to be celebrated, as a sign of the nation's renewed commitment to black freedoms, black soldiers were subject to a remarkable degree of injustice. Rather than coexisting in a mutually beneficial interdependence, romanticized at times as common liberation, the black soldier felt the coercive power of the military at its most extreme. As the war neared its conclusion, this disciplinary violence escalated. During the final year of the war, the Union army executed nineteen white and twenty-seven black men; in December 1865 six black soldiers were shot to death for mutiny in the last execution of the Civil War.[57]

Wood walks a fine line in his portrayal of the black recruit, suggesting that progress is a partial affair without abandoning a sense that there is something ennobling about the soldier's sacrifice. The disproportionate punishment of black soldiers at the hands of Union officers, however, demands a more radical reconsideration of the relationship between African American enlistees and the wartime state. Whether it appears to advocate white on black violence or to censure it, O'Sullivan's depiction of William Johnson's execution makes a mockery of the notion that black men freed themselves by fighting in the Civil War. To the contrary, it implies that the prospect of black agency required a swift and brutal response. If postbellum lynching represented, among other things, the efforts of Southern whites to reverse the gains of emancipation by terrorizing a newly enfranchised population, the history of military discipline suggests that excessive punishment inflicted on the black body functioned in the North as well as the South to foreclose the promised reciprocity between black male citizens and the federal state.

⚬ David Blight has recently described the conflict between "emancipationist" and "reconciliationist" accounts of the Civil War in the postbellum period. He argues that narratives of reconciliation that emphasized the "endearing mutuality of sacrifice among soldiers" as the basis for sectional healing eventually triumphed over (though never entirely erased) narratives of emancipation that presented "the liberation of blacks to citizenship and Constitutional equality" as the purpose and end result of the Civil War.[58] In Blight's view, the reconciliationist account of the war is, in essence, a sentimental fiction that substitutes pathos—the intense feeling generated by the white soldier's generic devotion—for recollection of the war's true causes. Blight identifies the celebration of self-sacrifice, which reaches a fever pitch by the century's end, as the primary mechanism of postbellum forgetfulness. By contrast, he considers the emancipationist vision, which promotes ideology over sentiment, to be firmly grounded in the war's reality.

Glory places the emancipationist narrative front and center, asking late-twentieth-century audiences to remember that the Civil War was fought to abolish slavery. At the same time, it questions the glorification of self-sacrifice that often characterizes *both* emancipationist and reconciliationist portraits of the war. The sight of the men of the 54th offering themselves, ready for drill, after learning that they will be executed upon capture, has its counterpart in the scene in which Shaw oversees the punishment of an ex-slave, Tripp. Tripp, who has gone to look for shoes that the army has failed to provide, is taken for a deserter, and Shaw commands that he be whipped in front of the other soldiers. When Colonel Hallowell, Shaw's second-in-command, objects, Shaw brushes him aside. When the drill sergeant takes Tripp's shirt off and reveals that his back is already covered with scars, Shaw hesitates. How can he inflict the same punishment, in the name of the Union army, that the slaveholder has already inflicted? When he regains his composure and orders the drill-sergeant to proceed, Tripp shoots him a look of disgust, and spits.

While the scene pays homage to abolitionist precedent by briefly focusing on Tripp's scarred back, it reverses course and offers an important revision of the conventional sentimental exchange. During the whipping we do not see Tripp's body. Instead, the camera shuttles between

Tripp's face and Shaw's as they gaze at one another. The camera moves in on each face in alternation until it comes to rest on Tripp's face as he watches Shaw watching him. Everything in his expression and his posture strains against the single tear that courses down his face; this tear is not an appeal for sympathy but, like spitting, an expression of revulsion. Dwelling on Tripp's controlled rage, rather than his suffering body, the scene functions as an accusation: the enlisted man's hateful stare focuses the viewer on the problem of Shaw's culpability and establishes his reaction as the object of our contemplation.

Glory takes the relationship between the black soldier's devotion to the cause and the discrimination he confronts in the Union army as its central subject. Tripp's defiance provides a stark contrast to the humble, long-suffering demeanor of the troops in the earlier scene. Throughout the film his hardheaded realism, presumably garnered from the experience of enslavement, is juxtaposed to Shaw's idealism. When Shaw reads the Confederate proclamation to the soldiers Tripp inserts a note of dissonance, asking the soldier standing next to him, "Still want that uniform?" Throughout, he wields the language of exchange, asserting that black soldiers are owed something in return for their service and assuming that this debt will go unpaid. When Shaw asks him to carry the regiment's flag into battle at Fort Wagner, he refuses. "I isn't fighting for you," he explains. "What about us, what are we going to get? You get to go back to that big house of yours, but what are we going to get?"

The evolution of Tripp's character provides something of a test case: if this man, who has experienced slavery's worst, can be brought to feel loyalty, anyone can. In the film's penultimate scene, black soldiers gather to sing and testify in anticipation of the next morning's battle. Awkward speaking in front of others, Tripp tearfully admits, "I love the 54th." His transformation is complete when, the following day, he sees Shaw killed in battle and changes his mind about carrying the flag. He takes up the flag, charges forward, and is immediately shot down. *Glory* concludes with a slow-motion shot of Tripp's body thrown into a mass grave; it lands on top of Shaw's corpse and the two men lie together. This image makes good not only on the homoerotic gaze that joins Shaw and Tripp in the whipping scene but also on the paternalist rhetoric that justifies harsh discipline as good fathering throughout. In this final shot, Tripp appears to be a child resting comfortably on his father's chest.

Reputedly, Confederates buried Shaw, without his uniform, in a trench with black soldiers as a way of dishonoring him. When Shaw's father learned of attempts to retrieve his son's body, he insisted that it be left where it was.[59] Speaking years later at the dedication of Augustus Saint-Gaudens's memorial to the Massachusetts 54th, William James helped to popularize the image of Shaw buried, unceremoniously, with "his dauntless negroes." "As for the colonel," he recounted, "not a drum was heard nor a funeral note, not a soldier discharged his farewell shot, when the Confederates buried him, the morning after the engagement. His body, half stripped of its clothing, and the corpse of his dauntless negroes were flung into one common trench together, and the sand was shoveled over them, without a stake or stone to signalize the spot. In death as in life, then, the Fifty-fourth bore witness to the brotherhood of man."[60] As I have argued, during the war the corpses of soldiers were routinely subject to the indignities that had long been inflicted on the corpses of marginalized people. These distressing conditions were elevated as the very anonymity of the mass dead, buried unceremoniously, came to signify the breadth and durability of collective remembrance. Representations of Shaw's body, buried alongside his black comrades, bring these developments full circle as his hasty, unobserved burial becomes an emblem of racial equality, or as James put it, "the brotherhood of man."

While the movie concludes with Tripp and Shaw lying together in a common grave, the credits roll against the backdrop of the Saint-Gaudens memorial. If the image of Shaw and Tripp buried side by side romanticizes the relationship between black and white soldiers, the monument stays true to racial and military hierarchy as Shaw, mounted on horseback, is positioned in front of a group of black foot soldiers. In keeping with its dual focus on subjection and liberation, the film concludes with two alternate ways of reading the alliance between the Boston Brahmin and the ex-slave turned war hero: is Tripp Shaw's equal or his subordinate? By extension, is his decision to carry the flag a sign that he has transcended his bitter experience or evidence of a misplaced optimism conceived in the heat of battle?

Staging mutually exclusive interpretations of black soldiering, Tripp's character reflects on the conflicted nature of the viewer's experience. Characterized by cynicism, Tripp stands in for the contemporary viewer who does not easily trust narratives of heroism and redemption. Indeed, the film provokes such skepticism by detailing the ugly features of military service even as it presents the valor and compassion of these ill-treated men as a source of heartfelt inspiration. In the end, Tripp's conversion is especially dramatic because it remains inexplicable. He knows that the war will not bring tangible reward—in his words, "ain't nobody gonna win"—but he grabs the flag anyway. Devotion triumphs over experience, thus proving the power of love. Likewise, what the viewer knows not only fails to qualify what she feels but, I would contend, enhances it. Having been offered ample evidence of the racism black soldiers encountered in the Union army, she still responds, unreservedly, to the contention that Tripp's death exemplifies the possibility of racial harmony.

Revisiting the problem of devotion by way of military discipline, the film not only teaches us a little bit about the conditions black soldiers faced in the Union army but also asks us to think critically about emancipationist narratives that continue to glorify their deaths. Using the scene of corporal punishment to frame the heroic commitment of black soldiers who turn their lives over to a principle that they know has no basis in reality, *Glory* considers the extent to which the soldier's faith is produced, and tempered, by the threat of violence.[61] Indeed, I would contend that the mystique surrounding black soldiers is similarly heightened by the depressing knowledge that black enlistment failed, in the long run, to rededicate the United States to the practice of equality. Keeping the memory of coercion alive, *Glory* demonstrates the stubbornness of belief—in the end our own—that embraces the spectacle of black men killed in battle as evidence of the value of war.

EPILOGUE GLORY

Violence is never senseless but always meaningful, because
violence in human culture always serves, one way or the other,
to make a point.—Joseph Roach, Cities of the Dead *(1996)*

Singing "John Brown's Body," soldiers imagined battlefield
death as a form of action and, in doing so, claimed the antislavery martyr's political agency for themselves. When Julia
Ward Howe wrote new lyrics for the tune, she put the power
to wage war in the hands of God. In place of the marching soldier, or his "mouldering" corpse, Howe's "Battle Hymn of the
Republic" describes an individual who is awed by the spectacle of divine vengeance: "Mine eyes have seen the glory
of the coming of the Lord." Calling on a tradition of female
mediumship in which the author is inspired by meanings
well outside her own experience, Howe renders the Civil
War as an expression of divine agency that dwarfs human
influence.[1]

As Howe's revision of "John Brown's Body" indicates, the
power of the dead to inspire or regenerate the living resides
in culture itself, as well-worn conventions, texts, and beliefs are reworked for new circumstances. My description of
Civil War culture takes its shape from these two songs, and
the process of revision that unites them. On the one hand,
artists and commentators derived the war's meaning from
the devotion of individual soldiers; dying in order to save
the Union and free slaves, soldiers rededicated the nation
to principle. Bearing out an evangelical rhetoric of compassion, these soldiers died, in imitation of Christ, so that others
might be saved. On the other hand, the war was often described as God's judgment on a slaveholding nation. This
narrative derives national identity not from individual courage but from common guilt, as God punishes all Americans
for their complicity in the sin of slavery.[2]

As Brown's body decays, his courage emboldens a mass

of fighting soldiers. "Battle Hymn" completes this process of abstraction: in this song, there are no bodies; apocalyptic violence—by definition total—leaves no wreckage behind. Extolling the conflict as the realization of biblical prophecy, Howe's song turns away from the problem of bodily suffering to revel in the glorious spectacle of God's vengeance. Yet if the apocalyptic scenario of divine retribution fulfills the urge to abstraction dramatized by "John Brown's Body," it also reverses the song's optimistic view of soldiering and war. While narratives of martyrdom exaggerate the individual's capacity for self-determination, narratives of divine retribution diminish individual agency to the vanishing point. In lieu of soldiers marching, fighting, or dying, Howe focuses on the plight of the civilian spectator who, unable to participate in the war, struggles to understand it.

Forty-two years old when the Civil War began, Howe had led a life characterized by intermittent success and significant frustration. An aspiring writer and intellectual, she was encumbered by a husband who fiercely opposed her independence and by the work of maintaining a household and bearing and raising six children. Marriage and motherhood were a constant drag on her energies, and, though she had achieved a degree of literary success by the time the war began, it fell short of her ambitions. In her *Reminiscences*, Howe describes "Battle Hymn" as an antidote to her sense of personal failure. Unlike other women who sent their sons or husbands to fight, she had sons too young and a husband too old for service. And while some women went to work in camps and hospitals, Howe lamented, "I could not leave my nursery to follow the march of our armies." She rejoiced, however, that "because of my sincere desire a word was given me to say, which did strengthen the hearts of those who fought in the field and of those who languished in prison."[3]

Accompanying her husband, Samuel Gridley Howe, on a trip to Washington, D.C., in the fall of 1861, Howe found a way to put her literary talents to work on behalf of the war effort. One November day, Howe went with friends to watch a review of the Union troops. A "sudden movement" of Confederate troops interrupted the exercises, and both soldiers and sightseers were forced to disband. Returning to Washington along crowded roads, Howe and her companions sang popular songs to entertain themselves and the soldiers. Their rendition of "John Brown's Body" got an especially enthusiastic response. The minister James Freeman Clark turned to Howe and asked, "'Why do you not write some good words for that stirring tune?'" (275). Howe woke up early the next morning, and as she waited for the sun to rise, the song began to take shape in her mind. She writes, "I sprang out of bed, and found in the dimness an old stump of a pen which I remembered to have used the day before. I scrawled the verses almost without looking at the paper. I had learned to do this when, on previous occasions, attacks of versification had visited me in the night, and I feared to have recourse to a light lest I should wake the baby, who slept near me. I was always obliged to decipher my scrawl before another night should intervene, as it was only legible while the matter was fresh in my mind. At this time, having completed my writing, I returned to bed and fell asleep, saying to myself, 'I like this better than most things I have written'" (275). The song was published in the *Atlantic Monthly* the following February and, like its antecedent, soon achieved tremendous popularity.

Like many Northern intellectuals and reformers, Howe was roused by Brown's courage. Writing to her sister Annie as Brown awaited execution, she explained, "The attempt I must judge insane but the spirit heroic. I should be glad to be as sure of heaven as that old man may be. . . . His death will be holy and glorious—the gallows cannot dishonor him—he will hallow it."[4] Unlike many of her contemporaries, however, Howe was personally acquainted with Brown, and his actions had an immediate impact on her life. When John Brown attacked Harpers Ferry in October 1859, Howe was seven months pregnant with her sixth child. Because her husband Samuel was one of the "secret six" that provided guns and money for Brown and his followers, Brown's raid and capture threw their household into crisis. Samuel, fearing that he would be prosecuted for his involvement with Brown, fled to Canada.[5] He returned home after Brown's execution, just in time for the birth of their son Sammy.

Howe idealized Brown as a man of action. And yet her revision of "John Brown's Body" canonizes the individual's insignificance in the face of war: "Battle Hymn" assumes the vantage point of a stationary observer who looks on as the events of war unfold. The song's narrator, a devout reader of the Old Testament, watches the war from a distance; applying the words of the "burning Gospel," she tries to interpret what she sees:

Mine eyes have seen the glory of the coming of the Lord:
He is trampling out the vintage where the grapes of wrath are stored;
He hath loosed the fateful lightning of His terrible swift sword:
   His truth is marching on.

I have seen Him in the watch-fires of a hundred circling camps,
They have builded Him an altar in the evening dews and damps;

I can read His righteous sentence by the dim and flaring lamps;
  His day is marching on.

I have read a fiery gospel writ in burnished rows of steel:
"As ye deal with my contemners, so with you my grace shall deal;
Let the Hero, born of woman, crush the serpent with his heel,
  Since God is marching on."

He has sounded forth the trumpet that shall never call retreat;
He is sifting out the hearts of men before His judgment-seat:
Oh, be swift, my soul, to answer Him! be jubilant, my feet!
  Our God is marching on.

In the beauty of the lilies Christ was born across the sea,
With a glory in his bosom that transfigures you and me:
As he died to make men holy, let us die to make men free,
  While God is marching on.[6]

With the exception of the fourth stanza—"be swift, my soul, to answer Him! be jubilant, my feet!"—"Battle Hymn" does not allude to fighting in war. Instead, the narrator searches out God's "righteous sentence" in the "flaring lamps" of campfires and "burnished rows of steel." Reading these lyrics, it is hard not to imagine the soldier who gazes into the fire looking for a sign, or Howe struggling to "decipher" her own text scribbled hastily in a dimly lit hotel room.

One might argue that as the war progressed and individual enthusiasm was exhausted, people increasingly drew on God's impenetrable authority to explain the horrifying expanse of the war. In the spring of 1863 Howe wrote, "The deep, terrible secret of the divine idea still lies buried in the burning bosom of the contest." "To interpret this," she continues, "is the first moral obligation of the situation."[7] In its emphasis on the process of interpretation, "Battle Hymn" transforms the war, wrought by human hands, into a message from God that must be scrutinized for an overarching moral purpose. In this way, the song retreats from a confident view of the individual's power to influence the course of events.

~ In 1861, Julia Ward Howe wrote a war anthem of unparalleled popularity and influence. Nine years later, she wrote *Appeal to Womanhood throughout the World*, which called on "Christian Women" to put an end to war. She wrote, "Arise, all women who have hearts, whether your baptism be that of water or of tears! Say firmly: 'We will not have great questions decided by irrelevant agencies. Our husbands shall not come to us, reeking with carnage, for caresses and applause. Our sons shall not be taken from us to unlearn all that we have been able to teach them of charity, mercy and patience. We, women of one country, will be too tender of those of another country, to allow our sons to be trained to injure theirs.'"[8] In the tradition of abolitionist sympathy, Howe employed the common suffering of mothers to build a political alliance that crossed national rather than racial boundaries. But unlike antebellum reform writing, Howe's *Appeal to Womanhood* does not imagine women bringing political change through identificatory sorrow or moral suasion. Instead, she hopes that women will negotiate peace among themselves. The *Appeal to Womanhood* concludes with a call for an international congress of women that would meet to "promote the alliance of the different nationalities, the amicable settlement of international questions, the great and general interests of peace" (303).

Howe's *Appeal to Womanhood* was translated into French, Spanish, Italian, German, and Swedish and widely circulated. She spent the next two years organizing what she later referred to as her "scheme of a worldwide protest of women against the cruelties of war."[9] She held meetings and lectured in New England and London, and corresponded with women throughout the world. In 1873, Howe organized a Mother's Day Peace Festival that was observed throughout the United States and can be considered a precursor to Mother's Day.[10] Her efforts met with little success, however, and after a few years of hard work she realized that "many steps were to be taken before one could hope to effect any efficient combination among women."[11]

How could Howe have written "Battle Hymn of the Republic" and *Appeal to Womanhood* in a single decade? While it is impossible to fully account for this transition without in-depth scrutiny of Howe's philosophical studies and writing in the intervening years, it is worth observing that in 1863 she lost her youngest child. From the first, Sammy was a favorite of both parents, and he was Julia's constant companion during the early years of the war. In May 1863, at the age of three and a half, he contracted diphtheria and died. Howe was blinded by grief. Attempting to cope in the aftermath of Sammy's death, she vacillated between despair and hope, between the Calvinism of her early childhood and the evangelical Christianity that was more comfortable to her as an adult. Writing to her sister Annie, she expressed her inability to comprehend Sammy's death: "I am alone, still fighting over the dark battle of his death, still questioning whether there is any forgiveness for such a death. Something must have been wrong somewhere—to find it out, I have tortured myself almost out of sanity. Now I must only say, it is, and look and wait for divine lessons which follow our bitter afflictions."[12] At some moments, however, Howe reassured herself that she and Sammy would eventually be reunited. In a letter written to Sammy after he died, she explains that although she does not see the end of her "loneliness and desolation," she knows that "Christ says we are to live again after this life, and I know that if I am immortal, God will not inflict upon me the pain of eternal separation from you."[13]

Did the sinner face an essential and impenetrable mystery when encountering the problem of human suffering, or did she turn to worship to find comfort and reassurance in times of trouble? In "Battle Hymn of the Republic," Howe leads with a spectacular rendering of God's awesome anger. Yet while the song revels in the outward signs of God's judgment, in the end it buckles under the weight of such majesty. The final verse retreats from the scene of total destruction, taking refuge in the interior landscape of spiritual transformation. Howe concludes by celebrating Christ's exemplary self-sacrifice, which has the power to "transfigure you and me," rededicating people to the cause of freedom. One wonders if the song, on balance, might have had a different emphasis if it had been written after Sammy's death, rather than before.

During the nineteenth century, death—and the difficulty of interpreting it—was generally viewed as a religious rather than a political problem. While private sorrow had long provided women a way to enter public life, during the Civil War the figure of the mourning mother functioned as a surrogate for collective grief. The mother's faith, tested and renewed by the untimely death of a beloved child, provided one model for a community tried and, in the end, restored by death in war. As long as Howe viewed war in heroic terms, women were exemplary in their devout response to the spectacle of male violence. When she decided that war was an abomination, however, maternal grief served to legitimate organized, political action. Imagining her congress of women, Howe writes, "Let them meet first, as women, to bewail and commemorate the dead." Then they will proceed to "solemnly take counsel with each other as to the means whereby the great human family can live in peace."[14] Having survived the death of her child, Howe turned to the challenges of public life with renewed determination.

If Howe's *Appeal to Womanhood* drew on a sentimental tradition that employs grief as a means to social transformation, it also indicated a growing tendency to view death as the abhorrent consequence of institutional power. An antebellum utopianism, which imagined the many ways that individuals, martyrs among them, might remake their world, was sorely tested by the carnage of war. In the aftermath of war, individuals appeared increasingly helpless, subject to forces—institutions, accidents, nature—beyond their control. This view, however, gave rise to new forms of resistance and critique. As faith in individual autonomy diminished, people could more easily identify violent death as a form of injustice characteristic of a badly organized society. In an antebellum context, mourning occasioned the affirmation of an expansive relatedness, or political love, that moved people to improve their world; in the decades and the century to follow, violent death often inspired political rage that pitted individuals against governing institutions.

During the Civil War, the state drew authority from the prospect of total annihilation. In the war's aftermath, however, the state's legitimacy derived, once again, from its power to curb violence and adjudicate the martyr's claim to power. Stanton, Lincoln's secretary of war, was determined not to let the assassin Booth become a martyr for the Southern cause. Shot in the neck by Sergeant Boston Corbett, John Wilkes Booth died early on the morning of April 26, 1865. Booth's body was wrapped in an old army blanket and taken to the ironclad *Montauk*, moored at the Washington Navy Yard.[15] Here Surgeon General Joseph K. Barnes, at Stanton's direction, performed an autopsy on Booth's body. The damaged vertebrae were removed from his neck and sent to the Army Medical Museum as specimens.[16] While Booth's body parts were put on display in a museum, his corpse was kept hidden from the public. After one woman succeeded in boarding the *Montauk* and clipping a lock of Booth's hair, Stanton worried that Booth's body might acquire mythic status if circulated among admirers. He had Booth's corpse removed from the *Montauk* and secretly buried, without ceremony, under the floor of a room in the Washington arsenal. The room was locked, and Stanton took possession of the key.[17]

Likewise, Stanton jealously guarded a single photograph of Booth's corpse. Alexander Gardner and his assistant, Timothy O'Sullivan, were brought on board the *Montauk*, again at Stanton's request, to photograph Booth's autopsy.[18] After Gardner developed the photograph, a government detective confiscated both the image and the photographic plate and turned them over to the War Department. Stanton's motivations for commissioning a photograph that he then either hid or destroyed remain a matter of speculation. It seems likely that he wanted to use the photograph to identify Booth and confirm that he was dead. Yet the fact that

Stanton suppressed the image suggests its residual function as a commemorative object that, like locks of hair, remained closely associated with Booth's person.[19]

If, at the war's end, the reign of God on earth still seemed remote, people had hopes for a renewed social order and a return to stability. While divine wrath provided an apt explanation for the indiscriminate violence of total war, once the war was over the deliberate punishment of selected traitors gave the federal government a chance to reassert its authority and reestablish order. If Stanton's treatment of Booth's body expressed a belief in the far-reaching influence of the martyr's corpse, the executions of Booth's coconspirators direct us toward new ways of interpreting violent death. Convicted of conspiring to murder Lincoln, David Herold, Mary Surratt, Lewis Powell (alias "Payne"), and George Atzerodt were hanged in the inner courtyard of Washington's Old Arsenal Penitentiary on July 7, 1865, with two hundred witnesses in attendance. Gardner and O'Sullivan were the only photographers invited to document the event. Unlike the clandestine image of Booth's autopsy, their photographs mark the birth of photojournalism: these are the first photographs taken of a public event as it unfolds in time.[20] Stanton kept the photograph of Booth's corpse secret because he believed, or recognized that others believed, in a potent form of identity that outlasted death and made the martyred body valuable and potentially dangerous. By contrast, Gardner and O'Sullivan's execution photographs dramatize the individual's powerlessness in the face of state authority.

These photographs are structured sequentially, conveying the event as a story with a beginning, middle, and end. The series begins with the crowd as it gathers to watch the execution and ends with the empty caskets that await the remains of the dead conspirators. At its center we witness the act of violence in the present tense: one photograph captures the bodies of the dead slightly blurred by the swaying of the rope. We are reminded of Melville's description of Brown's body, "Slowly swaying (such the law)." Equating this gentle movement with the rule of law, Melville dramatizes the oblique appearance of state power. In the context of photographic documentation, however, the swaying motion represents a stunning advance in the power of the photograph to record the impact of violence on the body. The deliberate character of the execution allowed for this breakthrough in documentary representation. Planned in advance and methodically orchestrated, the state's intentional violence allowed the photograph to take on new immediacy and dynamism.

At least one photograph suggests that the appropriate response to such violence was not sympathy but revulsion. It shows an attendant, William Coxshall, as he stands beneath the scaffold vomiting. As he recounted, "I became nauseated, what with the heat and the waiting, and taking hold of the supporting post, I hung on and vomited. I felt a little better after that, but not too good."[21] Unlike the flow of tears that manifests the imaginative alliance of spectator and victim in a sentimental context, vomiting expresses Coxshall's inability to assimilate what he sees. Far from internalizing the suffering of others, Coxshall doubles over, for a moment incapacitated by a singular discomfort that suggests the power of violence to isolate rather than unify.

Like photographs of the battlefield dead, these execution photographs portray the effect of violence on the body. Unlike the earlier photographs, however, they place these effects in context. Documenting the progress of the execution as well as the instruments and the people that inflict violence, these images describe violent death as the result of particular actions and agencies. In doing so, they invite us to view corpses as the expression of human rather than divine intentionality, and death as embedded in social circumstance.

⬱ When Mamie Till Bradley decided to hold an open-casket funeral for her murdered son, she called on a journalistic tradition that offered the corpse as a sign of social injustice and on a sentimental tradition that took mourning as an occasion to build political community in response to such injustice. Exposing her son's disfigured body to a national audience, she broke the silence surrounding the mutilation of black bodies. Gathering an African American community together to rage and sorrow over the murder of her child, she claimed the privileges of ritual commemoration that mutilation so often worked to foreclose.

Fourteen-year-old Emmett Till, a native of Chicago, had been kidnapped and brutally murdered by two white men while visiting relatives in Money, Mississippi, during the summer of 1955. While making a purchase at a local grocery, the African American boy supposedly made an inappropriate remark, or whistled, at Carolyn Bryant, who was working the cash register. Three days later, Bryant's husband Roy and his half brother J. W. Milam abducted Till from his uncle's home, beat him mercilessly, shot him in the head, and dumped his body in the Tallahatchie River. By the time Till's body surfaced, it was so bloated and disfigured that it could not be recognized. His uncle, Mose Wright, was able to identify the corpse, however, because Till wore a ring engraved with his father's initials.[22]

Not surprisingly, Mississippi authorities were eager to bury Till's body as quickly as possible. When Mamie Till Bradley got word that the sheriff was about to bury her son in a pine box without embalming or dressing the body, she recalls, "We got busy." "We called everybody we thought would be able to stop the burial of that body" because, she explained, "I wanted that body. I demanded that body because my thoughts were, I had to see it, to make sure, because I'd be wondering even now who was buried in Mississippi."[23] The sheriff agreed to return Till's body to Chicago, but he sent along an official order that the casket remain sealed.

If the law demanded that Till's casket stay closed, emotional prudence also dictated against viewing. Bradley's friends and relatives advised her not to look at Emmett's corpse. Bradley, however, wanted to see her dead son. She later recalled, "I looked at that horribly mangled monstrosity—the odor was terrible—what had been done to a human being created by God was a crime so foul, I don't have words to describe it. . . . It looked like something from outer space, and it seemed like a weird nightmare, not a part of me."[24] Having seen the body, Bradley decided that other people should see it too. Till's body lay in state in the Roberts Temple Church of God for three days while tens of thousands of people filed past and paid their last respects. Bradley also allowed cameramen from *Jet* magazine to photograph the corpse. A photograph of Till lying in his coffin—skull crushed, features obliterated, one eye missing—created an immediate sensation when it was published in *Jet* and reprinted in many African American newspapers and magazines.[25]

To those who saw Till's body, or read about it in the newspapers, Bryant and Milam's message rang loud and clear: white men were free to murder blacks when they pleased. The extreme violence they inflicted on Till was also intended to make another, related statement. As John Edgar Wideman observes, "It is not an accident that the hacked, dead face of Emmett Till looks inhuman. The point of killing and mutilating him, inflicting the agony of his last moments, was to prove he was not human."[26] When Bradley described her son's body as "something from outer space," she recognized this effect. As her actions demonstrated, however, she understood that the self-same signs of violence could be used to make a different point.

Bradley not only wanted the "whole world" to see Till's body; she wanted the whole world to see it through her eyes. While Till's battered face revealed the magnitude of racial hatred, his body, carefully laid out in a freshly starched white shirt, testified to the love offered up to the dead boy. This famous photograph simultaneously documents the alienating effects of violence on Till's body and the role of commemorative ritual in reclaiming that body for the black community. Bradley not only exposed the violence routinely inflicted on black people but also demanded access to the dead body, a privilege that had been strategically denied to black mourners.

Emmett Till would be another long-forgotten victim if his mother had not decided to hold an open-casket funeral and invite the press to photograph her son's corpse.[27] Till's disfigured face revealed a violence so powerful and so unnatural that it could annihilate a mother's capacity to recognize her own son. Yet by insisting, visibly and publicly, on laying claim to this alien form with no hint of shame or embarrassment, Bradley opened up a space for the public to claim their relatedness to the mutilated boy. Indeed, a number of young African Americans who viewed the famous photograph of Till's corpse recognized that his body could be their own, and the image has been credited with radicalizing a generation of African Americans.[28]

This book reexamines nineteenth-century views of violence, suffering, and death as they relate to the formation of political community. I come to the subject, however, by way of the recognition—fully realized in the twentieth century—that the body is subject to overpowering external forces. While we continue to regard death in war as an arena for personal distinction and a source of collective renewal, this view is more difficult to sustain in light of a countertradition that regards corpses as the result of systematic violence. To recognize, as Bradley did, that the corpse is available to various uses, that it can be crafted or remade to suit a political purpose, is to recognize that violence is a form of expression—as nuanced and embedded in circumstance and convention as any other sort of utterance. Emmett Till's funeral provides just one of many twentieth-century instances in which the public presentation, or representation, of the violated corpse leads an audience to reflect on social conditions.

Drawing inspiration from Mamie Bradley, and others, who have demanded attention for the violated dead, I have taken a look at some nineteenth-century corpses with an eye to social context. At the same time, I have tried not to abandon the impulse to abstraction at the heart of a sentimental tradition, in full bloom by the time the Civil War began, that takes mourning as the occasion to build communities dedicated to social and political change. Bradley used her son's corpse to expose the conventions of white on black violence in all their repulsive and enraging detail. She did not, however, forgo the power of abstraction.

Emmett Till's mother wanted to put an end to lynching and understood that sharing her grief with others was a place to begin. I write in the hope of a future, as yet impossible to envision, in which people give their attention to the effects of violence—pain, mutilation, and loss—and allow their actions to be transformed by what they learn.

NOTES

INTRODUCTION

1 Weiss was an outspoken opponent of slavery who published poetry, essays, and reviews in a number of magazines and may be best known for his *Life and Correspondence of Theodore Parker* (1863). John Weiss, "War and Literature," *Atlantic Monthly*, June 1862, 681.

2 Edmund Wilson, *Patriotic Gore: Studies in the Literature of the American Civil War* (New York: Oxford University Press, 1962), xxxi.

3 Throughout, I am indebted to Elaine Scarry's contention that the wounded body tends to augment the power of the state that inflicts pain. Because we experience certainty by way of the body, the corpse provides a sign of uncontestable reality. At points, the state can claim this very certainty as evidence of its own authority. See Elaine Scarry, *The Body in Pain: The Making and Unmaking of the World* (New York: Oxford University Press, 1985).

4 Joseph Roach, *Cities of the Dead: Circum-Atlantic Performance* (New York: Columbia University Press, 1996), 41.

5 The question of "political love" is at the heart of Benedict Anderson's study of nationalism. How do individuals come to feel an emotional attachment to fellow citizens that they will never meet as well as for the nation itself? In keeping with Anderson's analysis, my book sets out to investigate how the corpse—an object of commemorative practice and discursive meditation—helped nineteenth-century Americans develop and express love for one another in both familial and national contexts. I am also interested, however, in how the war dead reveal the limits of such devotion. While the abstractions used to commemorate dead soldiers inspired the living with a sense of belonging, at times the war dead presented a material challenge—they had to be identified, counted, and disposed of—that signified the failure of the national community to create lasting ties. Benedict Anderson, *Imagined Communities: Reflections on the Origin and Spread of Nationalism*, rev. ed. (New York: Verso, 1991), 9–12, 141–43.

6 Paul Finkelman, "Manufacturing Martyrdom: The Antislavery Response to John Brown's Raid," in *His Soul Goes Marching On: Responses to John Brown and the Harpers Ferry Raid*, ed. Paul Finkelman (Charlottesville: University Press of Virginia, 1995), 47.

7 Governor Wise seems to have given this idea some consideration. In response to a letter from New York mayor Fernando Wood asking if Wise had "nerve enough" to incarcerate Brown for life instead of hanging him, Wise wrote, "I have precisely the nerve enough to let him be executed with the certainty

of his condemnation." Wise may or may not have had Dr. Sayre's letter in mind when he continued, "He shall be executed as the law sentences him, and his body shall be delivered over to surgeons, and await the resurrection without a grave in our soil." Oswald Garrison Villard, *John Brown, 1800–1859; A Biography Fifty Years After* (1910; New York: Alfred A. Knopf, 1943), 502–4; Stephen B. Oates, *To Purge This Land with Blood: A Biography of John Brown* (New York: Harper and Row, 1970), 344.

8 For an excellent summary of nineteenth-century views of the corpse as they pertain to the afterlife, see Gary Laderman, *The Sacred Remains: American Attitudes toward Death, 1799–1883* (New Haven, Conn.: Yale University Press, 1996), 51–62. On death customs and beliefs more generally, see James Farrell, *Inventing the American Way of Death, 1830–1920* (Philadelphia: Temple University Press, 1980); Nancy Isenberg and Andrew Burstein, eds., *Mortal Remains: Death in Early America* (Philadelphia: University of Pennsylvania Press, 2003); Martha V. Pike and Janice Gray Armstrong, eds., *A Time to Mourn: Expressions of Grief in Nineteenth Century America* (Stony Brook, N.Y.: Museums at Stony Brook, 1980); Lewis O. Saum, "Death in the Popular Mind of Pre–Civil War America," in *Death in America*, ed. David Stannard (University of Pennsylvania Press, 1974), 30–48; Drew Gilpin Faust, "The Civil War Soldier and the Art of Dying," *Journal of Southern History*, 67 (February 2001): 3–38; Robert V. Wells, *Facing the 'King of Terrors': Death and Society in an American Community, 1750–1990* (Cambridge: Cambridge University Press, 2000).

9 See Mary Louise Kete, *Sentimental Collaborations: Mourning and Middle-Class Identity in Nineteenth-Century America* (Durham, N.C.: Duke University Press, 2000), and Esther Schor, *Bearing the Dead: The British Culture of Mourning from the Enlightenment to Victoria* (Princeton, N.J.: Princeton University Press, 1994).

10 Robert Leigh Davis writes, "The death of a beloved child is what slavery feels like, Stowe shows. It is the experiential analogue for what is otherwise wholly outside the subjectivity of her white audience. As long as her reader is willing to equate the death of the child with analogous forms of loss, grief forms the basis for a reunifying experience of sympathy." Robert Leigh Davis, *Whitman and the Romance of Medicine* (Berkeley: University of California Press, 1997), 78.

11 Harriet Beecher Stowe, *Uncle Tom's Cabin; or, Life among the Lowly* (1852; New York: Harper and Row, 1965), 90.

12 For wonderful discussions of this scene, see Davis, *Whitman and the Romance of Medicine*, 79–80, and Karen Sánchez-Eppler, "Then When We Clutch Hardest: On the Death of a Child and the Replication of an Image," in *Sentimental Men: Masculinity and the Politics of Affect in American Culture*, ed. Mary Chapman and Glenn Hendler (Berkeley: University of California Press, 1999), 66–67.

13 Walt Whitman, *Poetry and Prose*, ed. Justin Kaplan (New York: Library of America, 1996), 748.

14 Laderman, *Sacred Remains*, 55.

15 On the relationship between oppression and the treatment and conceptualization of the dead, see Russ Castronovo, *Necro Citizenship: Death, Eroticism, and the Public Sphere in the Nineteenth-Century United States* (Durham, N.C.: Duke University Press, 2001); Sharon Patricia Holland, *Raising the Dead: Readings of Death and (Black) Subjectivity* (Durham, N.C.: Duke University Press, 2000); Karla F. C. Holloway, *Passed On: African American Mourning Stories* (Durham, N.C.: Duke University Press, 2002); Ruth Richardson *Death, Dissection, and the Destitute* (1987; Chicago: University of Chicago Press, 2000); Roach, *Cities of the Dead*; Michael Sappol, *A Traffic of Dead Bodies: Anatomy and Embodied Social Identity in Nineteenth-Century America* (Princeton, N.J.: Princeton University Press, 2002).

16 John H. Brinton, *Personal Memoirs of John H. Brinton, Civil War Surgeon, 1861–1865* (1914; Carbondale: Southern Illinois University Press, 1996), 15.

17 On the Army Medical Museum, see Laderman, *Sacred Remains*, 145–48, and Katherine Kinney, "Making Capital: War, Labor, and Whitman in Washington, D.C.," in *Breaking Bounds: Whitman and American Cultural Studies*, ed. Betsy Erkkila and Jay Grossman (New York: Oxford University Press, 1996), 174–89.

18 Richard Scheidenhelm, ed., *The Response to John Brown* (Belmont, Calif.: Wadsworth, 1972), 144.

19 Louis Ruchames, ed., *John Brown: The Making of a Revolutionary* (New York: Grosset and Dunlap, 1969), 167.

20 James Moorhead argues that during the Civil War there was "virtual unanimity" among Northerners that the war was the "climactic test of the redeemer nation and its millennial role." This represented a significant shift from the prewar years, when "churches overwhelmingly believed America's mission to be one of moral persuasion with evangelical piety and democratic institutions offering a contagious example to the rest of the world." James Moorhead, *American Apocalypse: Yankee Protestants and the Civil War, 1860–1869* (New Haven, Conn.: Yale University Press, 1978), x. See also Ernest Lee Tuveson, *Redeemer Nation: The Idea of America's Millennial Role* (Chicago: University of Chicago Press, 1968).

21 Frederick Douglass, *The Civil War, 1861–1865*, vol. 3 of *The Life and Writings of Frederick Douglass*, ed. Philip S. Foner (New York: International Publishers, n.d.), 99.

22 Robert Alotta, *Civil War Justice: Union Army Executions under Lincoln* (Shippensburg, Pa.: White Mane, 1989), 6; William C. Davis, *The Guns of '62*, vol. 2 of *The Image of War, 1861–1865* (Garden City: New York: Doubleday, 1982), 201.

23 "The Execution of Johnson," *Harper's Weekly*, December 28, 1861.

24 Takashi Morizumi, *Children of the Gulf War* (N.p.: Global Association for Banning Depleted Uranium Weapons, 2002), 1.

CHAPTER ONE

1 "To John S. Clark, 1864," *New York Tribune*, April 20, 1865. Gary Alan Fine also takes up the legitimation, indeed the "veneration," of Brown's insurrectionary violence during the war years. He asks, "Given the low esteem in which violent insurgents are held, how is it that John Brown could become for many a model of courage and morality?" He argues that Brown's stature was facilitated by his links to cultural and political elites as well as by the secession of Southern states, which left "the reputational field open for Brown's supporters." Gary Alan Fine, "John Brown's Body: Elites, Heroic Embodiment, and the Legitimation of Political Violence," *Social Problems* 46 (May 1999): 1–2.

2 C. A. Browne, *The Story of Our National Ballads* (New York: Thomas Y. Crowell, 1919), 180. Some scholars claim that the John Brown of the song's title was a sergeant at Fort Warren in Massachusetts, not the John Brown of Harpers Ferry fame. Nonetheless, as soldiers began to take up this tune, they certainly had John Brown's historic martyrdom in mind. While there are countless versions of the song, all of them begin, "John Brown's body lies a-mouldering in the grave / His soul is marching on," and include the verse "He's gone to be a soldier in the army of the Lord, / His soul is marching on." On the genesis and development of "John Brown's Body," see ibid., 181–99, and Boyd Stutler, "John Brown's Body," *Civil War History* 4 (1958): 251–61.

3 A student of Civil War culture soon recognizes the extent to which "John Brown's Body" permeated army life. John Ketcham, a Union soldier, lost his brother Edward at Gettysburg. Describing Edward's burial to their mother, he wrote, "In a little grove behind the batteries, under an oak tree, in his soldier's uniform, wrapped in a shelter-tent, lies all the earthly remains of my brother. 'He has gone to be a soldier in the army of the Lord.'" Annette Tapert, ed., *The Brothers' War: Civil War Letters to Their Loved Ones from the Blue and Gray* (1988; New York: Vintage Books, 1989), 151.

4 Priscilla Wald and Kirk Savage discuss the tendency of nationalist art and rhetoric to exclude African Americans; both argue that representations of citizenship are shaped by these omissions. In Wald's view, "official narratives," which endow particular groups with citizenship, are "haunted" by the disenfranchised. The process of exclusion gives the lie to egalitarian rhetoric, making it obvious that rights are not natural but bestowed selectively. Addressing the dearth of public monuments to slavery and emancipation, Savage argues that the failure to represent black agency in postwar sculpture went hand in hand with the failure to institute a new "interracial order." This absence enabled the emergence of the white "citizen-soldier" that dominated postwar memorial sculpture. Similarly, I believe that representations of martyred slaves continued to exert influence as they were absorbed, and nearly eclipsed, by representations of martyred white soldiers. Priscilla Wald, *Constituting Americans: Cultural Anxiety and Narrative Form* (Durham, N.C.: Duke University Press, 1995), 1–13; Kirk Savage, *Standing Soldiers, Kneeling*

Slaves: Race, War, and Monument in Nineteenth-Century America (Princeton, N.J.: Princeton University Press, 1997).

5 Qtd. in Franklin Sanborn, ed., *The Life and Letters of John Brown, Liberator of Kansas, and Martyr of Virginia* (1885; New York: Negro Universities Press, 1969), 594, 610, 588.

6 Thoreau had been invited to attend a memorial service for Brown held in North Elba, N.Y., on July 4, 1860. Instead, he sent an essay, "The Last Days of John Brown," and it was read out loud at the ceremony. Henry Thoreau, *The Writings of Henry D. Thoreau: Reform Papers*, ed. Wendell Glick (Princeton, N.J.: Princeton University Press, 1973), 151.

7 Richard Scheidenhelm, ed. *The Response to John Brown* (Belmont, Calif.: Wadsworth, 1972), 37.

8 Brown found the notion of a biracial family, in which he figured as patriarch, compelling. In 1834, he told his brother Frederick that he would like to adopt and educate a slave boy. Always short of funds, Brown hoped that some "Christian slaveholder" would donate a child to his family. If not, however, he and his family would be willing to "submit to considerable privation in order to buy one." Years later, Brown led a raid on the homes of two Missouri planters and liberated their slaves. As the group retreated to Kansas, one of the fugitives gave birth to a boy who, according to Osborne Anderson, "the old Captain named . . . John Brown, after himself." Stephen B. Oates, *To Purge This Land with Blood: A Biography of John Brown* (New York: Harper and Row, 1970), 32; Osborne Anderson, *A Voice from Harper's Ferry: A Narrative of Events at Harper's Ferry* (1861; Freeport, N.Y.: Books for Libraries Press, 1972), 16–17.

9 John Stauffer uses the figure of a "black heart" to describe Brown's effort to identify so entirely with black people that he might "blur racial categories" and set the stage for universal equality. While Brown's attempt to acquire a "black heart" should not be interpreted as an instance of "blacking up," the performative nature of Brown's efforts to identify with black people suggests that his cultivation of racial indeterminacy is, among other things, a means to expanded public relevance. Eric Lott's analysis of blackface minstrelsy helps us to see Brown's investment in biracial identity as an attribute of whiteness and as a political variant on a history of white performance that stages the interpenetration of racial identities. John Stauffer, *The Black Hearts of Men: Radical Abolitionists and the Transformation of Race* (Cambridge, Mass.: Harvard University Press, 2002), 6; Eric Lott, *Love and Theft: Blackface Minstrelsy and the American Working Class* (New York: Oxford University Press, 1993). See also Louis Menand, "John Brown's Body," *Raritan* 22 (Fall 2002): 55–61.

10 Harriet Beecher Stowe, "The Story of 'Uncle Tom's Cabin,'" in *Uncle Tom's Cabin; or, Life among the Lowly* (1878; New York: Harper and Row, 1965), xix.

11 My account of Stowe's "The Story of Uncle Tom's Cabin," and of sentimental

method more generally, is indebted to Philip Fisher's *Hard Facts*. In Fisher's analysis, the responsive anguish of the witness to trauma—both characters in sentimental novels and readers of them—reproduces suffering across time and space. Arguing that sentimentality experiments with "the extension of full and complete humanity to classes of figures from whom it has been socially withheld," Fisher trains our attention on the spectator who, by virtue of identifying with socially marginalized figures, finds her sense of relatedness substantially expanded. Responding to Fisher's argument, Laura Wexler has pointed out that for the victim in question there is nothing radical or transformative about having her feelings acknowledged by others. Indeed, prisoners, madmen, children, and slaves can only feel bewildered by the sentimental spectator's sense of discovery as "primary feeling *is* their normal state." Wexler's comments underscore what Fisher's analysis acknowledges more obliquely—sentimental narration, while concerned with the plight of the oppressed, remains relatively uninterested in exploring the experience of victimization. Philip Fisher, *Hard Facts: Setting and Form in the American Novel* (1985; New York: Oxford University Press, 1987), 99; Laura Wexler, *Tender Violence: Domestic Visions in an Age of U.S. Imperialism* (Chapel Hill: University of North Carolina Press, 2000), 104–5.

12 Joan Hedrick, *Harriet Beecher Stowe: A Life* (New York: Oxford University Press, 1994), 219.

13 Stowe, *Uncle Tom's Cabin*, 415.

14 Elizabeth Margaret Chandler, *Essays, Philanthropic and Moral, Principally Relating to the Abolition of Slavery in America* (Philadelphia: L. Howell, 1836), 117, 118.

15 Glenn Hendler addresses this problem in his discussion of Louisa May Alcott's novel *Work*. He observes that, at its most extreme, sympathetic identification combines a nearly psychotic loss of self with narcissistic self-absorption. Glenn Hendler, *Public Sentiments: Structures of Feeling in Nineteenth-Century American Literature* (Chapel Hill: University of North Carolina Press, 2001), 120.

16 Shirley Samuels, "The Identity of Slavery," in *The Culture of Sentiment: Race, Gender, and Sentimentality in Nineteenth-Century America*, ed. Shirley Samuels (New York: Oxford University Press, 1992), 160.

17 Discussing the tendency of white feminist-abolitionists to appropriate the experience of slaves even as they agitated against oppression and exclusion, Karen Sánchez-Eppler concludes, "The discovery that these efforts to liberate the body result in its repression . . . attests to the difficulties and resistance inherent in acknowledging the corporeality of personhood." Karen Sánchez-Eppler, *Touching Liberty: Abolition, Feminism, and the Politics of the Body* (Berkeley: University of California Press, 1993), 49.

18 Considering the relationship between sentimentality and national identity, Lauren Berlant argues that far from eradicating violence, sympathetic identification provides the grounds for its proliferation. Sympathetic feeling—and claims of its world-transforming effects—conceals a self-congratulatory pas-

sivity that allows violence to spread. Although Fisher also sees the reader's passivity as a constitutive feature of sentimental narration, he views this inaction as an honest expression not only of the limits of sentimentality but of representation more generally. Limiting the "goal of art to the revision of images rather than to the incitement to action," sentimental narration may espouse "cautious and questionable" politics, but it "assumes a healthy and modest account of the limited and interior consequences of art." By claiming that sentimentality asks readers to dwell, at least momentarily, on the inadequacy of their own imaginative endeavor, I hope to suggest that, far from promoting self-congratulation, sentimental art may, in certain instances, cultivate dissatisfaction with representation as a means to political change. Lauren Berlant, "Poor Eliza," *American Literature* 70 (September 1998): 656–57; Fisher, *Hard Facts*, 122.

19 Elaine Scarry's analysis of the ways that pain can be detached from the body of the person who suffers provides a useful corrective to both a utopian nineteenth-century view of the benevolent consequences of identification and a contemporary tendency to view identification as a form of violence. Scarry makes valuable distinctions between those who appropriate the suffering of their victims as a source of their own authority and those who represent the pain of others in an effort to alleviate it. Viewing the separation of pain from the particular body as an essential attribute of human activity, and recognizing the abstraction of bodily pain as a source of political effect, Scarry invites us to deliberate on the consequences of this process in any given instance. See Elaine Scarry, *The Body in Pain: The Making and Unmaking of the World* (New York: Oxford University Press, 1985).

20 Oliver Wendell Holmes, *The Works of Oliver Wendell Holmes* (Boston: Houghton, Mifflin, 1892), 13:277.

21 Elizabeth Barnes, *States of Sympathy: Seduction and Democracy in the American Novel* (New York: Columbia University Press, 1997), 96.

22 Like Holmes, Lincoln dramatized the remarkable impact of *Uncle Tom's Cabin* when he allegedly greeted Stowe as "the little woman who made this great war." Elizabeth Young discusses the origin of this story and pursues its relevance to literary critics by proposing to "take Lincoln's tribute . . . seriously" and "interpret *Uncle Tom's Cabin* as a cultural artifact of, if not actually about, the Civil War." Elizabeth Young, *Disarming the Nation: Women's Writing and the American Civil War* (Chicago: University of Chicago Press, 1999), 29.

23 Scheidenhelm, *The Response to John Brown*, 36–37.

24 Oates, *To Purge This Land*, 24; Sanborn, *Life and Letters*, 91–93.

25 Wendell Phillips, "Address," December 15, 1859, in Scheidenhelm, *The Response to John Brown*, 63.

26 *Letters of Lydia Maria Child* (Boston: Houghton, Mifflin, 1882), 103–4. This was not the first time that Child had longed to rush to the bedside of a man wounded in the name of antislavery. After Massachusetts senator Charles Sumner was beaten nearly to death on the Senate floor by Representative

Preston Brooks of South Carolina, Sumner received a distraught letter from Child. "My first impulse," she writes, "was to rush directly to Washington, to ascertain whether I could not supply to you, in some small degree, the absence of a mother's or sister's care." As her letter continues, however, it seems that her desire to rush to Sumner's bedside expresses a frustrated urge toward more radical action. Child, like Sumner, feels a "burning indignation" over the war in Kansas. She writes, "I have so longed to seize a signal-torch, and rush over all the mountains, and through all the valleys, summoning the friends of freedom to the rescue!" In sympathy with Sumner, Child imagines herself lighting out on an expedition very similar to the one that Brown will undertake three years later. In reality, even Child's more temperate desire to nurse wounded heroes is thwarted by the responsibilities of domestic life: she is unable to visit Sumner as she is needed at the bedside of her own aging father. Child concludes her letter to Sumner with some bitterness: "At times, my old heart swells almost to bursting, in view of all these things; for it is the heart of a man imprisoned within a woman's destiny." *Lydia Maria Child, Selected Letters, 1817–1880*, ed. Milton Meltzer and Patricia G. Holland (Amherst: University of Massachusetts Press, 1982), 283.

27 *Letters of Lydia Maria Child*, 105–7. In early 1860, the American Anti-Slavery Society published, in New York, a volume that contained Child's correspondence with Wise, Brown, and Margaretta Mason, who, like Wise, objected to Child's proposed visit. *Correspondence between Lydia Maria Child and Gov. Wise and Mrs. Mason, of Virginia* sold an extraordinary 300,000 copies and was, in Child's estimation, "the most notable of all my anti-slavery doings." *Lydia Maria Child, Selected Letters*, 474.

28 *Lydia Maria Child, Selected Letters*, 329, 339.

29 Carolyn Karcher, *The First Woman in the Republic: A Cultural Biography of Lydia Maria Child* (Durham, N.C.: Duke University Press, 1994), 416.

30 Henry David Thoreau, "The Last Days of John Brown," in *The Writings of Henry David Thoreau: Reform Papers*, ed. Wendell Glick (Princeton, N.J.: Princeton University Press), 145 (hereafter cited as *Reform Papers*). For a collection of Northern speeches, poetry, letters, and sermons written in response to Brown's raid and execution, see James Redpath, ed., *Echoes of Harpers Ferry* (1860; New York: Arno Press, 1969). Addressing the reaction of transcendentalists, George Fredrickson argues that Brown helped Emerson and Thoreau reconcile inner vision with the practical demands of social life. At Harpers Ferry, John Brown proved that "action could be as sublime as thought." George Fredrickson, *The Inner Civil War: Northern Intellectuals and the Crisis of the Union* (1965; Urbana: University of Illinois Press, 1993), 40.

31 Brown asked Child not to visit him in prison. He suggested, however, that there was "another channel" through which her sympathy might reach him: he asked Child to raise money to help support his wife and children after his death. *Letters of Lydia Maria Child*, 118–19.

32 Thoreau, *Reform Papers*, 120.

33 *The Journal of Henry D. Thoreau*, ed. Bradford Torrey and Francis H. Allen, vol. 12 (Boston: Houghton Mifflin, 1906), 429.

34 Thoreau, *Reform Papers*, 119, 135.

35 Oates, *To Purge This Land*, 307, 322.

36 Scheidenhelm, *The Response to John Brown*, 144.

37 Abraham Lincoln, for example, dismissed Brown's raid, claiming that it did not interest the slaves that it was intended to liberate. In his Cooper Union Address, Lincoln points out that "John Brown's effort was not a slave insurrection. It was an attempt by white men to get up a revolt among slaves, in which the slaves refused to participate. In fact, it was so absurd that the slaves, with all their ignorance, saw plainly enough it could not succeed." Abraham Lincoln, *Speeches and Writings, 1859-1865*, ed. Don Fehrenbacher (New York: Library of America, 1989), 125.

38 Scheidenhelm, *The Response to John Brown*, 133.

39 These details are drawn from "Our Charlestown Correspondence," *New York Herald*, December 2 and 3, 1859, 1; "The Execution of John Brown," *New York Daily Tribune*, December 3, 1859, 7.

40 While Booth opposed Brown's cause and deplored his actions, he, like so many others, could not help admiring the man. Indeed, Booth described Brown to his sister Asia as "the grandest character of this century." Edward Steers, *Blood on the Moon: The Assassination of Abraham Lincoln* (Lexington: University Press of Kentucky, 2001), 36.

41 On the purpose of public executions and their disappearance, see Michel Foucault, *Discipline and Punish: The Birth of the Prison*, trans. Alan Sheridan (1977; New York: Vintage, 1995), 3-131; Karen Halttunen, *Murder Most Foul: The Killer and the American Gothic Imagination* (Cambridge, Mass.: Harvard University Press, 1998), 7-32; Louis P. Masur, *Rites of Execution: Capital Punishment and the Transformation of American Culture, 1776-1865* (New York: Oxford University Press, 1989); David Rothman, *The Discovery of the Asylum: Social Order and Disorder in the New Republic* (1971; Boston: Little, Brown, 1990), 3-108.

42 David Hunter Strother, "John Brown's Death and Last Words," MS 78-1, 11, Boyd B. Stutler Collection, West Virginia State Archives, Charleston, W.Va.

43 "Execution of John Brown," *New York Daily Tribune*.

44 Strother, "John Brown's Death," 11.

45 "Execution of John Brown," *New York Daily Tribune*. In addition, a number of journalists found ways to skirt checkpoints undetected by disguising themselves or relying on personal connections to get closer to the scaffold. See Boyd B. Stutler, "The Hanging of John Brown," MS 78-1, 5-6, Boyd B. Stutler Collection, West Virginia State Archives; and Edmund Ruffin, *The Diary of Edmund Ruffin*, ed. William Kauffman Scarborough, vol. 1. (Baton Rouge: Louisiana State University Press, 1972), 368-69.

46 Elizabeth Preston Allan, *The Life and Letters of Margaret Junkin Preston* (Boston: Houghton Mifflin, 1903), 114.

47 As Foucault has observed, the show of force enacted during public execu-

tions intimates the power of the state to make war against its enemies. The relationship between punishment and war is all too obvious at the scene of Brown's execution: in the context of the looming secession crisis, this display of military power expressed the intolerance of the federal government and the potential aggression of Southern states simultaneously. Foucault, *Discipline and Punish*, 48–50.

48 "Scenes in Charlestown," *New York Herald*, December 3, 1859, 1.

49 Herman Melville, *Battle-Pieces and Aspects of the War* (1866; New York: Da Capo, 1995), 11.

50 "Domestic Intelligence," *Harper's Weekly*, December 10, 1859, 794.

51 Louis Ruchames, *John Brown: The Making of a Revolutionary* (New York: Grosset and Dunlap, 1969), 167. This message, loosely paraphrased, was published in some Northern newspapers. It does not, however, appear to have been as widely reproduced or as influential as Brown's courtroom speech. According to Richard Slotkin, "There is no more succinct statement of that principle of regeneration through violence." Although Brown uses the "myth of blood atonement" to affiliate his own death with Christ's, Slotkin argues that in an American context the language of blood is also tied to theories of racial difference and thus implies "racially oriented violence" as the particular condition for collective redemption. Richard Slotkin, *The Fatal Environment: The Myth of the Frontier in the Age of Industrialization, 1800–1890* (New York: Atheneum, 1985), 275, 262.

52 Timothy Sweet helps us understand the logic of substitution as it applies to representations of war violence. Analyzing the "rhetorical operations" used during the Civil War to transform "the body of the soldier" into "the ideological discourse of the state," he observes that the rhetoric of national unity, specifically the galvanizing image of the body politic, is based on a substitution whereby "millions of actual bodies are transformed into a single, powerful figure." Timothy Sweet, *Traces of War: Poetry, Photography, and the Crisis of the Union* (Baltimore: Johns Hopkins University Press, 1990), 6, 12–13.

53 Fales Henry Newhall, "The Conflict in America: A Funeral Discourse Occasioned by the Death of John Brown of Osawatomie," in Redpath, *Echoes of Harper Ferry*, 203.

54 Sanborn, *Life and Letters*, 620.

55 Villard, *John Brown*, 646.

56 Lincoln, *Speeches and Writings, 1859–1865*, 405.

57 Lincoln, *Speeches and Writings, 1832–1858*, ed. Don Fehrenbacher (New York: Library of America, 1989), 35–36. As others have noticed, Lincoln's stated intention in this speech—to encourage obedience to the law and thus preserve the founders' legacy—is repeatedly undermined. The rhetorical energy he devotes to describing the mobs and tyrants that threaten national stability outstrips the persuasive power of his proposed solution. Scholars have interpreted Lincoln's halfhearted defense of the law as a sign his own "parricidal" urges: does he really want to play the part of the obedient son? Regarding Lincoln's meditation on the law as an expression of filial ambivalence, we may

fail to notice that Lincoln is confused not only about his relationship to the past but also about the role of law in the present. Is law the most effective way of defining political community? Might violence, if more costly, bind citizens more firmly to the state? Arguments that foreground genealogy domesticate the difficult questions this speech raises about Lincoln's attitudes toward the political uses of violence. See Russ Castronovo, *Fathering the Nation: American Genealogies of Slavery and Freedom* (Berkeley: University of California Press, 1995), 1-10; Eric Sundquist, "Slavery, Revolution, and the American Renaissance" in *The American Renaissance Reconsidered*, ed. Walter Benn Michaels and Donald E. Pease (Baltimore: Johns Hopkins University Press, 1985), 4-6; George Forgie, *Patricide in the House Divided: A Psychological Interpretation of Lincoln and His Age* (New York: Norton, 1979), 55-87.

58 Lincoln, *Speeches and Writings, 1859-1865*, 536.

59 Wald, *Constituting Americans*, 71.

60 Robert Penn Warren, *The Legacy of the Civil War* (1961; Cambridge, Mass.: Harvard University Press, 1983), 3-4.

61 Examining the work of historian James McPherson and filmmaker Ken Burns, Edward Ayers notes that the struggle and uncertainty of war recede as soldiers appear to "kill each other for the common purpose of discovering the depth and the nature of their nationalism." These narratives, and others like them, lend support to the notion that wars are "engines of beneficial social change" and that the Civil War was "good for the country in the long run." Edward Ayers, "Worrying about the Civil War," in *Moral Problems in American Life: New Perspectives on Cultural History*, ed. Karen Halttunen and Lewis Perry (Ithaca, N.Y.: Cornell University Press, 1998), 149, 157.

62 Villard, *John Brown*, 465-66. Dramatizing his complex relationship to Brown, as well as the volatility of political allegiances at this point in time, Wise organized a successful raid on the federal arsenal at Harpers Ferry on April 16, 1861. See Barton Wise, *The Life of Henry A. Wise of Virginia* (New York: Macmillan, 1899), 274-81.

CHAPTER TWO

1 Jonathan Sawday explains that "despite the fact that neither the protestant nor catholic churches regarded intact christian burial as a prerequisite for obtaining posthumous grace," people widely believed that the "denial of burial involved the punishment of the soul." Jonathan Sawday, *The Body Emblazoned: Dissection and the Human Body in Renaissance Culture* (London: Routledge, 1995), 280.

2 "Reminiscences of Robert James Christies, 1831-1853," 1432 THL, 20, Handley Library Archives, Winchester, Va.

3 Published in *Oberlin Evangelist*, January 4, 1860.

4 Drew Gilpin Faust, "The Civil War Soldier and the Art of Dying," *Journal of Southern History* 67 (February 2001): 10-13.

5 James Monroe, "A Journey to Virginia in December, 1859," in *Oberlin Thursday Lectures, Addresses, and Essays* (Oberlin, Ohio: Edward J. Goodrich,

1897), 158–84. John Copeland Sr. had written to Governor Wise before the execution requesting his son's body. Wise replied that he would let him have the body but that the elder Copeland must not come to Virginia himself; he would have to send a white man as a proxy. Wise was next contacted by A. N. Beecher, the mayor of Oberlin. Wise told Beecher that he had already promised the body to Copeland's father. According to the American Anti-Slavery Society's account of the event, Mayor Beecher then commissioned a "southern gentlemen" with proslavery sentiments to act as the elder Copeland's representative. When this gentleman called on the appropriate Southern authorities, however, he was arrested and detained for twelve hours before being allowed to return to his home in Washington. The "friends of Freedom, in Ohio," not to be discouraged, then sent Professor James Monroe of Oberlin College to "make another effort to obtain the bodies of the colored men." He was also unsuccessful. For accounts of these events, see Robert E. McGlone, "John Brown, Henry Wise, and the Politics of Insanity," in *His Soul Goes Marching On: Responses to John Brown and the Harpers Ferry Raid*, ed. Paul Finkelman (Charlottesville: University Press of Virginia, 1995), 250; *The Anti-Slavery History of the John Brown Year* (New York: American Anti-Slavery Society, 1861), 137; "The Body of Copeland—Remarkable Circumstances," *Liberator*, January 6, 1860.

6 Nicholas Marshall uses these statistics to argue that historians have underestimated the role of disease in prompting increased membership in Protestant churches during this period. He argues as well that scholars largely misapprehend the relationship between death and sentimental culture when they regard an "antebellum fascination with illness and death" as an "outgrowth" of sentimental culture. To the contrary, he maintains that a deep cultural investment in "sentiment and sympathy came from the real need to deal with death." Nicholas Marshall, "'In the Midst of Life We Are in Death': Affliction and Religion in Antebellum New York," in *Mortal Remains: Death in Early America*, ed. Nancy Isenberg and Andrew Burstein (Philadelphia: University of Pennsylvania Press, 2003), 186.

7 James Farrell, *Inventing the American Way of Death, 1830–1920* (Philadelphia: Temple University Press, 1980), 36–42.

8 Faust, "The Civil War Soldier," 10; Lewis O. Saum, "Death in the Popular Mind of Pre–Civil War America," in *Death in America*, ed. David Stannard (University of Pennsylvania Press, 1974), 41–43; Gary Laderman, *The Sacred Remains: American Attitudes toward Death, 1799–1883* (New Haven, Conn.: Yale University Press, 1996), 28.

9 Laderman, *Sacred Remains*, 31.

10 Laderman observes that evangelical Protestants downplayed the corruptibility of the body in favor of an idealized version of death that aimed to console survivors by emphasizing the continuity between life and death. He describes a "cult of memory that disguises death as it domesticates and beautifies the body, making the last image more palatable and therefore more emotionally conducive to the act of memorialization." Laderman, *Sacred Remains*, 55–56.

11 For a comprehensive analysis of the rise of anatomy in the United States, see Michael Sappol, *A Traffic of Dead Bodies: Anatomy and Embodied Social Identity in Nineteenth-Century America* (Princeton, N.J.: Princeton University Press, 2002). Sappol makes a compelling case for the tremendous influence of anatomical practice on the culture at large, devoting particular attention to its contribution to the formation of class identity.

12 Michel Foucault, *Discipline and Punish: The Birth of the Prison*, trans. Alan Sheridan (1977; New York: Vintage, 1995), 11, 33.

13 On the increasing importance of anatomy to medical inquiry, see James Cassedy, *Medicine in America: A Short History* (Baltimore: Johns Hopkins University Press, 1991), 40-42; Edward B. Krumbhaar, "The Early History of Anatomy in the United States," *Annals of Medical History* 4 (1922): 272-86; Geoffrey Marks and William K. Beatty, *The Story of Medicine in America* (New York: Charles Scribner's Sons, 1973), 73-97; Richard Harrison Shyrock, *Medicine in America: Historical Essays* (Baltimore: Johns Hopkins University Press, 1966), 210-11.

14 *The Introductory Lectures of Professors Pattison and Revere, Delivered in Jefferson Medical College, Philadelphia* (Philadelphia: Wm. F. Geddes, 1833).

15 On the racist character of medical experimentation, dissection, and grave robbing, see Robert Blakely and Judith Harrington, eds., *Bones in the Basement: Postmortem Racism in Nineteenth-Century Medical Training* (Washington: Smithsonian Institution Press, 1997); David Humphrey, "Dissection and Discrimination: The Social Origins of Cadavers in America, 1760-1915," *Bulletin of the New York Academy of Medicine* 49 (September 1973): 819-25; Todd Savitt "The Use of Blacks for Medical Experimentation and Demonstration in the Old South," *Journal of Southern History* 48 (August 1982): 331-48.

16 Steven Wilf observes that New York's anatomy act "introduced dissection into America's retributive apparatus." He asks why this harsh measure was introduced during a period marked by penal reform, noting that the law fell into disuse less than a decade after it was enacted. Because the public was nearly as incensed by the dissection of criminals as it was by the dissection of law-abiding citizens, judges hesitated to apply the sentence of postmortem dissection for fear of inciting further mob violence. Steven Wilf, "Anatomy and Punishment in Late-Eighteenth-Century New York," *Journal of Social History* 22, no. 3 (Spring 1989): 507. On the Doctors' Riot, see also James Walsh, *History of Medicine in New York: Three Centuries of Medical Progress*, vol. 2 (New York: National Americana Society, 1919), 378-91.

17 Walsh, *History of Medicine in New York*, 386-87.

18 In *Death, Dissection, and the Destitute*, Ruth Richardson takes the same transformation, as it unfolded in Britain, as her subject. With the passage of the Anatomy Act in 1831, "what had for generations been a feared and hated punishment for murder became one for poverty." Ruth Richardson, *Death, Dissection, and the Destitute* (1987; Chicago: University of Chicago Press, 2000), xv. On the advent of anatomy legislation in the United States, and

especially the uses of the category "unclaimed," see Sappol, *A Traffic of Dead Bodies*, 98–135.

19 On the evolution of anatomy legislation, see John Blake, "The Development of American Anatomy Acts," *Journal of Medical Education* 30 (August 1955): 431–39; Horace Montgomery, "A Body Snatcher Sponsors Pennsylvania's Anatomy Act," *Journal of the History of Medicine* 21 (October 1966): 374–93.

20 In the climate of increased official sanction and enduring public disapproval, anatomists themselves took a romantic view of their pursuit of knowledge. Lecturing medical students in the 1830s and 1840s, professors of anatomy celebrate the expansion of medical schools by narrating the troubled history of their discipline. Anatomists of old, who persevered in the face of popular prejudice and legal hostility, emerge as outlaw heroes. Anatomists view their predecessors as rebels willing to break the law and endure the violence of an ignorant public in order to advance medical knowledge. As the law comes to accommodate physicians, however, the public is transformed from an actual menace into an abstract recipient of the physician's practical knowledge, and the doctor emerges as a servant who works to "alleviate the miseries of mankind." Joseph Pancoast, *An Introductory Lecture Delivered at the Commencement of the Winter Course of Anatomy for 1834-5* (Philadelphia: W. P. Gibbons, 1835), 5.

21 See Marks and Beatty, *The Story of Medicine in America*, 94–95; Montgomery, "A Body Snatcher Sponsors Pennsylvania's Anatomy Act," 390–92.

22 John Blake speculates that the Civil War revealed to the public the "ghastly inadequacy of American surgeons," and that consequently anatomy acts were passed in the interest of improving medical education. It is also possible that, as Gary Laderman argues, the enormous losses of the Civil War created an indifference toward death that made it easier to regard the corpse as a useful object. Blake, "The Development of American Anatomy Acts," 435; Laderman, *Sacred Remains*, 136–43.

23 Sharon Patricia Holland argues that during the nineteenth century, medical science played an important role in constructing the dead as alien, contributing to our own tendency to view life and death as fundamental opposites. In turn, the polarization of the living and the dead provided "the beginning binary" on which other "dichotomous systems such as black and white or straight and queer" are modeled. The very notion that death represents the end of life and thus its antithesis—an assumption that Holland means to challenge—informs our habit of using opposing categories to envision and describe other forms of marginality. Likewise, Joseph Roach argues that the "segregationist taxonomies" of the Enlightenment take root in the increasing separation between the living and the dead. Sharon Patricia Holland, *Raising the Dead: Readings of Death and (Black) Subjectivity* (Durham, N.C.: Duke University Press, 2000), 32; Joseph Roach, *Cities of the Dead: Circum-Atlantic Performance* (New York: Columbia University Press, 1996), 50.

24 On racial science, see Robert Bieder, *Science Encounters the Indian, 1820–1880* (Norman: University of Oklahoma Press, 1986); George Fredrickson, *The Black Image in the White Mind: The Debate on Afro-American Character and Destiny, 1817–1914* (1971; Middletown, Conn.: Wesleyan University Press, 1987); Reginald Horsman, *Race and Manifest Destiny: The Origins of American Racial Anglo-Saxonism* (Cambridge, Mass.: Harvard University Press, 1981); Samuel Otter, *Melville's Anatomies* (Berkeley: University of California Press, 1999).

25 Monogenesists, by contrast, believed in a single act of creation and viewed racial difference as the result of environment. Fredrickson cautions us against exaggerating the difference between these schools. Although monogenesists regarded racial difference as the result of environment, they often maintained that these differences were irreversible. Fredrickson, *The Black Image*, 83.

26 Thomas Jefferson, *Notes on the State of Virginia* (1787; New York: W. W. Norton, 1972), 143. On Jefferson and racial science, see Alexander Boulton, "The American Paradox: Jeffersonian Equality and Racial Science," *American Quarterly* 47 (September 1995): 467–92.

27 It is worth noting that Jefferson tested a smallpox vaccine on his own slaves in 1801. Todd Savitt, *Medicine and Slavery: The Diseases and Health Care of Blacks in Antebellum Virginia* (Urbana: University of Illinois Press, 1978), 294–97.

28 On *Crania Americana*, see Horsman, *Race and Manifest Destiny*, 125–27; and Otter, *Melville's Anatomies*, 102–18.

29 Morton was not the only doctor looking for Indian skulls, and soon enough collecting Indian crania had become a thriving frontier business. In 1859, the surgeon general asked the United States Army to collect Native American remains in the West. Hundreds of skeletons were later sent to the Army Medical Museum in Washington, D.C., and then moved to the Smithsonian. Grave robbers continued to raid the burial grounds of Native Americans throughout the nineteenth century. In 1990, activists secured passage of the Native American Graves Protection and Repatriation Act, which, among other things, restores collected remains to their tribes of origin. On the exploitation of Native American remains, see Bieder, *Science Encounters the Indian*, 64–67; Matthew Dennis, "Patriotic Remains: Bones of Contention in the Early Republic," in Burstein and Isenberg, *Mortal Remains*, 136–48; Dan Monroe, "The Politics of Repatriation," in *American Indian Studies: An Interdisciplinary Approach to Contemporary Issues*, ed. Dane Morrison (New York: Peter Lang, 1997), 391–401.

30 Otter, *Melville's Anatomies*, 120.

31 Ibid., 112–16.

32 J. Monroe, "A Journey to Virginia," 170–71.

33 Duane Schultz, *Over the Earth I Come: The Great Sioux Uprising of 1862* (New York: St. Martin's Press, 1992), 1–6.

34 William Hartley and Ellen Hartley, *Osceola: The Unconquered Indian* (New York: Hawthorn Books, 1973), 248–49. See also Mab Segrest, *Memoir of a Race Traitor* (Boston: South End Press, 1994), 1–4.

35 *The Piazza Tales and Other Prose Pieces, 1839–1860*, vol. 9 of *The Writings of Herman Melville*, ed. Harrison Hayford, Hershel Parker, and G. Thomas Tanselle (Evanston: Northwestern University Press, 1987), 46.

36 Maggie Montesinos Sale, *The Slumbering Volcano: American Slave Ship Revolts and the Production of Rebellious Masculinity* (Durham, N.C.: Duke University Press, 1997), 170.

37 David Walker, *David Walker's Appeal to the Coloured Citizens of the World* (New York: Hill and Wang, 1995), 2. Published privately by Walker in 1829, the *Appeal* went through two more editions in the next nine months. I have relied on the third edition, published in June 1830, edited by Charles Wiltse in 1965, and reprinted with slight alterations and an introduction by Sean Wilentz.

38 James McCune Smith and William Wells Brown both published attacks on Jefferson that resemble Walker's in important ways. Juxtaposing Jefferson's comments on racial difference to his sexual history, both authors argue that far from being separate species blacks and whites are bound by blood ties. Reproducing passages from Jefferson's writings, scrutinizing their flaws, and using them to advance their analysis, Brown and Smith, like Walker, accentuate the importance of context in determining truth. In doing so, they not only expose the contradictions in Jefferson's life and work but also question claims to objective knowledge. James McCune Smith, "On the Fourteenth Query of Thomas Jefferson's Notes on Virginia," *Anglo-African Magazine* 1, no. 8 (August 1859); William Wells Brown, *Clotel; or, The President's Daughter* (1853; New York: University Books, 1969). See also Adélékè Adéèkó's discussion of *Clotel* as Brown's response to American ethnologists, "Signatures of Blood in William Wells Brown's *Clotel*," *Nineteenth-Century Contexts* 21, no. 1 (1999): 115–34.

39 Eric Sundquist, *To Wake the Nations: Race in the Making of American Literature* (Cambridge, Mass.: Harvard University Press, 1993), 9. As Maggie Sale observes, however, it was the new primacy of the idea of whiteness as it came to justify both enslavement and expansion that made the appeal to an inclusive founding rhetoric of universal, natural rights especially subversive. Sale, *The Slumbering Volcano*, 17.

40 On the impact of Walker's radical treatise, see Sean Wilentz, "The Mysteries of David Walker," introduction to *David Walker's Appeal*, vii–xxiii; and Vincent Harding, *There Is a River: The Black Struggle for Freedom in America* (New York: Harcourt Brace Jovanovich, 1981), 92–94.

41 Houston Baker, *Long Black Song: Essays in Black American Literature and Culture* (Charlottesville: University Press of Virginia, 1972), 47.

42 Discussing the conflation of death and liberty in both pro- and antislavery writing, Russ Castronovo warns us against assuming that adopting the voice of the dead is a form of opposition. He argues that the association between

death and freedom that "saturates nineteenth-century culture" posits an "inert" or ahistorical freedom as a model for national citizenship and thus does not readily advance liberation from the material constraints of enslavement. Russ Castronovo, *Necro Citizenship: Death, Eroticism, and the Public Sphere in the Nineteenth-Century United States* (Durham, N.C.: Duke University Press, 2001), 36.

43 Harding, *There Is a River*, 93–94.

44 On the connections between Walker's *Appeal* and Turner's insurrection, see Harding, *There Is a River*, 75–100; and Mary Kemp Davis, *Nat Turner before the Bar of Judgment: Fictional Treatments of the Southampton Slave Insurrection* (Baton Rouge: Louisiana State University Press, 1999), 15–41.

45 *"The Confessions of Nat Turner" and Related Documents*, ed. Kenneth Greenberg (Boston: St. Martin's Press, 1996), 10.

46 Douglas Egerton argues that dismemberment, particularly decapitation, was a form of punishment reserved for slaves and especially insurrectionaries. He contributes a discussion of African death rituals to our understanding of the value attached to the integrity of the dead body. He writes, "Africans, and many African Americans, believed that an unnatural death, or the failure to observe proper burial rites, doomed the soul to wander forever in the desolate waste of the damned, unable to serve as that protecting ancestor to whom later generations might appeal for assistance." Slaveowners, well aware of these beliefs, sought to deter rebellion by punishing slaves with a "form of retribution *beyond death*." Douglas Egerton, "A Peculiar Mark of Infamy: Dismemberment, Burial, and Rebelliousness in Slave Societies," in Isenberg and Burstein, *Mortal Remains*, 149, 153.

47 F. Roy Johnson, *The Nat Turner Slave Insurrection* (Murfreesboro, N.C.: Johnson, 1966), 199–200. See also Harding, *There Is a River*, 99–100; and Henry Irving Tragle, *The Southampton Slave Revolt of 1831: A Compilation of Source Material* (Amherst: University of Massachusetts Press, 1971), 165.

48 Sundquist, *To Wake the Nations*, 71.

49 Tony Horwitz, "Untrue Confessions," *New Yorker*, December 13, 1999, 82.

50 Debate over the status of Turner's subjectivity raged in the twentieth century after William Styron published his novel *The Confessions of Nat Turner* (1967). Styron imagined that Turner's uprising was the consequence of his frustrated lust for Margaret Whitehead, a young white woman. Incensed black intellectuals reacted to Styron's attempt to pathologize Nat Turner: in *William Styron's Nat Turner: Ten Black Writers Respond*, ed. John Henrik Clarke (1968; Westport, Conn.: Greenwood Press, 1987), some set the historical record straight while others questioned the very urge to fathom Nat Turner's "true self." John Oliver Killens put it most pointedly when he wrote, "What's the big mystery about Nat's motivation? He was a slave, PERIOD" (37). Significantly, Thomas Wentworth Higginson made the same point a century earlier when, in his 1861 essay on Turner's rebellion, he observed, "The biographies of slaves can hardly be individualized; they belong to the class. We know bare facts; it is only the general experience of human beings in like con-

dition which can clothe them with life." Applying this observation to Turner himself, Higginson asserted that "what his private experiences and special privileges or wrongs may have been, it is therefore now impossible to say." Thomas Wentworth Higginson, *Black Rebellion; a Selection from "Travellers and Outlaws"* (1889; New York: Arno Press, 1969), 280-81.

51 William Sidney Drewry, *The Southampton Insurrection* (Washington, D.C.: Neal, 1900), 19-20.

52 Peter Wood, "Nat Turner: The Unknown Slave and Visionary Leader," in *Black Leaders of the Nineteenth Century*, ed. Leon Litwack and August Meier (Urbana: University of Illinois Press, 1988), 40. See also Davis, *Nat Turner before the Bar of Judgment*, 279.

53 Published in *Oberlin Evangelist*, December 21, 1859.

54 Copeland was not alone in turning to Crispus Attucks as an exemplar of black resistance: the revolutionary hero figured significantly in abolitionist polemics at midcentury. Describing the celebration of Crispus Attucks Day in Boston in 1858, Stephen Browne argues that African American writers and orators claimed Attucks as a martyr "not so much to American independence as to African American emancipation." In this way, they laid claim to Revolutionary principles while criticizing the Revolution's outcome. Stephen H. Browne, "Remembering Crispus Attucks: Race, Rhetoric, and the Politics of Commemoration," *Quarterly Journal of Speech* 85 (May 1999): 183.

55 Monroe, "A Journey to Virginia," 175.

CHAPTER THREE

1 Walt Whitman, *Leaves of Grass* (Brooklyn, N.Y., 1856), 202-5.

2 See Katherine Kinney, "Making Capital: War, Labor, and Whitman in Washington, D.C.," in *Breaking Bounds: Whitman and American Cultural Studies*, ed. Betsy Erkkila and Jay Grossman (New York: Oxford University Press, 1996), 174-89.

3 Neil Schmitz, "Refiguring Lincoln: Speeches and Writings: 1832-1865," *American Literary History* 6 (Spring 1994): 104.

4 See Phoebe Lloyd, "Posthumous Mourning Portraiture," in *A Time to Mourn: Expressions of Grief in Nineteenth Century America*, ed. Martha V. Pike and Janice Gray Armstrong (Stony Brook, N.Y.: Museums at Stony Brook, 1980), 71-106; and Jay Ruby, *Secure the Shadow: Death and Photography in America* (Cambridge, Mass.: MIT Press, 1995).

5 As the war progressed, attempts to identify the dead and bury them in marked graves were increasingly successful. Many bodies, however, never received an adequate burial. In the aftermath of the conflict the War Department placed white wooden headboards on more than 300,000 graves, and these were replaced during the 1870s with more durable marble and granite markers. See David Sloane, *The Last Great Necessity: Cemeteries in American History* (Baltimore: Johns Hopkins University Press, 1991), 114.

6 On the discontinuity between antebellum death ritual and the "impersonal and disembodied national narrative" used to commemorate the dead during

wartime, see Lisa Long, "'The Corporeity of Heaven': Rehabilitating the Civil War Body in *The Gates Ajar*," *American Literature* 69 (December 1997): 794.

7 Betsy Erkkila, *Whitman the Political Poet* (New York: Oxford University Press, 1989), 205, 214.

8 Walt Whitman, *Poetry and Prose*, ed. Justin Kaplan (New York: Library of America, 1996), 800.

9 James Dawes, *The Language of War: Literature and Culture in the U.S. from the Civil War through World War II* (Cambridge, Mass.: Harvard University Press, 2002), 29, 32.

10 My thanks to Stephen Cushman for this observation.

11 Qtd. in Sloane, *The Last Great Necessity*, 115.

12 Henry Sweetser Burrage, *Gettysburg and Lincoln: The Battle, the Cemetery, and the National Park* (New York: G. P. Putnam's Sons, 1906), 91.

13 In *Lincoln at Gettysburg: The Words That Remade America* (New York: Simon and Schuster, 1992), 19–40, Garry Wills describes the aftermath of the battle of Gettysburg, the design of the national cemetery, and the occasion of Lincoln's famous speech.

14 Abraham Lincoln, *Speeches and Writings, 1859–1865*, ed. Don Fehrenbacher (New York: Library of America, 1989), 536.

15 As Elizabeth Young has argued in response to Aaron and others, this represented absence is a critical fiction that exposes the process of canonization as it works to elevate certain texts and eliminate others. Young draws our attention to a longstanding critical preoccupation with the (failed) representational efforts of white male authors that has facilitated the glaring absence of women's war writing from this canon. Like wartime writers who claimed that the war could not be described, critics have taken the silence of certain authors as testimony to the war's immensity and significance while sidelining an enormous body of wartime writing. Like Young, Kathleen Diffley and Alice Fahs also take Aaron's "unwritten war" as the point of departure for their investigations of the vast and diverse popular culture of the Civil War. Daniel Aaron, *The Unwritten War: American Writers and the Civil War* (New York: Alfred A. Knopf, 1973), xix; Elizabeth Young, *Disarming the Nation: Women's Writing and the American Civil War* (Chicago: University of Chicago Press, 1999), 2–3; Kathleen Diffley, *Where My Heart Is Turning Ever: Civil War Stories and Constitutional Reform, 1861–1876* (Athens: University of Georgia Press, 1992); Alice Fahs, *The Imagined Civil War: Popular Literature of the North and South, 1861–1865* (Chapel Hill: University of North Carolina Press, 2001).

16 Jahan Ramazani discusses modern poets who reshape the elegy by working against the grain of its idealizing conventions. Taking the work of Geoffrey Hill as his example, Ramazani discusses Holocaust poems that "refuse the closure, rebirth, and substitution traditional in the elegiac genre, lest they seem to impose sense and purpose on mass murder." Jahan Ramazani, *Poetry of Mourning: The Modern Elegy from Hardy to Heaney* (Chicago: University of Chicago Press, 1994), 8. On twentieth-century war writing, see also Allyson

Booth, *Postcards from the Trenches: Negotiating the Space between Modernism and the First World War* (Oxford: Oxford University Press, 1996); Dawes, *The Language of War*; Margot Norris, *Writing War in the Twentieth Century* (Charlottesville: University Press of Virginia, 2000).

17 Susan Sontag beautifully describes this ambivalence when she writes, "Though far from enthusiastic about this war, which he identified with fratricide, and for all his sorrow over the suffering on both sides, Whitman could not help but hear war's epic and heroic music. This ear kept him martial, albeit in his own generous, complex, amatory way." Susan Sontag, *Regarding the Pain of Others* (New York: Farrar, Straus and Giroux, 2003), 52.

18 Michael Moon, *Disseminating Whitman: Revision and Corporeality in "Leaves of Grass"* (Cambridge, Mass.: Harvard University Press, 1991), 173.

19 Whitman, *Poetry and Prose*, 416.

20 Stephen Cushman describes the "discrepancy" between "loud belligerence" and "quieter watching" that characterizes *Drum-Taps*. Like Erkkila and Schmitz, Cushman is interested in the impact of photography on Whitman's wartime writing and believes that the best poems in *Drum-Taps* are distinguished by their visual emphasis. He cautions, however, against the view that the Civil War "engendered" either photographic or literary realism, suggesting that "it makes much more sense to say that some of the conditions that combined to produce war in North America during the nineteenth century also combined to produce realism there." Stephen Cushman, *Bloody Promenade: Reflections on a Civil War Battle* (Charlottesville: University Press of Virginia, 1999), 236, 240.

21 Whitman made his last revisions of *Drum-Taps* for the 1881 edition of *Leaves of Grass*.

22 Erkkila, *Whitman the Political Poet*, 212.

23 Whitman, *Poetry and Prose*, 438–39.

24 Erkkila, *Whitman the Political Poet*, 213.

25 Whitman, *Poetry and Prose*, 457.

26 C. A. Browne, *The Story of Our National Ballads* (New York: Thomas Y. Crowell, 1919), 216.

27 Benedict Anderson, *Imagined Communities: Reflections on the Origin and Spread of Nationalism*, rev. ed. (New York: Verso, 1991), 11.

28 Lincoln, *Speeches and Writings, 1859–1865*, 659–60.

29 James McPherson, *Battle Cry of Freedom: The Civil War Era* (1988; New York: Ballantine Books, 1989), 859.

30 Lincoln, *Speeches and Writings, 1859–1865*, 536.

31 Ibid., 505. Likewise, Lincoln argued that the suspension of the writ of habeas corpus was a military necessity aimed at detaining agitators intent on discouraging recruitment. See "To Erastus Corning and Others, June 12, 1863," 454–63.

32 Walt Whitman, *"Memoranda during the War" [and] "Death of Abraham Lincoln,"* ed. Roy P. Basler (Bloomington: Indiana University Press, 1962), 12.

33 Whitman, *Poetry and Prose*, 799.

34 Gary Laderman informs us that although Lincoln's body was embalmed it began to show signs of putrefaction while on display. The paradoxical relationship between decay and continuity was inscribed on the president's corpse through the partial failure, or incomplete success, of this new technology. Once again, the nationalist abstraction of undying continuity, meant to deny the material effects of violence, played out against the backdrop of the body's decomposition. Laderman, *Sacred Remains*, 160-63.

35 Edward Steers estimates that 7 million people—one in four Americans— turned out to pay their respects to the dead president. For descriptions of the funeral tour, see Ralph Borreson, *When Lincoln Died* (New York: Appleton-Century, 1965), 78, 103; Dorothy Meserve Kunhardt and Philip B. Kunhardt Jr., *Twenty Days: A Narrative in Text and Pictures of the Assassination of Abraham Lincoln and the Twenty Days and Nights That Followed* (New York: Harper and Row, 1965); Steers, *Blood on the Moon: The Assassination of Abraham Lincoln* (Lexington: University Press of Kentucky, 2001), 293.

36 Borreson, *When Lincoln Died*, 69.

37 Sallie Brock, *The Southern Amaranth* (New York: Wilcox and Rockwell, 1869).

38 Mary Louise Kete, *Sentimental Collaborations: Mourning and Middle-Class Identity in Nineteenth-Century America* (Durham, N.C.: Duke University Press, 2000). See also Mary Loeffelholz, "The Religion of Art in the City at War: Boston's Public Poetry and the Great Organ, 1863," *American Literary History* 13 (Summer 2001): 212-41.

39 Aaron, *The Unwritten War*, xv.

40 Oliver Wendell Holmes, "The Poetry of War," first delivered to the Dowse Institute, Cambridge, Mass., November 21, 1865, Special Collections Department, University of Virginia, Charlottesville, Va.

41 See Mark L. Walston, "Voices of the Holy War: Occasional Verse of the American Civil War," *Victorians Institute Journal* 15 (1987): 93-104.

42 Henry Howard Brownell, *Lyrics of a Day; or, Newspaper-Poetry* (New York: Carleton, 1864), iii.

43 Richard White, *Poetry Lyrical, Narrative, and Satirical, of the Civil War* (New York: American News Company, 1866), vi-vii.

44 Ibid., vii. Likewise, Walston argues that the mediocrity of Civil War poetry— characterized by "diffuseness, contradiction, or repetition"—establishes it as a reflection of "the unrehearsed feelings of Americans in a period of great upheaval" and provides an unmediated expression of "the character of a people at war." Walston, "Voices of the Holy War," 103.

45 *War Lyrics and Songs of the South* (London: Spottiswoode, 1866).

46 I have not found any account of the notebook or its author. The notebook is held at Brown University's John Hay Library. As it is unpaginated, I will not refer to page numbers here.

47 After September 11, the streets of New York were again full of occasional poetry and art. Dan Barry, reporting for the *New York Times*, described messages written in the dust that covered the area near ground zero: "Perhaps a

formal memorial will be built someday. For now there are the walls and windows of Lower Manhattan, where thousands of messages have been inscribed in the gray snow of destruction that fell two weeks ago today." Dan Barry, "Ephemeral Notes from a World Lost Bear Witness to the Unspeakable," *New York Times*, September 25, 2001.

48 An anthology of poetry written in response to Lincoln's death sounds similar themes and provides an interesting companion to this notebook. See *Poetical Tributes to the Memory of Abraham Lincoln* (Philadelphia: J. B. Lippincott, 1865).

49 Kevin Henkin, *City Reading: Written Words and Public Spaces in Antebellum New York* (New York: Columbia University Press, 1998), 3.

50 Qtd. in Henkin, *City Reading*, 98.

51 Herman Melville, *Battle-Pieces and Aspects of the War* (1866; New York: Da Capo, 1995).

52 Timothy Sweet, *Traces of War: Poetry, Photography, and the Crisis of the Union* (Baltimore: Johns Hopkins University Press, 1990), 167.

53 Sweet argues that Melville's war poems reflect critically on the tendency of other wartime artists, most especially Whitman, to "aestheticize the effects of violence and to evade questions about the historical contingency of politics." Melville, by contrast, rejects "conventional inscriptions that harmonize nature, the human body, and ideology." Sweet, *Traces of War*, 165.

54 Michael Rogin, *Subversive Genealogy: The Politics and Art of Herman Melville* (1979; Berkeley: University of California Press, 1985), 260.

55 Melville, preface to *Battle-Pieces*, v.

56 On the function of these bulletin boards in relation to the circulation of information during the Civil War, see Menahem Blondheim, *News over the Wires: The Telegraph and the Flow of Public Information in America, 1844–1897* (Cambridge, Mass.: Harvard University Press, 1994), 29; Fahs, *The Imagined War*, 19; Henkin, *City Reading*, 168–70.

57 Norris, *Writing War*, 24–25.

58 My account of these photographs, housed at Yale University's Medical Library, is indebted to Kathy Newman's essay "Wounds and Wounding in the American Civil War: A (Visual) History," *Yale Journal of Criticism* 6 (Fall 1993): 63–86.

59 Alan Trachtenberg also juxtaposes Melville's *Battle-Pieces* with medical photographs of wounded soldiers. He finds a determined objectivity, which aims to capture the part rather than the whole, in the episodic quality of Melville's volume and in the "sullen" gaze of soldiers who "watch themselves being watched." These provide examples of the fragmentation that characterizes representations of the Civil War. The unusual portrait of John Miller's leg bone allows me to argue that this kind of observation occasionally produced images of fragmentation so intense that they are able to convey the impossibility of trying to comprehend, let alone narrate, the war. Alan Trachtenberg, *Reading American Photographs: Images as History, Mathew Brady to Walker Evans* (Hill and Wang, 1989), 116.

CHAPTER FOUR

1 William Stapp, "To . . . Arouse the Conscience, and Affect the Heart," in *An Enduring Interest: The Photographs of Alexander Gardner*, ed. Brooks Johnson (Norfolk, Va.: Chrysler Museum, 1991), 23–24. Pat Hodgson writes, "There was an authenticity to a photograph which convinced people that here was reality at last. . . . It is difficult for us today to understand the impact that these first photographs made. Their veracity was never doubted." Pat Hodgson, *Early War Photographs* (Boston: New York Graphic Society, 1974), 11.

2 Barthes takes as his example Alexander Gardner's photograph of Lewis Powell (alias "Payne") awaiting execution for his role in the conspiracy to assassinate Abraham Lincoln. Thus Barthes draws our attention to the way that a death sentence, like an old photograph, produces a subject that is at once dead and alive. Roland Barthes, *Camera Lucida: Reflections on Photography*, trans. Richard Howard (New York: Hill and Wang, 1981), 96.

3 Discussing Walter Benjamin's description of the "decline of photography," Eduardo Cadava writes that while early photographs have a "phantasmatic, instantaneous, hallucinatory" quality that conveys the individual's sense of helplessness when confronted with time passing, later photographs are "marked by an increasingly mimetic ideology of realism, an ideology reinforced by advances in the technical sophistication of the camera." My argument assumes, by way of Barthes, Benjamin, and Cadava, that at its inception the photograph embodied distance and that as photographic technology improved the power of the photograph to convey incomprehension became less evident. Eduardo Cadava, *Words of Light: Theses on the Photography of History* (Princeton, N.J.: Princeton University Press, 1997), 13–14.

4 On efforts to determine these dates, see William Frassanito, *Antietam: The Photographic Legacy of America's Bloodiest Day* (1978; Gettysburg, Pa.: Thomas Publications, 1997), 71–73; and D. Mark Katz, *Witness to an Era: The Life and Photographs of Alexander Gardner* (New York: Viking Penguin, 1991), 44–45.

5 It appears that the first photograph of war corpses was taken by Felix Beato in 1858. Taken four months after the siege of Lucknow in which Indian troops (led by the British) defeated Hindu and Muslim rebels, this photograph shows the skeletons of the dead "mutineers," whose bodies had been left unburied as a form of punishment. Frances Fralin, *The Indelible Image: Photographs of War, 1846 to the Present* (New York: Harry N. Abrams, 1985), 34–37. On war photographs taken before the Civil War, see also Hodgson, *Early War Photographs*, 11–60; Jorge Lewinksi, *The Camera at War: A History of War Photography from 1848 to the Present Day* (New York: Simon and Schuster, 1978), 37–43; Susan Sontag, *Regarding the Pain of Others* (New York: Farrar, Straus and Giroux, 2003), 48–51.

6 Discussions of the exhibit and its impact reliably return to three sources: the review in the *New York Times*; reproductions of the photographs in *Harper's Weekly* and an accompanying essay; Oliver Wendell Holmes's brief discussion of the exhibit in his *Atlantic Monthly* essay "Doings of the Sun-

beam" (July 1863). The absence of any mention of the exhibit in other New York newspapers calls into question the assertion that these photographs had a tremendous impact. It is not only impossible to gauge the effects of these photographs but also difficult to determine their popularity. William Frassanito maintains that Gardner's Antietam photographs sold at a steady pace throughout the war and provided incentive to other photographers who hoped to make money with similar views. By contrast, William Stapp notes that after the Antietam exhibit efforts to photograph the conflict went unremarked in national newspapers and photographic journals. He also observes that of the "hundreds of illustrations deriving from photographs that were published in the illustrated press during the Civil War, only about two dozen were from views taken in the field; the remainder were almost all studio portraits." Frassanito, *Antietam*, 286; Stapp, *An Enduring Interest*, 24, 118.

7 "Brady's Photographs: Pictures of the Dead at Antietam," *New York Times*, October 20, 1862. Although Gardner and Gibson made these photographs, credit went to their employer, Mathew Brady.

8 Jay Ruby, *Secure the Shadow: Death and Photography in America* (Cambridge, Mass.: MIT Press, 1995), 63–74.

9 Karen Sánchez-Eppler, "'Then When We Clutch Hardest': On the Death of a Child and the Replication of an Image," in *Sentimental Men: Masculinity and the Politics of Affect in American Culture*, ed. Mary Chapman and Glenn Hendler (Berkeley: University of California Press, 1999), 70.

10 Fisher explains, "It is particularly important for sentimentalism that there be two victims rather than one, and that they be the essence of the family, mother and child tied by the quintessential bond of feeling, maternal love. The primary victim is not the child who undergoes physical destruction, but the mother who must be present when all she values most is torn from her and destroyed." Fahs discusses the importance of the mother in Civil War poetry and song. She observes that fathers rarely appear in these texts and accounts for this absence by noting that "war demanded that soldiers be loyal to a new patriarchal authority, the state." Philip Fisher, *Hard Facts: Setting and Form in the American Novel* (1985; New York: Oxford University Press, 1987), 106; Alice Fahs, *The Imagined Civil War: Popular Literature of the North and South, 1861–1865* (Chapel Hill: University of North Carolina Press, 2001), 107.

11 Alexander Gardner, *Gardner's Photographic Sketch Book of the Civil War* (1866; New York: Dover Publications, 1959).

12 Katz, *Witness to an Era*, 28–31.

13 Timothy Sweet, *Traces of War: Poetry, Photography, and the Crisis of the Union* (Baltimore: Johns Hopkins University Press, 1990), 110.

14 Indeed, the bill appropriating funds to construct a telegraph line was accompanied by a rider that requested funds for experiments in mesmerism. For a discussion of these developments, see Menahem Blondheim, *News over the Wires: The Telegraph and the Flow of Public Information in America, 1844–1897* (Cambridge, Mass.: Harvard University Press, 1994), 31. On Morse's telegraph as it pertains to the development of national identity, see Jill Le-

pore, *A Is for American: Letters and Other Characters in the Newly United States* (New York: Alfred A. Knopf, 2002), 139-61.

15 David Mindich, "Edwin M. Stanton, the Inverted Pyramid, and Information Control," in *The Civil War and the Press*, ed. David B. Sachsman, S. Kitrell Rushing, and Debra Reddin van Tuyll (New Brunswick, N.J.: Transaction Publishers, 2000), 197. Diffley notes that this development encouraged Lincoln's "partisan use" of the Associated Press. Kathleen Diffley, *Where My Heart Is Turning Ever: Civil War Stories and Constitutional Reform* (Athens: University of Georgia Press, 1992), xliii.

16 Qtd. in Blondheim, *New over the Wires*, 38.

17 Bernard A. Weisberger, *Reporters for the Union* (1953; Westport, Conn.: Greenwood Press, 1977), 74-124.

18 Elaine Scarry, *The Body in Pain: The Making and Unmaking of the World* (New York: Oxford University Press, 1985), 115.

19 William Frassanito, *Gettysburg: A Journey in Time* (Gettysburg, Pa.: Thomas Publications, 1975), 187-92.

20 William Stapp, "'Subjects of Strange and Fearful Interest,' Photojournalism from Its Beginnings in 1839," in *Eyes of Time: Photojournalism in America*, ed. Marianne Fulton (Boston: Little, Brown, 1988), 27-28; Ruby, *Secure the Shadow*, 13.

21 Miles Orvell, *The Real Thing: Imitation and Authenticity in American Culture, 1880-1940* (Chapel Hill: University of North Carolina Press, 1989), 77.

22 Frassanito, *Gettysburg*, 192.

23 Whitman, *Poetry and Prose*, 436.

24 Laura Wexler's discussion of "the production of domestic images in the age of American imperialism" is relevant here. Discussing Frances Benjamin Johnston's photographs of sailors on board the *Olympia* in 1899, Wexler observes, "Within the sentimental construct, home boys must in some sense be mamma's boys, which prevents them from being arsonists, rapists, looters, lynchers." Even when the subject of the photograph is an enemy corpse, domestic conventions work to obscure the violence perpetrated by soldiers. Laura Wexler, *Tender Violence: Domestic Visions in an Age of U.S. Imperialism* (Chapel Hill: University of North Carolina Press, 2000), 21, 35.

25 Oliver Wendell Holmes, "The Stereoscope and the Stereograph," *Atlantic Monthly*, June 1859; reprinted in *Photography: Essays and Images*, ed. Beaumont Newhall (New York: Museum of Modern Art), 60.

26 John Tagg warns us against assuming that photographs reflect a prior reality. He argues that, instead, they must be viewed in relation to the material, institutional, and historical contexts in which they are produced. Although I would not disagree with this assertion, I think Tagg underestimates the photograph's particular claim on the material world. As I see it, photographs show us objects, places, and bodies in a way that reproduces our own routine visual encounters with identical or similar scenes. For this reason, they impart a keen sense of verisimilitude. This sense of familiarity is complicated, however, by the static nature of the photograph: we see familiar things but

we often see them in the absence of the contextualizing knowledge that we bring to daily life. Thus the question is not whether photographs capture an unmediated reality, but how they describe the viewer's relationship to that reality. Often, photographs demand that we contemplate our disorientation in the face of an object world that appears untouched by change. Recontextualizing them, we run the risk of neutralizing this weird effect. John Tagg, *The Burden of Representation: Essays on Photographies and Histories* (Minneapolis: University of Minnesota Press, 1993).

27 Cadava, *Words of Light*, 3.

28 Alan Trachtenberg, *Reading American Photographs: Images as History, Mathew Brady to Walker Evans* (New York: Hill and Wang, 1989), 75.

29 In the context of war photography, it is tempting to assume that this intensity prompts viewers to question the necessity of war or turns them against it altogether. For example, Susan Moeller argues that photographic coverage of war has led to increasing skepticism among Americans that has, in turn, influenced military policy. Recent studies by George Roeder and Barbie Zelizer ask us to reconsider this assumption. Examining photographs of World War II, Roeder maintains that the government published previously censored images of the dead in order to "intensify public commitment to the war effort." Considering "atrocity photographs" of Holocaust victims published in the weeks following the liberation of Nazi internment camps, Zelizer argues that the conventions spawned by these images have worked to desensitize audiences to more recent acts of genocide. She observes that "coverage has not prevented atrocity's recurrence." Susan Moeller, *Shooting War: Photography and the American Experience of Combat* (New York: Basic Books, 1989), 6–7; George Roeder, *The Censored War: American Visual Experience during World War Two* (New Haven, Conn.: Yale University Press, 1993), 6; Barbie Zelizer, *Remembering to Forget: Holocaust Memory through the Camera's Eye* (Chicago: University of Chicago Press, 1998), 203.

30 Mindich, "Edwin M. Stanton," 179–208. According to Blondheim, "During the war the Associated Press assumed the position of a semi-official medium for the distribution of information emanating from sources in the administration." Blondheim, *News over the Wires*, 130.

31 At the time, Roche was employed by E. and H. T. Anthony and Company. On Roche's wartime work, see Susan Williams, "'Richmond Again Taken': Reappraising the Brady Legend through Photographs by Andrew J. Russell," in *Virginia Magazine of History and Biography* 110, no. 4 (2002): 437–60. For a brief overview of Roche's career, see the obituary published in *Anthony's Photographic Bulletin* 26 (1895): 367.

32 This intimate focus, however, made it "virtually impossible to pinpoint the exact site of any of the photographs in the Fort Mahone series." In his collections of Civil War photographs, Frassanito tries to figure out exactly where a shot was taken and then juxtaposes the original photograph with a contemporary image of the same spot. This technique provides a sense of conti-

nuity that connects the present to the past in a comforting way. In the case of the Fort Mahone series, however, Frassanito was unable to include any modern views. "In the absence of further pertinent information," he writes, "the photographs will essentially speak for themselves." William Frassanito, *Grant and Lee: The Virginia Campaigns, 1864–1865* (New York: Scribner, 1983), 344.

33 Susan Sontag describes "being a spectator of calamities taking place in another country" as a "quintessential modern experience." She refuses, however, to attribute the inattention that results from this onslaught of disturbing images to apathy alone. Instead, she suggests that consumers "turn off not just because a steady diet of images of violence has made them indifferent but because they are afraid." Sontag, *Regarding the Pain of Others*, 18, 100.

CHAPTER FIVE

1 *Glory*, dir. Edward Zwick (Tri-Star Pictures, 1989).

2 See Jim Cullen, *The Civil War in Popular Culture: A Reusable Past* (Washington: Smithsonian Institution Press, 1995), 158–59.

3 The idea that military discipline was good for black soldiers—a means to manhood and self-determination—has made its mark on historiography as well. For example, Joseph Glatthaar writes, "Despite the excesses of some officers, discipline more than any single thing converted a mob of black males into soldiers in the United States Army." Joseph Glatthaar, *Forged in Battle: The Civil War Alliance of Black Soldiers and White Officers* (New York: Free Press, 1990), 120.

4 Kirk Savage, *Standing Soldiers, Kneeling Slaves: Race, War, and Monument in Nineteenth-Century America* (Princeton, N.J.: Princeton University Press, 1997), 167.

5 William Wells Brown, comp., *The Anti-Slavery Harp: A Collection of Songs for Anti-Slavery Meetings* (1848; Wilmington, Del.: Scholarly Resources, 1970). Reason is best known for his variant on the image of the supplicant female slave who kneels, chained hands clasped, as she appeals to an implicitly white audience for assistance. See Jean Fagan Yellin, *Women and Sisters: The Antislavery Feminists in American Culture* (New Haven, Conn.: Yale University Press, 1989), 15–17.

6 Benjamin Rush, *Enquiry into the Effects of Public Punishments upon Criminals and upon Society* (Philadelphia: Joseph James, 1787), 6.

7 Richard Brodhead observes that in many abolitionist texts the scene of whipping figures the "whole structure of relations that identify Southern slavery as a system." In sum, "whipping means slavery." Richard Brodhead, *Cultures of Letters: Scenes of Reading and Writing in Nineteenth-Century America* (Chicago: University of Chicago Press, 1993), 14.

8 J. Hector St. John de Crevecoeur, *Letters from an American Farmer* (1782; Oxford: Oxford University Press, 1997), 66.

9 Rush, *Enquiry into the Effects of Public Punishments*, 7.

10 Paul Gilje describes the transition from ritualized punishments, designed to

humiliate the offender, to more violent forms of abuse meant to inflict pain and sometimes death. Paul Gilje, *Rioting in America* (Bloomington: Indiana University Press, 1996).

11 On the relationship between mob violence and the conflict between pro- and antislavery forces, see Leonard Richards, *Gentlemen of Property and Standing: Anti-Abolition Mobs in Jacksonian America* (New York: Oxford University Press, 1970).

12 Abraham Lincoln, *Speeches and Writings, 1832–1858*, ed. Don Fehrenbacher (New York: Library of America, 1989), 29.

13 Taken to its rhetorical extreme, the conflation of public life and citizen misrule provides the basis for hyperbolic claims about an essentially "American" penchant for violence. When, in 1905, James Elbert Cutler dubbed lynching "our national crime," he followed Lincoln's lead by at once denouncing racist violence and mining it as a source of collective distinction. Lincoln, *Speeches and Writings, 1832–1858*, 32; James Elbert Cutler, *Lynch-Law: An Investigation into the History of Lynching in the United States* (1905; New York: Negro Universities Press, 1969), 1.

14 "The Execution of Johnson," *Harper's Weekly*, December 28, 1861.

15 For a description of military executions that largely conforms to accounts in the popular press, see Robert Alotta, *Civil War Justice: Union Army Executions under Lincoln* (Shippensburg, Pa.: White Mane, 1989), 37–43.

16 William C. Davis, *The Guns of '62*, vol. 2 of *The Image of War, 1861–1865* (Garden City, N.Y.: Doubleday, 1982), 201; Alotta, *Civil War Justice*, 6.

17 Alotta, *Civil War Justice*, 43.

18 "Execution of Deserters," *Harper's Weekly*, September 12, 1863.

19 The first private execution in the United States took place in Pennsylvania in 1834; by 1845, public executions had been abolished in New England and the mid-Atlantic states. Louis P. Masur, *Rites of Execution: Capital Punishment and the Transformation of American Culture, 1776–1865* (New York: Oxford University Press, 1989), 94.

20 Captain Benét was the ancestor and namesake of Stephen Vincent Benét, author of the Pulitzer Prize–winning narrative poem *John Brown's Body* (1928). Qtd. in Alotta, *Civil War Justice*, 38.

21 Davis, *The Guns of '62*, 201; Alotta, *Civil War Justice*, 38–39.

22 Karen Halttunen qualifies accounts of the privatization of punishment when she observes that the public still clamored for access to private executions; increasingly, people turned toward textual renderings of the scene to satisfy a seemingly insatiable appetite for state murder. Karen Halttunen, *Murder Most Foul: The Killer and the American Gothic Imagination* (Cambridge, Mass.: Harvard University Press, 1998), 71–72.

23 This is especially true of illustrations of hangings. While sketches of shootings also feature military pageantry, they tend to focus on the confrontation between the firing squad and the condemned man. On the differences between the conventions governing the two types of executions, see Alotta, *Civil War Justice*, 37–42.

24 Gary Laderman, *The Sacred Remains: American Attitudes toward Death, 1799-1883* (New Haven, Conn.: Yale University Press, 1996), 99.

25 Alice Fahs, *The Imagined Civil War: Popular Literature of the North and South, 1861-1865* (Chapel Hill: University of North Carolina Press, 2001), 43.

26 Michel Fabre, "Popular Civil War Propaganda: The Case of Patriotic Covers," *Journal of American Culture* 3 (Summer 1980): 223-25.

27 On the origins and history of the Uncle Sam icon, see "Uncle Sam" at the American Studies at the University of Virginia website: <http://xroads.vir ginia.edu/~CAP/SAM/home.htm> (August 16, 2003).

28 Frederick Douglass, "Address to the People of the United States, Delivered at a Convention of Colored Men," in *Reconstruction and After*, vol. 4 of *The Life and Writings of Frederick Douglass*, ed. Philip Foner (New York: International Publishers, n.d.), 379.

29 On the relationship between lynching in the South during the Civil War and after, see Fitzhugh Brundage, ed., *Under Sentence of Death: Lynching in the South* (Chapel Hill: University of North Carolina Press, 1997), 78-80.

30 My thanks to Ken Moon for bringing these images, and the history of their reproduction, to my attention. On the execution and the resulting images, see Ervin Jordan Jr., *Black Confederates and Afro-Yankees in Civil War Virginia* (Charlottesville: University Press of Virginia, 1995), 272, and William Frassanito, *Grant and Lee: The Virginia Campaigns, 1864-1865* (New York: Scribner, 1983), 216-22. Frassanito notes that the death of Private William Johnson was not among the 267 executions reported by the military in its "List of US Soldiers Executed by United States Military Authorities during the Late War." On the difficulty of calculating how many soldiers were executed during the Civil War, and the possibility that the numbers are larger than historians have estimated, see Alotta, *Civil War Justice*, 186-87.

31 When we take into consideration the fact that Confederate soldiers were encouraged to watch Johnson's execution and that two photographic concerns took time to record it, the men relaxing in the background of one of these photographs point toward the commodification of lynching in the postbellum period when newspapers advertised lynchings, special trains were scheduled to convey spectators to the event, vendors sold food and drink, and photographers did a brisk business in commemorative images. See Grace Hale, *Making Whiteness: The Culture of Segregation in the South, 1890-1940* (New York: Pantheon, 1998), 203.

32 Aside from these photographs of William Johnson, I have been able to locate only one other photograph of the Union army executing a soldier. It depicts the execution of a soldier outside Petersburg in August 1864 and portrays the event from a great distance. In addition, two photographs taken near Corinth, Mississippi, document the execution of a white civilian identified as a spy. In the first he faces the firing squad, while the second shows him lying dead beside his coffin. See Davis, *The Guns of '62*, 252, and William C. Davis, *Fighting for Time*, vol. 4 of *The Image of War, 1861-1865* (Garden City, N.Y.: Doubleday, 1983), 131. My thanks to Gary Gallagher, Randy Hackenburg, and

William Davis for helping me to determine the scarcity of photographs of military executions.

33 Discussing lynching photographs, Jacqueline Goldsby observes that, in contrast to the long view taken by most photographs of Civil War corpses, lynching photographs collapse the distance between photographer and victim in order to "allow the camera to probe, prod, and pierce the victim's body and command its subjugation to the photograph's gaze." The consequent "unsightliness" of the image, she argues, substantiates both "the unlimited range of the mob's rule and African Americans' perceived unfitness as citizens deserving of state protection." Jacqueline Goldsby, "A Spectacular Secret: The Cultural Logic of Lynching in American Life and Literature" (unpublished MS, 2003), 30, 25. See also Robyn Wiegman, *American Anatomies: Theorizing Race and Gender* (Durham, N.C.: Duke University Press, 1995), 81–100.

34 Ira Berlin, Joseph P. Reidy, and Leslie S. Rowland, eds., *Freedom's Soldiers: The Black Military Experience in the Civil War* (New York: Cambridge University Press, 1998), 19.

35 Abraham Lincoln, *Speeches and Writings, 1859–1865*, ed. Don Fehrenbacher (New York: Library of America, 1986), 586.

36 Lincoln's Emancipation Proclamation reiterated the terms of the Second Confiscation Act, freeing slaves in the seceding states and authorizing them to serve in the Union army. For summaries of these events and discussion of the recruitment and enlistment of African American soldiers, see David Blight, *Frederick Douglass' Civil War: Keeping Faith in Jubilee* (Baton Rouge: Louisiana State University Press, 1989), 150–53; James McPherson, *Battle Cry of Freedom: The Civil War Era* (1988; New York: Ballantine Books, 1989), 353–66, 499–502; Ira Berlin, Joseph Reidy, and Leslie Rowland, eds., *The Black Military Experience*, Freedom: A Documentary History of Emancipation, 1861–67, ser. 2 (New York: Cambridge University Press, 1982), 1–34; Gail Buckley, *American Patriots: The Story of Blacks in the Military from the Revolution to Desert Storm* (New York: Random House, 2001), 86–87.

37 Kathleen Diffley argues that the perceived reciprocity between the federal state and emancipated slaves threatened to encroach on local and familial ties long used to structure political relations both practically and metaphorically. Thus the figure of the black soldier became a flash point for conflict over the expanded powers of the wartime state. During the Draft Riots of July 1863, this tendency to associate state power with the interests of black men took a vicious turn as white rioters, angry about the draft, murdered black bystanders. Kathleen Diffley, *Where My Heart Is Turning Ever: Civil War Stories and Constitutional Reform, 1861–1876* (Athens: University of Georgia Press, 1992), 25–30.

38 Fahs, *The Imagined Civil War*, 169.

39 "Addresses of the Hon. W. D. Kelley, Miss Anna E. Dickinson, and Mr. Frederick Douglass, at a Mass Meeting, Held at National Hall, Philadelphia, July 6,

1863, for the Promotion of Colored Enlistments," African-American Pamphlet Collection, 1824–1909, Library of Congress.

40 *Narrative of the Life of Frederick Douglass, An American Slave*, ed. Houston Baker (New York: Penguin Books, 1982), 105.

41 Frederick Douglass, "Address for the Promotion of Colored Enlistments," in *The Civil War, 1861–1865*, vol. 3 of *The Life and Writings of Frederick Douglass*, ed. Philip S. Foner (New York: International Publishers, n.d.), 362.

42 Blight, *Frederick Douglass' Civil War*, 164.

43 Ibid., 156.

44 Douglass, "Address for the Promotion of Colored Enlistments," 362. Conversely, white citizens were promised that if they supported black enlistment, fewer white men would have to go into service. A letter addressed to the "People of New York" by "The Association for Promoting Colored Volunteering" urges, "Other States are fast taking our men to fill their quotas, especially our colored men. Several thousands of these may be added to the strength of our army, and also saved to the quota of our State, by a prompt and vigorous movement. Our country's interest and self-interest here unite." See "First Organization of Colored Troops in the State of New York, to Aid in Suppressing the Slave-holders' Rebellion," African-American Pamphlet Collection, 1824–1909, Library of Congress.

45 Douglass, "Men of Color, To Arms!," in *The Civil War*, vol. 3 of *Life and Writings*, ed. Foner, 319.

46 Douglass, "Address for the Promotion of Colored Enlistments," 366.

47 While *Glory* ends with the men of the Massachusetts 54th mowed down in battle, the illustrious history of the 54th largely unfolded in the following months as enlisted men refused to accept unequal pay. When the state of Massachusetts proposed making up the difference between the seven dollars a month offered to black soldiers and the thirteen dollars white soldiers received, the men of the 54th refused the offer. They would only accept full pay from the federal government, as anything less implied that they were not equal to other federal troops. It was not until July 1864 that black soldiers who had been free at the start of the war were granted equal pay retroactive from their first day of service. Those who were slaves at the beginning of the war were granted equal pay in March 1865. As Donald Yacovone observes, "The regiment's successful eighteen-month campaign for equal pay and the recognition of racial equality that victory implied represented the unit's most important achievement." Donald Yacovone, "The Pay Crisis and the 'Lincoln Despotism,'" in *Hope and Glory: Essays on the Legacy of the 54th Massachusetts Regiment*, ed. Martin H. Blatt, Thomas J. Brown, and Donald Yacovone (Amherst: University of Massachusetts Press, 2001), 35.

48 See Alotta, *Civil War Justice*, 26–27; Buckley, *American Patriots*, 93; Berlin, Reidy, and Rowland, *Black Military Experience*, 30.

49 Blight, *Frederick Douglass' Civil War*, 165.

50 Lincoln, *Speeches and Writings, 1859–1865*, 484–85.

51 Douglass, "Address for the Promotion of Colored Enlistments," 367.

52 See Iver Bernstein, *The New York City Draft Riots: Their Significance for American Society and Politics in the Age of the Civil War* (New York: Oxford University Press, 1990).

53 Douglass, "The Commander-in-Chief and His Black Soldiers," in *The Civil War*, vol. 3 of *Life and Writings*, ed. Foner, 370.

54 Qtd. in Natalie Spassky, *A Catalogue of Works by Artists Born between 1816 and 1845*, vol. 2 of *American Paintings in the Metropolitan Museum of Art* (New York: Metropolitan Museum of Art, 1985), 198.

55 These figures are drawn from Glatthaar, *Forged in Battle*, 118, 115. According to Alotta 72.22 percent of all mutiny convictions and 50 percent of all rape convictions involved black soldiers. Alotta, *Civil War Justice*, 26, 30. On the practice of impressment, see Jordan, *Black Confederates and Afro-Yankees*, 267–69.

56 Berlin, Reidy, and Rowland, *Black Military Experience*, 437–42; Glatthaar, *Forged in Battle*, 113–17.

57 Alotta, *Civil War Justice*, 207–8, 189.

58 David Blight, *Race and Reunion: The Civil War in American Memory* (Cambridge, Mass.: Harvard University Press, 2001), 5, 2.

59 Lincoln Kirstein, *Lay This Laurel* (New York: Eakins Press, 1973), sec. 3: n.p.; Buckley *American Patriots*, 99.

60 William James, "Robert Gould Shaw," in *Memories and Studies* (New York: Longmans, Green, 1911), 54.

61 I borrow the term "soldier's faith" from David Blight, who borrowed it from the title of the Memorial Day address that Oliver Wendell Holmes Jr. delivered at Harvard University in 1895. Holmes's affirmation of unthinking obedience illustrates the underside of the romance of white heroism, thus strengthening Blight's critique. Holmes writes, "There is one thing I do not doubt . . . and that is that the faith is true and adorable which leads a soldier to throw away his life in obedience to a blindly accepted duty, in a cause which he little understands, in a plan of campaign of which he does not see the use." Qtd. in Blight, *Race and Reunion*, 210.

EPILOGUE

1 Ernest Lee Tuveson notes that Howe, who believed in "the law of progress, and the perfectibility of human nature," seems an unlikely "poet of the American apocalyptic faith." He maintains that the fact that she wrote "Battle Hymn" indicates "how deeply such ideas must have penetrated the national mind." Similarly, Howe biographer Deborah Clifford writes, "The lines that rolled out so easily from Julia's mind onto that scrap of paper in Willard's Hotel were inspired by a thorough familiarity with the temper of the northern mind." Ernest Lee Tuveson, *Redeemer Nation: The Idea of America's Millennial Role* (Chicago: University of Chicago Press, 1968), 198; and Deborah Clifford, *Mine Eyes Have Seen the Glory: A Biography of Julia Ward Howe* (Boston: Little, Brown, 1978), 147.

2 In her discussion of the song, Mary Loeffelholz observes that "the abiding power of 'The Battle Hymn,' after all, lies in its conscription of thundering Puritan biblical eloquence to celebrate the North's mass national discipline in the Civil War." Mary Loeffelholz, "The Religion of Art in the City at War: Boston's Public Poetry and the Great Organ, 1863," *American Literary History* 13 (Summer 2001): 220.

3 Julia Ward Howe, *Reminiscences, 1819–1899* (1899; New York: Negro Universities Press, 1969), 272–73.

4 Laura E. Richards and Maude Howe Elliott, *Julia Ward Howe, 1819–1910*, 2 vols. (Boston: Houghton Mifflin, 1916), 1:177.

5 On the circumstances of Samuel Howe's involvement with Brown and his flight to Canada, see Mary Grant, *Private Woman, Public Person: An Account of the Life of Julia Ward Howe from 1819 to 1868* (Brooklyn, N.Y.: Carlson, 1994), 133–34.

6 Julia Ward Howe, "The Battle Hymn of the Republic," *Atlantic Monthly*, February 1862, 10, available at <http://www.theatlantic.com/issues/1862feb/batthym.htm> (July 24, 2003).

7 Richards and Elliott, *Julia Ward Howe*, 193.

8 Ibid., 302.

9 Howe, *Reminiscences*, 341.

10 Clifford, *Mine Eyes*, 185–87.

11 Howe, *Reminiscences*, 336. It is worth noting that, despite her initial frustration, Howe's efforts continue to have an impact. On Mother's Day in 2003 the women's antiwar group Codepink circulated an edited version of Howe's *Appeal* online. Codepink presented the document as a "timeless reminder of the profound loss and pain war creates for all mothers," while recognizing that "from such loss and pain can come a fierce determination and power within all mothers, to join each other, and give rise to the birth of peace!" <http://www.codepinkalert.org/Get_Involved!_Mothers_Day_Proclamation.shtml> (July 24, 2003).

12 Richards and Elliott, *Julia Ward Howe*, 184.

13 Ibid., 183. She also took comfort from imagining Sammy's proximity to John Brown in heaven. "The time of your birth," she wrote, "was a sad one. It was the time of the imprisonment and death of John Brown, a very noble man, who should be in one of the many mansions of which Christ tells us, and in which I hope, dear, that you are nearer to Him than any of us can be" (179).

14 Richards and Elliott, *Julia Ward Howe*, 302.

15 Edward Steers, *Blood on the Moon: The Assassination of Abraham Lincoln* (Lexington: University Press of Kentucky, 2001), 204–6.

16 Ibid., 262.

17 For a description of these events, see Fletcher Pratt, *Stanton: Lincoln's Secretary of War* (New York: W. W. Norton, 1953), 424–25; and Benjamin P. Thomas and Harold M. Hyman, *Stanton: The Life and Times of Lincoln's Secretary of War* (New York: Alfred A. Knopf, 1962), 420–21.

18 Gardner was involved in documenting the aftermath of the assassination at

every point. He made copies of photographs of three conspirators that were used in the manhunt, photographed locations related to the assassination, documented Booth's autopsy, and made portraits of the conspirators. D. Mark Katz, *Witness to an Era: The Life and Photographs of Alexander Gardner* (New York: Viking Penguin, 1991), 149–71.

19 An illustration of the autopsy was published in *Harper's Weekly* on May 13, 1865. It is important to note that Stanton also suppressed a photograph of Lincoln's corpse. Jeremiah Gurney photographed Abraham Lincoln's body as it lay in state in New York City on April 24, 1865. Stanton read in the paper that the photograph had been taken and demanded that it be seized and destroyed. A single print survived, however, and resurfaced in 1952. Katz, *Witness to an Era*, 161, 200–201.

20 Naomi Rosenblum, *A World History of Photography* (New York: Abbeville Press, 1984), 200. Images of the execution circulated as *cartes de visite* and provided the basis for sketches published in *Harper's Weekly* on July 22, 1865.

21 Qtd. in Katz, *Witness to an Era*, 184.

22 Emmett Till's father, Louis, was executed by the U.S. military for raping two women and murdering a third while stationed in Italy during World War II. Describing the execution of Till's father as a "terrible and grotesque coincidence," Stephen Whitfield notes that "in Europe during World War II, ninety-five soldiers were hanged for the crimes of rape or murder of unarmed civilians. Statistically improbable as it may seem, eighty-seven of those executed were black." Stephen Whitfield, *A Death in the Delta: The Story of Emmett Till* (1988; Baltimore: Johns Hopkins University Press, 1991), 116–17.

23 Henry Hampton and Steve Frayer, comps., *Voices of Freedom: An Oral History of the Civil Rights Movement from the 1950s through the 1980s* (New York: Bantam Books, 1990), 5.

24 Mamie Till Bradley, as told to Ethel Payne, "Mamie Bradley's Untold Story," *Chicago Defender*, April–June 1956, in *The Lynching of Emmett Till: A Documentary Narrative*, ed. Christopher Metress (Charlottesville: University Press of Virginia, 2002), 227.

25 Jacqueline Goldsby argues that this photograph takes on immense significance in light of the absence of representations of Till's actual death. She writes, "There is no visual record of either the moment of his exchange with Carolyn Bryant or the struggle with his attacker that ended his life. . . . In the photographic void created by those acts, the images that do exist do so *in their stead*, as compensation for what cannot be rendered as visible evidence of the cause of the event." Jacqueline Goldsby, "The High and Low Tech of It: The Meaning of Lynching and the Death of Emmett Till," *Yale Journal of Criticism* 9, no. 2 (1996): 263.

26 John Edgar Wideman, "The Killing of Black Boys" (1997), in Metress, *Lynching of Emmett Till*, 280.

27 In her analysis of newspaper photographs of dead black boys published during the 1990s, Deborah McDowell argues that a tendency to focus on the grieving mother "shrinks the larger network of familial relations to one." She ob-

serves, however, that some mothers, "continuing a tradition begun by Mamie Till[,] . . . refuse to be relegated to roles as passive mourners." Instead, they demand public attention on the basis of their grief, building a large community of mourners as they agitate for reform. Deborah McDowell, "Viewing the Remains: A Polemic on Death, Spectacle, and the [Black] Family," in *The Familial Gaze*, ed. Marianne Hirsch (Hanover, N.H.: University Press of New England, 1999), 158, 169. For a detailed discussion of Mamie Till Bradley's role in shaping public response to the murder and trial, see Ruth Feldstein, "'I Wanted the Whole World to See': Race, Gender, and Constructions of Motherhood in the Death of Emmett Till," in *Not June Cleaver: Women and Gender in Postwar America, 1945-1960*, ed. Joanne Meyerowitz (Philadelphia: Temple University Press, 1994), 263-303.

28 For example, Anne Moody recalls, "Before Emmett Till's murder, I had known the fear of hunger, hell, and the Devil. But now there was a new fear known to me—the fear of being killed just because I was black. This was the worst of my fears." Anne Moody, *Coming of Age in Mississippi* (1968; New York: Dell, 1976), 125.

INDEX

Baker, Houston, 58
Barnes, Elizabeth, 22
Barnes, Joseph K., 171
Barthes, Roland, 105
Battlefield dead: abstraction of, 1–2, 6, 16, 36–39, 71–79, 165–66, 175, 177 (n. 5), 186–87 (n. 57); classification of injuries causing, 8; commemorating en masse, 78–79; compared with executed soldiers, 11, 144–45; dealing with as national project, 71–72, 78; freezing to death, 98; inability to mourn individual, 3, 5–6, 74, 78–79, 113–15, 194–95 (n. 6); inspiring and regenerating the living, 16, 165; lack of proper burial, 3, 5–6, 8, 74; living soldiers dealing with, 107–9; medical dissection of, 8; Melville's poetic treatment of, 96–99, 102; mothers' response to, 113–15, 124–25, 170, 200 (n. 10); silence in response to, 72–73, 79; unidentified corpses, 5, 74, 76, 194 (n. 5); and Walt Whitman, 6, 71–72, 73, 75–78, 80–83, 87–88, 102, 130, 196 (nn. 17, 20), 198 (n. 53). *See also* Corpses; Death; Decomposition; Photographs, Civil War
"Battle Hymn of the Republic" (Howe): abstraction of death in, 165–66; full text of song, 167–68; inspired by "John Brown's Body," 2, 166; portraying Civil War as divine retribution, 165–68, 208 (n. 1), 209 (n. 2). *See also* Howe, Julia Ward; "John Brown's Body"
Battle-Pieces and Aspects of the War (Melville), 96–99
Benét, Stephen Vincent, 142
"Benito Cereno" (Melville), 42, 53–54, 70
Bennett, James Gordon, 118

"Bit of War History, A" (painting) (T. W. Wood), 155–59
Blackhead Signpost, 61
"Black Laws" of Reconstruction, 148
Black soldiers: account of in movie *Glory*, 132–33, 134, 161–64, 207 (n. 47); and Confederate army, 132, 149, 154–55, 162–63; enlistment of in Union army, 10, 132, 133–34, 150–54, 206 (nn. 36–37), 207 (n. 44); enlistments as contrabands, 150–51, 156–57; and excessive discipline of in Union army, 133, 134, 148, 160–61, 164, 203 (n. 3); and lack of equal pay for, 154, 207 (n. 47); need for manpower of in Union army, 150–51; in Revolutionary War, 68, 194 (n. 54); as symbols of emancipation, 58, 132, 151, 206 (n. 37); triptych of, 155–59; oppression of, 133–35, 156, 160, 161–62. *See also* African Americans; Executions; Lynching; Slavery
Blight, David, 154, 161
Blood: Copeland's use of, 68–69; Brown's use of, 18, 23–24, 27, 35–36, 186 (n. 51)
Bontecue, Reed, 99
Booth, John Wilkes: death of, 171–72, 210 (n. 19); and John Brown, 14, 17, 29, 185 (n. 40)
Bradley, Mamie Till, 173–76
Brady, Mathew, 119, 148; exhibition of photographs at gallery of, 106–10, 113–15, 199–200 (n. 6)
Brinton, John Hill, 8–9
Brock, Sallie, 90
Brown, John: black coconspirators, fate of, 7, 40, 42–44, 51–52, 67–70, 187–88 (n. 5); compared with Nat Turner, 60; compared with Uncle Tom, 22; courtroom speech, 18, 22–24, 30, 36; effect on Julia Ward

Howe, 167, 209 (n. 13); as enemy
of the state, 9, 14, 16; energizing
abolitionists in the North, 16–17,
25–28, 39, 184 (nn. 30–31); execution of, 16–18, 28–36, 39, 143,
172, 185 (n. 45); and John Wilkes
Booth, 14, 17, 29, 185 (n. 40);
martyrdom of contributing to wartime nationalism, 14, 15–17, 39, 180
(n. 1); speech at scaffold, 9–10, 34–
36, 186 (n. 51); struggle over corpse
of, 4, 7, 177–78 (n. 7); sympathy
with slaves, 16, 18, 22, 23–24, 27,
35–36, 181 (nn. 8–9), 186 (n. 51);
and Thoreau, 18, 26–27, 181 (n. 6).
See also Harpers Ferry, insurrection at; "John Brown's Body"
Brown, John, Jr., 23
Brown, Mary, 7
Brown, William Wells, 135, 192
(n. 38)
Brownell, Henry Howard, 92, 93
Bryant, Carolyn, 173
Bryant, Roy, 173, 174
Butler, Benjamin, 150

Cadava, Eduardo, 126
Campbell, Thomas, 135–36
Cemeteries, at battlefields, 78–79
Censorship, 116, 118–19, 127
Chandler, Elizabeth Margaret, 20, 23
Child, Lydia Maria, 24–26, 27, 28,
183–84 (nn. 26–27), 184 (n. 31)
Christian Commission, Headquarters
of, 116
Christies, Robert, 41
Cities of the Dead (Roach), 165, 190
(n. 23)
City Reading (Henkin), 96
Civil War: and artists' response to, 6,
73–74, 79, 134, 195 (n. 15); causing
changes in attitude toward dis-
section, 47–48, 190 (n. 22); and
national culture, 1, 6, 38, 83, 87,

187 (n. 61); defined as a war for
emancipation, 10, 151, 161, 165; as
divine retribution for slavery, 9–12,
35, 57–58, 165–68, 208 (n. 1), 209
(n. 2); as divine test of redeemer
nation, 9–10, 179 (n. 20); expansion of federal authority during,
86; and postwar realism, 74, 75, 79.
See also Battlefield dead; Nationalist culture; Wartime nationalism
Clark, James Freeman, 166
Coconspirators of John Brown, 7, 40,
42–44, 51–52, 67–70, 187–88 (n. 5)
Coconspirators of John Wilkes
Booth, 172
"Come Up from the Fields Father"
(Whitman), 124
Commemorative objects, 4–6; of
Brown at abolitionist meetings, 26;
clippings of hair, 4, 74, 171; compared with dissection, 9; and John
Wilkes Booth, 171–72; postmortem
photographs, 4, 44, 74, 104, 110–13,
123, 126–27, 174–75, 210 (n. 25)
Confederate army: and black sol-
diers, 132, 149, 154–55, 162–63;
photographs of dead soldiers of,
108–10, 119–21, 128–30; and right
to confiscate slaves from, 150–51
Confessions of Nat Turner, The
(Gray), 42, 59–67; questions of
authorship, 61–63, 65–66
Confiscation Acts, 150–51, 206 (n. 36)
Contrabands, 150–51, 156–57. *See
also* Black soldiers; Union army
"Contrast: Federal buried, Confederate unburied, where they fell
on the Battle-field of Antietam, A"
(photograph) (Gardner), 108–10
Cook, John, 7
Copeland, John: prison letters of,
42, 43, 67–69; struggle to retrieve
corpse of, 7, 40, 43-44, 51–52, 69,
187–88 (n. 5)

Dissection: affront to religious beliefs, 7, 40-41, 44; changes in attitudes toward after Civil War, 47-48, 190 (n. 22); denying social nature of corpse, 7-9, 40-41, 45, 69-70, 190 (n. 23); of marginal people, 7-8, 40-43, 46-47, 51-53, 67, 179 (n. 15), 189 (n. 16), 189-90 (nn. 18-19); possibility of John Brown's body undergoing, 7, 177-78 (n. 7); public controversy over, 46-47; as punishment after death, 3, 41-43, 52-53, 61, 67; and scientific racism, 41-42, 46, 67, 189 (n. 15); and utilitarian attitude toward the dead, 41, 45, 48. *See also* Anatomy, study of; Anatomy legislation

"Donelson" (Melville), 97-98, 102

Douglass, Charles, 152

Douglass, Frederick, 19, 148; and black enlistment, 10, 152-55; disillusionment with black enlistment, 154-56; response to slavery, 55, 64, 65, 153

Douglass, Lewis, 152

Draft: Draft Riots, 142, 155, 206 (n. 37); and enlistment of African Americans, 133-34; justification of by Lincoln, 86-87

Drewry, William, 67

Drum-Taps (Whitman), 80-81, 82-83, 96, 97, 115, 119, 124

Drum-Taps and Sequel to Drum-Taps (Whitman), 81-82

Emancipation: black soldiers as symbols of, 58, 132, 151, 206 (n. 37); leads to new forms of coercion, 150, 156-61; proclaimed in order to recruit blacks for Union army, 87, 150

Emancipation Proclamation, 86, 87, 132, 150, 206 (n. 36)

Emerson, Ralph Waldo, 36

Enquiry into the Effects of Public Punishments (Rush), 137

Erkkila, Betsy, 75

Ethnology, pioneering days of, 49-51, 61, 63, 64

Executions: by firing squad, 11, 141, 144, 154, 204 (n. 23), 205-6 (n. 32); by hanging, 27, 32-33, 143, 145-50, 172-73, 204 (n. 23); of John Brown, 16-18, 28-36, 39, 143, 172, 185 (n. 45); military, 10-11, 141-47, 204 (nn. 15, 19); military, of black soldiers, 148-50, 154, 156, 160, 205 (nn. 30-31), 208 (n. 55), 210 (n. 22); military presence at, 29, 31-33, 34, 185-86 (n. 47); of Native Americans, 42, 52; newspaper accounts of, 143-44, 204 (n. 22); newspaper illustrations of, 30, 32-33, 143-45, 204 (n. 22); photographs of, 148-50, 172-73, 205-6 (nn. 31-32); as public show of force against disobedience, 10-11, 29, 134-35, 142-43, 172-73; spectators at, 17, 29, 34, 142-44, 148-50, 172-73, 185 (n. 41), 204 (n. 22-23)

Exhibition of photographs of war dead, New York, 106-10, 113-15, 199-200 (n. 6)

Fahs, Alice, 145, 151

Faust, Drew G., 5

Fenton, Roger, 106

"Field Where General Reynolds Fell" (photograph) (Gardner), 119-21

Firing squads, 11, 141, 144, 154, 204 (n. 23), 205-6 (n. 32)

First Confiscation Act (1861), 150-51

"First O Songs for a Prelude" ("Drum-Taps") (Whitman), 81

Fisher, Philip, 114

Fort Donelson, 97-98

Fort Hudson, 155
Fort Mahone, photographs from, 128–30, 202–3 (n. 32)
Fort Monroe, 150
Fort Sumter, 8
Fort Wagner, 132, 155, 162
Fort Warren, 14
Foucault, Michel, 45
Frank Leslie's Illustrated Newspaper, 32–33, 143, 144
Frassanito, William, 122, 129
Freedmen's Bureau, 86

Gardner, Alexander: Antietam photographs, 106–10, 113–15, 124, 199–200 (n. 6); and Booth's corpse photograph, 171–72, 209–10 (n. 18); execution photographs, 148, 172–73; *Sketch Book* photographs, 115–17, 119–25
Gardner's Photographic Sketch Book of the Civil War (Gardner), 115–17, 119–25
Gettysburg Address, 37–38, 79, 195 (n. 13); compared with John Brown's courtroom speech, 36
Gettysburg cemetery, 78–79, 123, 195 (n. 13)
Gibbons, James Sloan, 83–85, 88
Gibson, James, 106, 115
Gliddon, George R., 50
Glory (film), 132–33, 134, 161–64, 207 (n. 47)
Golden Rule, 23, 36
Gordon (slave), 151–52
Government Printing Office, 118
Grave robbing: for bodies of marginalized people, 7, 40–41, 51–52, 189 (n. 15); declared an offense in New York State, 46; of Native American burial grounds, 49, 191 (n. 29); as response to demand for corpses at medical schools, 46–47. *See also* Dissection

Gray, Thomas, 59–63, 65–66
Green, Shields, 7, 40, 42, 69–70

Habeas corpus, 86, 196 (n. 31)
Hanging, execution by, 27, 32–33, 143, 145–50, 172–73, 204 (n. 23)
Harewood Hospital, 99
Harpers Ferry, insurrection at, 16–17, 23, 67, 185 (n. 37); abolitionists' response to, 24–26; Governor Wise's response to, 27–28; Howe family involvement in, 167. *See also* Brown, John
Harper's Weekly, 34, 106, 108, 141, 143, 151–52
"Harriet Gould's Book," 91, 96
"Harvest of Death, A" (photograph) (Gardner), 119
Henkin, Kevin, 96
Herold, David, 172
Holmes, Oliver Wendell, 22, 92, 125
"Home of a Rebel Sharpshooter, The" (photograph) (Gardner), 119, 121–25
Horwitz, Tony, 62
Howe, Julia Ward: mobilizing women against war, 168–70; son's death, 169–70, 209 (n. 13); writing of "Battle Hymn of the Republic," 2, 165–67, 208 (n. 1)
Howe, Samuel Gridley, 166, 167
Humphrey, Luther, 18

Incarceration, 139, 148. *See also* Corporal punishment
Indigenous Races of the Earth (Nott and Gliddon), 50
Insurrection: Denmark Vesey's, 42; dissection of African Americans and Native Americans executed for, 41–43, 51–53; at Harpers Ferry, 16–17, 23–28, 67, 167, 185 (n. 37); interiority of insurgents, 42, 54, 59–67, 70, 193–94 (n. 50); mob

33, 161–63, 207 (n. 47); beginnings of, 152–53; at Fort Wagner attack, 155

Mayo, William Worral, 52

Mayo Clinic, 52

McPherson, James, 86

Medical schools: competition between, 46; and grave robbing, 7, 40–41, 46–47, 51–52

Melville, Herman: *Battle-Pieces and Aspects of the War*, 96–99, 102; "Benito Cereno," 42, 53–54, 70; poetry of contrasted with Whitman's, 97–98, 102, 198 (n. 53); "Portent, The," 34, 172

Mental metempsychosis, 20–21. *See also* Sentimentality; Sympathy

Mesmerism, 117, 200–201 (n. 14). *See also* Telegraph

Milam, J. W., 173

Millennialism, 26

Miller, John, 99–102

"Million Dead, Too, Summ'd Up, The" (Whitman), 75–77

Mindich, David, 127

Monroe, James: and John Copeland's corpse, 40, 43–44, 51–52, 69, 187–88 (n. 5); and Shields Green's corpse, 69–70

Montauk (ironclad ship), 171

Moon, Michael, 81

Morse, Samuel F. B., 118

Morton, Samuel George, 49, 50

Mother's Day Peace Festival, 169

Mott, Valentine, 52

Mourning: disrupted during Civil War, 5–6, 74, 113–14; of Lincoln's death, 87–89, 94–96, 198 (n. 48); and mothers, 111–15, 170, 210–11 (n. 27); paraphernalia, 45; poetry as form of, 90–91, 94–96, 197–98 (nn. 47–48); prewar customs of, 4–5, 9, 74, 78, 178 (n. 8), 188 (n. 6); prewar versus postwar,

5–6, 74–75, 78, 113–15; religious beliefs behind, 7, 40–41, 44; as unifying social structure, 4–6, 175; use of beautified corpses, 4–5, 44–45, 74, 110–13, 174–75. *See also* Battlefield dead; Corpses; Death; Decomposition; Photographing the dead

Narrative of the Life of Frederick Douglass (Douglass), 64, 153

National Era, 19

Nationalist culture: centrality of self-sacrifice, 15–16, 37–38, 163–64, 208 (n. 61); excluding African Americans from, 180–81 (n. 4); strengthened by Lincoln's death, 87–89; of violence, as predicted by John Brown, 35; war as divine test of redeemer nation, 9–10, 179 (n. 20); war as way to revitalize national identity, 1–2, 6, 38, 83, 175, 187 (n. 61). *See also* Civil War; Violence; Wartime nationalism

Native Americans, 3; collecting skulls of, 41–42, 49–50, 191 (n. 29); dissection of, 41–42; executions of insurgents, 42, 52; scientific racism against, 41–42, 48–51

Newhall, Fales Henry, 35

Newspapers: accounts of executions in, 29–33, 143–45, 204 (n. 22); homogeneity in news coverage with advent of telegraph, 118, 201 (n. 15), 202 (n. 30); and objectivity, rise of in press reporting, 127; reporting of Civil War using telegraph, 118–19, 127, 200–201 (n. 14); reporting of Civil War through bulletin boards, 98, 198 (n. 56)

New York, poetry in streets of, 94–96, 197–98 (n. 47)

New York Daily Tribune, 40

42-43; in light of Declaration of Independence, 48, 55-56, 192 (n. 39); study of skulls in pursuit of, 41-42, 49-51, 67, 191 (n. 29); theories of racial inferiority, 41-42, 48-49, 190-91 (nn. 23-25); Thomas Jefferson's pursuit of, 48-49, 54-56, 191 (n. 27), 192 (n. 38)

Second Confiscation Act (1862), 151, 206 (n. 36)

Secret Service, 116, 119

Sentimentality: about death, prewar, 111-13, 125, 175, 188 (n. 6), 200 (n. 10), 201 (n. 24); abstracting death, 19-20, 34; and antislavery authors and orators, use of, 19-22, 34, 170, 181-82 (n. 11), 182-83 (nn. 17-18); lack of in *The Confessions of Nat Turner*, 64; real and fictional people blur in use of, 22; in wartime poetry, 72, 76, 91. *See also* Sympathy

"Sharpshooter's Last Sleep, A" (photograph) (Gardner), 119, 122

Shaw, Robert Gould, 132, 161-62

"Sight in Camp in the Daybreak Gray and Dim, A" (Whitman), 82

Silence: as way to deal with battle-field deaths, 72-73, 79, 82; as literary response, 79-80, 195 (n. 15)

Sioux Indians, 42

Skulls, and study of in pursuit of sci-entific racism, 49-51, 54, 67, 191 (n. 29)

Slavery: abolitionists advocating vio-lent resistance to, 17, 39, 55, 153; black soldiers as symbols of free-dom from, 58, 132, 151, 206 (n. 37); Civil War as divine retribution for, 9-12, 35, 57-58, 165-68, 208-9 (nn. 1-2); compared with army life for black soldiers, 133-35, 156, 160, 161-62; compared with suffering soldiers, 3, 11-12, 39; compared

with violence to dead by scientific racists, 42-43; and contraband slaves, 150-51, 156-57; Douglass's response to, 55, 64, 65, 153; John Brown's identification with, 16, 18, 22, 23-24, 27, 35-36, 181 (nn. 8-9), 186 (n. 51); and mob violence leading up to Civil War, 139-40, 203-4 (nn. 10-11); no mention of in "John Brown's Body," 16; op-pression of continued after death, 7-8, 40-43, 67, 179 (n. 15); seek-ing to evoke sympathy for slaves by conveying pain of, 5, 12, 18-22, 35-36, 39, 42, 138, 170, 178 (n. 10), 183 (n. 19); and self-possession, 9; whipping symbolizing excesses of, 11, 135-39, 151-53, 203 (n. 7). *See also* African Americans; Anti-slavery authors and orators

Southampton insurrection, 59-67. *See also* Turner, Nat

South Carolina Sea Islands, 151

Southern Amaranth, The (Brock), 90

Specimen Days (Whitman), 6, 75, 77, 80

Spiritualism, 117

Stanton, Edwin, 118, 127, 151, 171-72

Stapp, William, 103

Stearns, George, 152, 155

Stowe, Harriet Beecher, 5, 12, 19-20, 22, 23, 181-82 (n. 11)

Strother, David Hunter, 29

Sumner, Charles, 183-84 (n. 26)

Sundquist, Eric, 56, 61

Surgical History of the Rebellion (Brinton), 8

Surratt, Mary, 172

Sweet, Timothy, 116-17, 186 (n. 52)

Sympathy: abolitionists seeking to evoke, through conveying pain, 5, 12, 18-22, 35-36, 39, 42, 138, 170, 178 (n. 10), 183 (n. 19); and affec-tive power of self-sacrifice, 16-17,

35, 39; as ideal basis for social order, 11; and mental metempsychosis, 20–21; and renewal, individual and collective, 24–26, 183–84 (n. 26); seen as source of sectional strife, 24–26, 28; with slaves, John Brown's, 16, 18, 22, 23–24, 27, 35–36, 181 (nn. 8–9), 186 (n. 51)

Technology of war, 1, 12–13, 74, 79–80, 125; of Union army, 115–16; use of telegraph, 116, 118–19, 127, 200–201 (n. 14)
Telegraph, 116, 118–19, 127, 200–201 (nn. 14–15), 202 (n. 30). *See also* Newspapers
Third South Carolina Volunteers, 154
Thirteenth Amendment, 148
"This Compost" (Whitman), 72, 102. *See also* "Poem of Wonder at the Resurrection of the Wheat" (Whitman)
Thoreau, Henry David, 28; and John Brown, 18, 26–27, 181 (n. 6)
Till, Emmett, 173–76
"Too Good to Be Lost" (Confederate poem), 94
To Wake the Nations (Sundquist), 56
Trachtenberg, Alan, 126, 198 (n. 59)
Travis, Joseph, 65
Treatise on Military Law (Benét), 142
Turner, Nat, 42, 59–67; and authorship questions of *Confessions*, 61–63, 65–66; believing he is chosen by God, 63–65; fate of corpse of, 67; and refusal to repent, 60, 62
"Turn O Libertad" (Whitman), 83
Types of Mankind (Nott and Gliddon), 50
"Typical Negro, A," 151–52, 155

Uncle Sam, 147, 205 (n. 27)
Uncle Tom's Cabin (Stowe), 5, 12,

19–20; political effect of, 22, 183 (n. 22); "The Story of 'Uncle Tom's Cabin'" (Stowe), 19
Union army: black soldiers in, 10, 132–34, 148–55, 160–64, 203 (n. 3), 206 (nn. 36–37), 207 (n. 44); corporal punishment in, especially of black soldiers, 10–11, 133, 134, 148, 160–61, 164, 203 (n. 3); executions within, 10–11, 141–47, 204 (nn. 15, 19); executions within, of black soldiers, 148–50, 154, 156, 160, 205 (nn. 30–31), 208 (n. 55); inspired by "John Brown's Body," 2, 15–17, 37–39, 180 (nn. 2–3); presence of at executions representing the state, 29, 31–33, 34, 185–86 (n. 47); technology and efficiency of, 115–16. *See also* Battlefield dead; Black soldiers; Confederate Army; Executions; Photographs, Civil War
United States Colored Troops, 154
United States Topographical Engineers, 119
Unwritten War, The (Aaron), 79

Vesey, Denmark, 42
Vicksburg, Miss., lynchings in, 140
"Vigil Strange I Kept on the Field One Night" (Whitman), 82, 83
Violence: abstraction of by sympathy and nationalism, 16–17, 35, 39; advocated by abolitionists, 17, 39, 55, 153; early ethnological studies highlighting, 50–51; as evidence of badly organized state, 171; executions as form of state violence, 10–11, 18; literary responses to, 79–80, 195–96 (nn. 15–16); mob violence leading up to Civil War, 25, 139–40, 203–4 (nn. 10–11); and photojournalism, 106, 119, 126–27, 130–31, 202 (n. 29), 203 (n. 33);

pictorial envelopes as critique of state violence, 145–48; racial, against blacks during Draft Riots, 155, 206 (n. 37); racial, dissection and dismemberment as forms of, 3, 7, 41–43, 52–53, 61, 67, 179 (n. 15), 193 (n. 46); racial, executions of black soldiers as form of, 148–50, 154, 156, 160, 205 (nn. 30–31), 208 (n. 55); racial, lynchings developing as, 140, 147–48, 160, 173, 204 (n. 13), 205 (nn. 29, 31), 206 (n. 33); use of corpse to make political statements about, 175–76, 211 (n. 28); of war, uniquely captured by photographs, 106; and war as way to revitalize national identity, 2–3, 35–36, 37, 38, 72, 83, 187 (n. 61); and women organizing against war, 169, 209 (n. 11). *See also* Battlefield dead; Civil War; Nationalist culture; Wartime nationalism

Walker, David, 42, 54–59; death of, 59
Walker, William, 154
War Department, 78, 116, 171; and numbers dying in Civil War, 75–76; and pay for black soldiers, 154
War Lyrics and Songs of the South, 93–94
Warren, Robert Penn, 38
Wartime nationalism: abstracting death, 1–2, 6, 16, 36–39, 71–79, 86, 165–68, 175, 177 (n. 5), 186–87 (n. 57); based on ideal of self-sacrifice, 16–17, 38, 39; culture of affected by song "John Brown's Body," 15–17, 180 (n. 3); and inexhaustible resources for Civil War, 84–85, 87–88; martyrdom of John Brown contributing to, 14, 16–17, 39, 180 (n. 1); and need to assert

nation's legitimacy, 8, 85–86; war as divine test of redeemer nation, 9–10, 179 (n. 20); war as way to revitalize national identity, 1–2, 6, 38, 83, 86–87, 175, 187 (n. 61). *See also* Civil War; Nationalist culture; Violence
Washington, George, 68
"We Are Coming, Father Abraham, Three Hundred Thousand More" (Gibbons), 83–84
Weedon, Frederick, 52
Weiss, John, 1
Wellcome Institute for the History of Medicine, London, 69
"What tho' These Limbs" (Confederate poem), 93–94
Whipping, 23; as military punishment, 10–11, 160, 161; symbolizing slavery for abolitionists, 11, 135–39, 151–53, 203 (n. 7). *See also* Corporal punishment
White, Richard, 92–93
Whitehurst, Daniel Winchester, 52
Whitman, Walt, 94, 96; and death of Lincoln, 87; *Drum-Taps,* 81–83, 96, 97, 115, 119, 124; and inexhaustible numbers of soldiers, 87–88; *Leaves of Grass,* 81–82; poetry of embracing death as transcendent, 6, 71–72, 73, 75–78, 80–83, 130; poetry of embracing war as means to national unity, 72, 80–83, 91, 97–98, 102, 196 (nn. 17, 20); poetry of contrasted with Melville's, 97–98, 102, 198 (n. 53); *Specimen Days,* 6, 75, 77, 80. *See also individual poems*
Wideman, John Edgar, 174
Wills, David, 78
Wilson, Edmund, 1
Winchester Medical College, 7, 40, 41, 51–52, 69
Wise, Henry: and corpses of exe-

cuted Harpers Ferry insurgents, 4, 7, 40, 187-88 (n. 5); and decision to allow John Brown's execution, 9, 24-25, 27-28, 39, 177-78 (n. 7), 187 (n. 62); and organizing John Brown's execution, 29-33, 34

Wood, Peter, 67

Wood, Thomas Waterman, 155-59, 160

"World's Homage, The" (Holmes), 22

Wright, Mose, 173

Zwick, Edward, 132-33, 135